The end of conceit

About the author

PATRICK CHABAL is currently professor in the department of history at King's College London. He was educated at Harvard, Columbia and Cambridge, where he was a research fellow. He has been a visiting professor in Italy, France, Switzerland, India, Portugal, the USA, Venezuela and South Africa. He is engaged in a long-term project combining the study of culture in comparative politics with a focus on Africa and an enquiry into the theory of the human and social sciences. His books include *Africa: The Politics of Suffering and Smiling* (2009), *Angola: The Weight of History* (2008), *Culture Troubles: Politics and the Interpretation of Meaning* (2006), *A History of Postcolonial Lusophone Africa* (2002), *Africa Works: Disorder as Political Instrument* (1999), *Power in Africa* (1992 and 1994) and *Amílcar Cabral* (1983 and 2002), a number of which have been translated into other European languages.

The end of conceit

Western rationality after postcolonialism

PATRICK CHABAL

Zed Books
LONDON | NEW YORK

The End of Conceit: Western Rationality after Postcolonialism was first published
in 2012 by Zed Books Ltd, 7 Cynthia Street, London N1 9JF, UK
and Room 400, 175 Fifth Avenue, New York, NY 10010, USA

www.zedbooks.co.uk

Copyright © Patrick Chabal 2012

The right of Patrick Chabal to be identified as the author of this work
has been asserted by him in accordance with the
Copyright, Designs and Patents Act, 1988

Designed and typeset in Monotype Fournier
by illuminati, Grosmont
Cover designed by Rogue Four Design

All rights reserved. No part of this publication may be
reproduced, stored in a retrieval system or transmitted in any
form or by any means, electronic, mechanical, photocopying or
otherwise, without the prior permission of Zed Books Ltd.

A catalogue record for this book is available from the British Library
Library of Congress Cataloging in Publication Data available

ISBN 978 1 84813 558 1 hb
ISBN 978 1 84813 557 4 pb

Contents

PREFACE vii

Introduction 1
West and non-West 4
Western rationality and postcolonialism 13
Rationality, theory and thinking 23

ONE The problem 35
At home 39
Abroad 76

TWO Identities 114
Who are we? 119
Who are the 'others'? 132
Why is the West more 'advanced'? 147
Why is the non-West a 'threat'? 162

THREE Ideas 178
Individual 186
Society 191
Freedom 197

Faith 204
Market 215
Change 222

FOUR Interpretations 235
    To think is to theorise 247
    To theorise is to explain 261
    To explain is to act 275
    To act is to think (again) 290

EPILOGUE Three questions 316
    Secularism 318
    Human rights 321
    Sovereignty 328

BIBLIOGRAPHY 336

INDEX 365

Preface

THIS BOOK is a personal essay, a reflection on the world in which we live. Although it centres on Europe and North America, those parts of the world in which I have been educated and spent my professional life, it is in fact the outcome of my long-standing research on Africa. For me the book represents the logical end product of an academic career devoted to the study of that continent, which has for too long been dubbed 'dark'. In the process of trying to understand, and explain, why Africa is what it is, I came to realise that the Europe in which I live has been deeply influenced by its contact with that part of the world we call the South – or, as in the book, the non-West. Indeed, I believe that casting a gaze on Europe from a non-European perspective – in my case African – makes it possible to think about ourselves differently. Whilst it is obviously not possible for a European to pretend to be anything other than a European, it is possible for a European to try to look at himself, and at his peers, from a non-European standpoint and in this way to question a number of assumptions that are normally taken for granted.

It is the attempt to make sense of the problems we face in Europe that made me realise that the instruments we use are no longer fit for the job. Those instruments – that is, the social sciences we employ to explain what is happening domestically and overseas – are both historically and conceptually out of date. Historically, they belong to the late nineteenth and early twentieth centuries, when we sought to explain the broad trends of the evolution of European societies. Conceptually, they derive from the belief that the social sciences can become more 'scientific' if they follow the path cleared for them by the physical (or so-called hard) sciences. However, a reflection on the West from a non-Western perspective has helped me to understand that we need to approach the question of the human and social sciences from a different angle.

In order to show more clearly what that might mean I have in this book moved from the concrete to the more abstract. Starting from a discussion of a number of issues that are of concern to us today, I have tried to explain how the way we approach them is determined by the assumptions of social science theories we have internalised. I show that these theories are now obstacles to the understanding of what is going on in our societies and what we can do about it. It is because they have formatted us to think in a certain way that we keep going down avenues that often turn out to be dead ends – whether it is in thinking about 'multiculturalism' at home or the protection of human rights abroad. As I make clear in the book, it is in fact theory that gets in the way of thinking. So it is our thinking we must change if we are to approach these questions more fruitfully.

This book has been written in difficult circumstances and I owe a large debt of gratitude to those who have made it possible. I am thankful to my colleagues in the History Department at King's College London, who have been understanding and accommodating. I am particularly grateful to Paul Readman, the department's head, who has given me every support. I am also obliged to Peter Burke, with whom I have over the years had very illuminating conversations. I am grateful to the Institute for Advanced Study in Princeton, which invited me to spend a very productive year in an environment that was both intellectually open and very conducive to thinking outside the box. It provided the setting where I was able to begin to write this book. I benefited greatly from my discussions with David Scott, Joan Scott and Rosalind Morris. Heartfelt thanks to George, who will know why. I am grateful to Zed Books for agreeing to publish what is in effect a very personal essay at a time when such writing is not in fashion. It is gratifying to realise that there are still publishers who are prepared to make possible the publication of unorthodox books – books which do not fit the templates of social science textbooks. Long may this last. But, as ever, it is Farzana and Emile who have provided the intellectual and personal support I needed to undertake, and complete, such an unwise project. Whilst many doubted the undertaking was feasible, or even sensible, they never wavered in the belief it was worthwhile. And so it is to them that the book is dedicated.

For Emile and Farzana, again

Introduction

ABOUT TEN YEARS AGO, when she was still a teenager, a French girl living in the south of the country converted to Islam. It was a quiet affair: she did not tell her parents, who were non-practising Christians, nor did she share the news with anyone except a couple of very close friends. It was difficult for her since she knew her parents would disapprove.

Eventually, she confided in her mother. She knew her father, who came from a French family once settled in Algeria, would rebuke her but her mother had been active in the anti-discrimination campaign in France and had many French Muslim friends. She had never objected to her daughter's socialising with *beur* (French of North African origin) teenagers. The mother agreed to keep quiet on condition that her daughter would not wear the scarf. It did not satisfy the daughter. Once she went away to university, she wore the full *hijab*.

Her friends were all second-generation Muslim *beurs* or converts to Islam. She met and fell in love with a local Muslim boy of Moroccan origin but decided they could not move in together unless they had been blessed by the *imam*. The boy was puzzled:

he was not religious and his family was secular. But the girl insisted and so they eventually had a 'Muslim ceremony' – effectively a Muslim wedding. Today this girl wears the *hijab* (sometimes the *jilbab* or *chador*) and fulfils her Muslim obligations to the letter. She has told her mother's family about her conversion and they have accepted it. Her father's family have disowned her.

Still, her life is dichotomised: she wants to be a good Muslim but she has to be careful lest her attire draws racist comments and restricts her professional options. She has not become a fundamentalist; her story is much more interesting than that. She sees herself as an emancipated woman, who wants to keep her full autonomy. She is working and does not envisage her future as a housewife. She hopes to do a Ph.D. and, in time, would like to do social science research. So why is she wearing a *hijab*, which is not an actual requirement in Islam and in the French context means she is likely to face a life of discrimination?

Much has been written about the sociological and psychological factors behind the conversion of European girls to Islam – a trend that shows no sign of abating.[1] These studies all point to relevant issues, which need to be understood and addressed, but they often omit one simple hypothesis: that conversion is actually the result of a deep personal choice. However, what interests me here is not primarily why individuals choose to convert to Islam but, rather, how our Western societies explain it.

A gut reaction is that such behaviour is quite simply 'irrational'. It does not make sense. Why would a 'Western' girl want to subject herself to such 'backward' practices? In the media, these girls are often said either to be the 'victims' of fundamentalist males or to court attention because it makes them feel special. But the media should not be pilloried for being simplistic. It merely reflects, more

---

1. See, for instance, Silvestri, 2011.

Introduction 3

or less crudely, what society thinks. So what do these explanations tell us about ourselves in the West?

For one thing, it shows there is now confusion in our societies about the meaning of 'rationality'. Indeed, why should it be irrational to convert? Or, to put it another way, failure to make sense of conversion to Islam may have to do with the end of certainty: Western societies are no longer sure of how to see themselves. And the issue of Islam has exacerbated the underlying sense of ambiguity. How should the West accommodate Islam?[2]

Further, the issue of Islam brings to the fore the question of the influence of the outside world. Is it benign or baleful? It all depends – does it not? – on how we construe who we are. So, let me start at the beginning: how do we define who we are? And, first, what does it mean to say that some are from the West and others from the non-West?

I tackle this question from three different angles. First, I discuss what West and non-West mean in the context of this book. I then address the notion of Western rationality, meant here simply as how Western societies explain and justify what they do both domestically and in the international arena. Finally, I show how in Western rationality 'theory' often gets in the way of 'thinking'. Or, to put it differently, this Introduction is an attempt to discuss why our ways of thinking, particularly about the contemporary social and political world, are hampered by our belief that to be rational means to be scientific.

---

2. Conversion to Islam is nothing new. What is of interest is how Western societies react to such conversions. For an interesting example from the late nineteenth century, see the life of a Swiss woman 'explorer', Isabelle Eberhardt, which is recounted in Kobak, 1998.

West and non-West

The West of which I speak is the West in which I stand – that is, broadly, that part of the world from which imperial expansion started in the fifteenth century. Perhaps this is vague but the point here is less to identify a specific geographical area than to discuss the construction of modern rationality in those societies that went on to industrialise first and then to colonise the rest of the world. My concern is to see how these peoples imagined the universe they came to control, how they sought to tame nature and what effects these imperial and scientific achievements had on their way of thinking.

Of course, there is a difference between Western Europe and the former dominions of Australia and North America, which were built as lands of immigration and have long seen themselves as melting pots. Yet, the question of West and non-West is today as pressing there as it is in Europe. It is what Huntington's well-known *The Clash of Civilizations*[3] is all about: the world is divided between groupings based on cultural and religious divisions, of which the so-called 'Christian West' is the principal one.[4] Indeed, Huntington's last book (*Who Are We?*) was all about the 'Hispanic challenge' to American identity.[5] The author became convinced that the foundations of Western societies lay in the values they held and that the other, in his view largely religiously informed, groupings held other values that were not compatible with Western ones. And from his perspective, that challenge was both distinctly non-Western *and* definitely a threat to the West. Conflicts were inevitable.

---

3. Huntington, 1996.
4. For a critical discussion of the concept as applies to Islam, see Hansen et al., 2009.
5. Huntington, 2004.

Introduction 5

So the perception of what West and non-West are does in fact impinge on what is going on today in our societies. For one thing, the West seems to be suffering a crisis of identity that requires us explicitly to define who we are – something we never had explicitly (even less defensively) to do in our imperial heyday. We have now come face to face with the need to look at ourselves a little more insistently. The truth of the matter is that when we think about who we are today, it is most often formulated in terms of who we are not. Unthinkingly perhaps, we tend to view ourselves not simply in terms of what is specific to us but how different (better?) we are from 'others'.

Now, a sense of superiority is certainly not new: all empires have seen themselves as the centre of the universe – as the Chinese so clearly did in the fifteenth century. But in the case of the West, it is backed by several centuries of world domination, which give us today a certain view of the rest of the world – and in particular of what I call the non-West. That term is a catch-all category but it is not wholly arbitrary. There is a History course at the University of Cambridge widely (albeit colloquially) referred to as "The West and the Rest" – no doubt part clever pun but also part legacy of the time when History was thought of in those terms (how much has it changed?). So the first definition of the non-West is very simple and covers, undifferentiated, the whole of the rest of the world: Asia, Africa, the Middle East and Latin America – a large portion of which is now often called the South.

But in popular imagination and in the media, the non-West tends to be more specific: it is that part of the world that has migrated to the West; people from the former colonies for those who had colonies (e.g. Britain, France, Portugal, Spain and Belgium) and from the countries of labour recruitment for the others (e.g. Germany, Italy, the USA, Australia). Again, there is nothing new about migrants into Western Europe, but there are today two distinct aspects. Many of those immigrants are perceived as racially distinct – as opposed to the Poles who went to France or the Italians who went to the USA in the early twentieth century. And then there is a sense that the more recent migrants cannot, or do not want to, integrate – precisely because they come from the non-West.

Many problems in the West are laid at the feet of these more recent migrants, but in fact they reflect an uncertainty in Western countries about the nature of 'national identity'. This is as true, albeit in different ways, in Western Europe as it is in the USA and the former dominions. Everywhere, the question of a country's distinctiveness is entangled with the vague but forceful perception that there are too many non-Western immigrants – a notion sometimes extended to those coming from Eastern Europe! What disturbs may be different – race, colour, culture, language, attitude, competence – but it is usually obscured under a discourse of social integration and criminality. Newly arrived migrants – whether Albanians, Angolans or Algerians – are now seen to destabilise the Western societies into which they settle.

The idea that the world is divided between the two – West and non-West – permeates our thinking. Not surprisingly, the rest of the world has reacted to this aggressive and exclusivist vision – as reflected both in the media and in more scholarly publications like Huntington's. Within Western countries too there has emerged a marked irritation among the offspring of immigrants, who are perceived somehow to challenge the identity of the Western country in which they were born, educated, where they live and to which, clearly, they belong. Are they not of the West too? How many generations have to elapse before the descendants of immigrants become locals?

The division of the world between West and non-West, now replicated domestically by a division between locals and 'immigrants', has brought about a strong sense of mutual antagonism. It has created, or deepened, hostility between different countries – the non-West is especially suspicious of the West – and within our own societies – the descendants of earlier non-Western migrants are becoming angry at the discrimination they believe they continue to suffer. And more and more often they look to the non-West in order to (re)construct their own sense of identity. Perhaps this helps explain the renewed commitment to Islam among second-generation descendants of secular immigrants to Western Europe.

The *popular* perception right across the Western world is that it is now increasingly besieged.[6] Not only is there a continuous flow of would-be migrants trying to make their way to the West but the growing numbers of illegal immigrants are perceived to create problems internally. In all Western countries the question of (legal and illegal) immigration has risen to the very top of the political agenda. Even in the Netherlands and Scandinavia, long seen as immigration havens because of their relatively open border policies and their liberal attitudes to foreigners, the issue has become acute. In these countries, there is now open racism where before there was not.

Paradoxically, then, whilst the original migrants often claim they feel relatively well integrated and relatively content with their lives in the West, it is their Western-born children who appear to suffer the greater sense of alienation and discrimination. So, two further questions inevitably arise. When is a migrant no longer a migrant? And what in fact is national identity – since all countries, especially in the West, are populated by peoples

---

6. See the popular reaction in Germany to the publication of Thilo Sarrazin's book *Deutschland schafft sich ab* (Germany is 'doing away' with itself), which became a bestseller. The book argues that there are too many Muslims in Germany and that their presence threatens German identity.

from mixed origins? Is the claim that today's immigrants cannot integrate because they do not want to?

The very fact that we need to ask these questions shows not just that they can never be answered once and for all but also that the answers are conditioned by the way in which we think about the problems in the first place. When West Indians came to Britain, Algerians to France and Mexicans to the USA in the middle of the last century, they were perceived very differently. Then they were the hard-working labourers required by a confident and economically booming West.[7] Today, migrants from the very same parts of the world are cast as (illegal) economic migrants threatening the jobs of the locals.

The perception that foreigners in the West might even be dangerous – a notion that spiralled out of control after 9/11 – is the latest incarnation of the branding of the non-Western 'other' as unsuited to the West. It also links, if in a fairly nebulous way, the sense of domestic unease with the feeling that the non-West (rather than the communist world) is now the 'enemy'. So the West's need to curtail immigration goes hand in hand with the popular view that, in some vague way, the non-West is a threat to the Western way of life, as we will see later in the book.

For its part, the non-West (or perhaps more precisely the people of non-Western origins who live in the West) sees itself as both misunderstood and bullied. This perception comes in different guises, all of them understandable, and there are some considerable variations between different parts of the world. Within the former European empires, there is a distinction between Asia and Africa. Latin America no longer sees itself primarily in colonial terms; its main problem is with its giant neighbour in the North. More acutely, Latin American societies continue to

---

7. Although they were not immune to racism. On West Indian migrants to Britain, see Phillips and Phillips, 2009.

be beset with the question of discrimination against the 'natives' and the descendants of the slaves, who form a substantial part of their populations.

South Asians are connected with the mother country, Britain, in myriad ways that are further complicated by the presence in the West of millions of migrants, now settled there permanently. The former British colonies, though now largely emancipated from British influence, continue to be disaffected by their perception of the treatment their migrants (and their descendants) receive in the West. India and Pakistan are sensitive to the way Britain, and the rest of Europe, continue to cast aspersions on their 'poorly assimilated' diaspora, which is often seen to suffer unfair discrimination. In addition, Pakistan resents the label of terrorist that now seems to attach to all its citizens, no matter how economically successful or integrated they are in the West. Indians, Bangladeshis, Pakistanis and Sri Lankans obviously react differently to their image in the West but they share a strong sense of being misunderstood, when not vilified, because of their own domestic social and political problems.

East Asian societies, including China, particularly those that were not colonised, feel that the West is both arrogant and unduly ignorant of the complexities of local societies. They too see themselves as misunderstood. The points of contention are more cultural and political than economic since all of these countries are admired in the West for their ability to achieve high rates of economic growth. The criticisms are levied against the authoritarian systems, which East Asians defend on the ground that Western-style democracy is both alien and unworkable in practice. Whatever the merit of these arguments, which are disputed, East Asians often feel they are caricatured and belittled by Western countries, which themselves have a long past of human and political abuse, and even extreme violence.

In the Middle East, the sense of grievance against the West combines strong resentment about the effects of imperial rivalry and colonial rule with a generalised disquiet about Western prejudice against Islam. And, given the overwhelming importance of oil in many of these countries, there is also a sense that the region is treated by the West merely as a 'fuel reservoir'. Cajoled or bullied according to circumstances, these countries often see themselves locked into geopolitical constraints imposed by the West, regardless of the impact such policies have at the local level. Indeed, the West is seen to support or overthrow authoritarian regimes at will according to its self-interest, which is castigated as hypocritical. Caught between the remnants of a Western orientalist gaze upon the region, which covers a multitude of tired clichés and prejudices, and the perception of a racist form of Western anti-Islam, people from the Middle East frequently feel they are treated unfairly.

But it is in Africa that the sense of grievance is greatest. There, the accumulated memory of the wrongs committed by the West since the fifteenth century and the perception that the failures of postcolonial development are largely the result of outside forces make for a potent mix. Most Africans harbour a profound sense of injustice over the enslavement of their peoples and the colonisation of their lands. An acknowledgement of the need for continued aid is tinged by the resentment of the continued dependence that such assistance fosters. Africans also often feel that this injustice has been aggravated by Western racism, which discriminates most potently against black people. In what they see as a continuation of the Western theories of racism elaborated in the nineteenth century, they believe that the West continues to place black people at the bottom of the social pyramid.

As if this were not enough there is today the perception that rampant globalisation tends to sharpen further the gap between the West and non-West. Contrary to expectations of a more integrated world, globalisation is generating strong local reactions against the 'outside' world. It is seen to work to the advantage of the West, which controls the levers of capitalism, and advocates worldwide deregulation in order to consolidate its economic advantage. The strength of this market-based process reinforces the perception that the West is exploiting the non-West: globalisation is but the latest attempt of the imperialist West to secure its dominance.

This generates two potent and contradictory reactions, which contribute to the growing rift between West and non-West. On the one hand, the effects of globalisation are universal and the phenomenal progress in telecommunications brings the lure of modernity to every corner of the globe. Everywhere, people can partake of the wonderful new world garishly displayed on their television screen and on the Internet. On the other hand, the intrusion of globalisation into every community highlights the precarious nature of local identity and rationality. Not only does the globalised message peddle a vision of a Western-type future in which everyone might become a contented Westerner but it leaves little place for the culture, values and beliefs of non-Western peoples. Globalisation appears to mean enforced Westernisation.

As a consequence, this local reaction against the 'other' fuels parochial and chauvinistic beliefs. In many parts of the non-West, the effect of globalisation has been to rekindle interest in the defence of the local, now seen to embody the virtues of those who feel battered by the waves of technological and cultural 'modernity' washing from the centres of Western economic powers. In many ways, then, the prophets of globalisation have it wrong: the more globalised the economic system is, the more resistant the local is to the effects of social, political and cultural homogenisation.

Of course, there is no denying the globalisation of popular culture brought about by the revolution in telecommunications and transport. A certain form of culture – especially in music, film and fashion – is now almost universal, even if it has local variants. Big Brother and Brazilian *telenovelas* are seen everywhere in the world, and they attract big audiences. Dreadlocks are fashionable in Slovakia, not just Jamaica. Mobile phone tunes are instantly shared across the world. Indian designs are produced in some of the best-known fashion houses in the West. There is much to give the impression that globalisation is shrinking the world to a 'big village'. But this is misleading.

This apparent cultural homogenisation has not brought about a universal acceptance that what we share is now greater than what separates us. Quite the opposite. What it has done is to insert the global into the local. In other words, this cultural melting pot has brought West and non-West into close proximity everywhere in the world, even in countries where there was no significant previous contact with the West. But beyond a superficial adoption of some features of global culture, especially by young people, this more intimate proximity with 'others' has generated fears and rekindled ancient hostility against foreigners and foreign cultures.

For example, rap (originally a black American ghetto music) has now been adopted and adapted everywhere in the world. Superficially, then, rap is now king. In the West, it is most often used by those who want to challenge or shock, *épater les bourgeois*, and is therefore often perceived by them as a threat to their values and customs – witness the debate about the 'glorification' of violence. However, in the non-West, rap has been dissociated from its social and political origins; it is but a fashionable musical style. In the West, rap is sometimes cast as a non-Western intrusion into a 'local' musical tradition, even if it is no more so than jazz, today seen as a mainstay of Western music. Elsewhere, as for example in Africa, rap is merely the vehicle for a music that sounds Western but usually conveys local concerns.

Western rationality and postcolonialism

But what is at issue? Why this long digression on West and non-West? What I am trying to capture here, awkward as the terms might be, is a sense of why the Western world has now entered an age of uncertainty. And the reasons for this have to do not just with the influx of non-Western immigrants or the Islamist threat but, much more profoundly, with the fact that the non-West poses today a distinct challenge to Western rationality as developed in the last three centuries. In turn, this confusion about the meanings of rationality has to do with what Weber called the disenchantment of the world, or, as some might see it, the challenge to the Enlightenment.

What the use of the concept of *rationality* points to here is not some abstract philosophical concept but, much more concretely, the everyday ways in which societies explain and think through the problems they confront: what is happening to us and what can we do about it? There is inevitably a large cultural component to this process, but in the West there are two aspects that merit special mention. The first is that rational and irrational are seen in dichotomously sharp terms. One is either rational or irrational. Explanations are either rational or irrational. We are not comfortable either with the in-between or with the idea that one could be both rational and irrational at the same time. I return to this question in the third part of this Introduction. The second aspect is that rationality is assumed to be rooted in the scientific approach.

Without doubt, there is in the West a belief that the type of secular and scientific methods evolved since the Enlightenment have generated rational social and political models, which make possible a better understanding and more efficient institutional organisation of society than existed before. It is this belief that is now challenged by the realisation that there might be other ways of conceptualising and doing things. And this realisation has brought about a loss of nerve. The West is beginning to lose the confidence (arrogance?) that the Western way is the better (the only?) way. In this book, I want to explore the reasons why some certainties have been breached and how this may be undermining Western rationality.

Far from the present (post-communist and post-bipolar) global age marking in any way the 'end of history',[8] it is in fact the beginning of the age of uncertainty – or what I call *the end of conceit*. Why this is so and what it might mean for the West will form the body of the book. Here I want to highlight three important aspects of this loss of confidence and explore briefly what the consequences might be. The first is what I call the postcolonial burden of history. The second is a discussion of the meanings of Western rationality. The third will touch on what I see as the limits of social, economic and political explanation in the West.

The postcolonial burden of history

What I mean by the postcolonial burden of history is the impact in the West of the legacy of the imperial past. This does not simply involve the present domestic effects of the former colonial countries' overseas colonisation but more broadly the relevance of the encounter between the Western imperialists and the indigenous peoples they met, conquered and subjugated. Therefore, this includes virtually all the Western countries (however they may see themselves today), since in some way they were all involved in this expansion, whether directly or indirectly by means of trade. And in the Americas, as well as in the dominions, Westerners went on to subdue, exploit and often exterminate the native 'others'.

---

8. Fukuyama, 1992.

Until now the term 'postcolonialism' has mainly referred to the critique by intellectuals of non-Western origin (most of whom, however, living in the West) of the West's past sins and its continued intellectual, cultural and political arrogance. It has focused primarily on how Westerners continue to hold the non-Western 'others' in contempt and how this attitude permeates what the West does both domestically and abroad. Therefore much has been written to expose the assumptions and prejudices that still govern the attitudes of Westerners and influence the behaviour of Western countries in the world. By far the most influential critique has been that of Edward Said, who made manifest how the West continued to view the Rest in 'exotic' terms and in this way cast the non-West in guises that served to reinforce its own sense of superiority.

If that critique has been useful in forcing a reconsideration of the West's presumption, it has also served to bring about a re-appreciation of the non-West. A clever film title, *The Empire Strikes Back*, captures the essence of the postcolonial project: to redeem non-Western culture and attack the foundations of the West's claim to superiority.[9] This postcolonial critique has had some considerable effect on the cultural and intellectual life of Western countries. Indeed, in some areas – cultural studies, literary criticism, visual arts, even history – the postcolonial approach has become, if not dominant, at least an integral part of the mainstream. And when it comes to the study of non-Western 'minorities', where the colonial legacy weighs most heavily, it has virtually become the new orthodoxy.

The reason for the impact of postcolonial critique is not difficult to fathom: the West today is expiating the crimes of the centuries of violence and exploitation that marked the expansion

---

9. *The Empire Strikes Back* is the second film in the *Star Wars* trilogy. The title was then used by Thompson, 2005 and Ashcroft et al., 2002.

of Europe, slavery, imperialism and colonial rule. Accepting the full cruelty of that history and trying to work out how best to make it good has led to a great deal of soul-searching and a willingness, sometimes an eagerness, to accept the postcolonial burden under which Western societies must now labour. This has been fertile ground for those non-Western intellectuals who have built a career on berating the West but, as I will show later, their critique mirrors rather than subverts Western rationality. Be that as it may, the impact of postcolonial studies has certainly been to reinforce the sense of uncertainty and the loss of confidence that now pervade the West.

It is the end of the 1960s and early 1970s that mark the beginning of the West's reckoning with the burden of history. The Second World War had exposed the folly of Europe's expansionist dreams, but the success of post-war reconstruction, with its thirty years of 'economic miracle', obscured the fact that Europe was losing its imperial grip. Indeed, it is India's independence, the fiasco of the Vietnamese and Algerian wars, the 1956 Suez idiocy, and the decolonisation of Africa that made real the end of the West's imperial pretensions – even if it did little to affect the non-territorial form of American imperialism. And it is with the sudden economic slowdown of the 1970s that the immigration of colonial 'subjects', who had been necessary to the reconstruction of Europe, began to be perceived as an 'intrusion' into Western societies.

It is at that time, therefore, that the West's history finally caught up with its peoples, who had been taught for centuries to see themselves at the apex of civilisation. History could no longer merely be the carrier of the West's dominance over the world – a story of unbroken success and progress (despite the very Western horrors of the Second World War). Instead it began to be perceived as a burden, if not a millstone. The end of formal colonial rule put into question the identity of the former imperial powers, which had until then visualised a future in which their worldwide reach would continue to prevail. It also made manifest to Western Europeans the unquestionable dominance of the USA, which now exercised its ascendancy by means of economic, political and cultural power (the new imperialism?) rather than by direct conquest.

This change ushered in a period of critical self-questioning, which challenged or even overturned many of the long-standing certainties on which the West's identity was predicated. Here, it is the oil crisis of 1973 and the American defeat in Vietnam, rather than the student explosions of 1968, which sealed the end of the West as the centre of gravity of worldwide events. From then on the West was only one part of that world, which it had controlled for so long and on whose domination it had refined a sense of its own superiority. If the USA appeared as the uncontested leader, the traumatic end of the Vietnam War and the constant threat of Soviet aggression ensured that it had to be mindful of how 'relative' its dominance was. So it too had to begin to cope with historical blowback, which it did in typical fashion by vacillating between an isolationist and an aggressively expansive mode.

This burden of history was felt differently in different parts of the West but it began to weigh more insistently everywhere, affecting both the ways in which societies evolved and how people began to think of their predicament. The consciousness of what the end of colonialism entailed and the effects of the postcolonial discourses were twofold. The one exposed the West's normality, its mortality as it were: for the first time in centuries the West was on the retreat. The other, the postcolonial critique, began to insinuate itself into the interstices of the age-old certainties of Western superiority. Western progress had been at the expense of the colonised world and if the empire struck back – as OPEC did in the 1970s – then the West's onward march to progress was in jeopardy.

The meanings of Western rationality

This was indeed the historical context within which the question of rationality began to surface more explicitly. There began to arise doubt in Western societies about both the substance of what passes for 'the rational' and the fact that Western-style rationality must necessarily result in the best possible outcomes. That such doubt would arise was not at first evident. The flower power 'revolution' of the 1960s and the turn towards Eastern religion – yogi Hinduism or Buddhism – appeared to be no more than the pastime of an idle Western youth that had few worries about their economic future. Similarly, the absorption of large number of immigrants (Africans, Asians or South Americans) willing to work hard and integrate seemed to comfort the idea that the future lay in the West. And Western economic expansion was not about to stop.

The recognition of the weight of the postcolonial world and the concentration of Western attention on the communist threat also appeared to confirm the West's realism and its acceptance of its new geopolitical standing. The flexibility of Western capitalism, now spreading rapidly to the rest of the world, particularly Southeast Asia, exposed the failures of the socialist command economy and seemed to bear out the West's advantage. This ability to adapt, economically and politically, and the visible attraction of a Western way of life, to which more and more of the world's population aspired, strengthened the notion that Western rationality in science and technology, but also in social and political engineering, was the true measure of its dominance.

Although there were some voices warning against the logic of Western developments (*Small is Beautiful*,[10] for instance, raised the environmental alarm), this was certainly the heyday of the belief in the superiority of Western rationality. The consecration of the

---
10. Schumacher, 1973.

Western way of thinking, which had been adumbrated by the end of the Second World War, when scientists and social scientists from Europe energised the USA's research, academic and intellectual scene, appeared to be validated in the late 1980s as the communist foe finally collapsed. Whatever else *The End of History*[11] was, it was first and foremost the declaration by an American (of non-Western origin!) that there was but one desirable outcome: the Western liberal model, which was the product of the full application of Western socio-political rationality upon the world. In retrospect, this argument appears as understandable if ill-founded hubris.

The challenge to Western rationality has been multilayered. In the political arena, it now seems clear that Western democracy (a quintessential expression of Western political rationality) is not, and cannot be, the single model of accountability that will suit the whole world, even if it embodies many aspects that are slowly being adopted everywhere. Perhaps what has happened in Afghanistan is the best illustration of this problem.[12] Economically, the Chinese experience shows both that a country can embrace capitalism without democracy and that the emerging relationship between politics and economics can differ from the Western model. In geopolitical terms, the notion that a unipolar world would be safer and more peaceful in the face of a single world policeman has turned out to be wrong. The very existence of a self-appointed single superpower has generated enormous (often violent) resistance across the globe. US policy with regard to Latin America, or the Middle East, has provoked strong anti-American resentment.

Culturally and socially, the impact of globalisation has rekindled or reinvented forms of local identity and culture that defy homogenisation. In Africa, for example, there have emerged powerful

---

11. Fukuyama, 1992.
12. Originally the Western powers declared they wanted to bring democracy to that country. Now they no longer speak of democracy. They would be content with an Afghan government that could ensure peace in the country.

and vicious movements of 'autochthony' – that is, discrimination on the part of the so-called 'indigenes' against foreign 'others'.[13] More generally, there has developed strong resistance to the universal discourse of human rights, which is often seen as the arbitrary imposition of Western values. Finally, the environmental threat has invalidated the expectation that rationality, in the form of new technology, would always find answers to the downside of technological progress. In order to combat global warming and ecological disaster, the West has now become dependent on the rest of the world, which claims not unreasonably that it is the Western form of capitalist development that has triggered this environmental threat.

The limits of Western socio-economic and political explanation

This questioning of rationality is most pronounced, and most critical, when it comes to explaining what is happening within our own societies. Why, in other words, does the West seem to suffer from a large number of problems, which appear not to be amenable to simple rational socio-economic solutions?

Returning to the French example: why has the country that prides itself on being the land of Cartesian rationality not been able to work out an answer to the increasingly disturbing conundrum of the *banlieues*?[14] The problem is complex, touching as it does on issues of social deprivation, youth alienation, straightforward racism and political disenfranchisement. Indeed, it could be said that the very problem of the *banlieues* was itself the outcome of the application of an all-too rational, albeit narrow-minded, form of social engineering. Combining an attempt to provide low-cost

---

13. See Geschiere, 2009.
14. The term *banlieue*, which means suburb, is now mostly used in France to refer to those troubled suburbs where immigrants live.

modern accommodation with the housing of migrants where it was easiest to do so, the state embarked on a programme of suburban urbanisation which has effectively created social and racial ghettoes.

The issue of the French *banlieues* is as clear-cut an example as can be found of the limits of the application of social, economic and political 'theories' to the understanding of contemporary Western societies. In the French case, this type of housing policy derived from a belief that the best form of integration involved treating migrants as though they were fully fledged French *citizens*, who would over time assimilate and overcome the social and cultural habits of their countries of origin. This assumption is clearly derived from a typical form of Western rationality, which consists in believing that modernisation must foster Westernisation. In this case, it was presumed that, once in France, foreign migrants, regardless of origins or socio-economic circumstances, would slowly but surely become French men and women. What that meant was not really thought through since it seemed so utterly self-evident.

As a result, questions of identity (who did these migrants *think* they were?), religion (did the notion of secularism and private faith make *sense*?) and of integration (what did these migrants actually *want*?) were never systematically considered. Furthermore, there was little thought given to the pitfalls of housing migrants together with other socially disadvantaged and economically fragile groups in poorly provided urban conurbations far away from the main cities, where the jobs were to be found. Whatever view one may take of the evolution of the *banlieues* – including the cynical perspective of those who argue that the creation of ghettoes out of harm's reach was deliberate – it is clear that the consequences of such policies have been catastrophic. The *banlieues* have struck back and now affect the country's very social fabric – at great cost to society.

It is interesting to see how the French government is handling what has become a real crisis. On the one hand, it continues to stress the message that these problems are not due to questions of identity or religion – all French citizens are treated the same – and there is no need, therefore, to address them in terms of the special needs of different 'communities'. As of today, all attempts (including Sarkozy's more incisive efforts) to keep records on ethnicity have been defeated. A majority of the French do actually believe that the mere statistical acknowledgement of ethnic diversity would create even more intractable social divisions. Multiculturalism, which is seen as an 'Anglo-Saxon' delusion, is not for France.

On the other hand, successive French governments have continued to insist that the issue is fundamentally one of economic deprivation, which can be amenable to various forms of social engineering. This ranges from increased welfare support for those who are unable to work to a large number of state-sponsored job-creation schemes. What these policies have in common is the assumption that the problem is primarily one of socio-economic integration *and* that it is the state's responsibility to devise policies that will facilitate such integration. The French dream, unlike the American, is one that sets the state, rather than the individual, as the keeper of social values and as the ultimate social engineer. And the French state is without question the ultimate expression of French rationality, the only actor capable of resolving those intractable problems.

I shall return later to the question of how the West has tried to cope with the multiracial and multicultural character of present-day societies; or, to put it differently, how Western societies have sought to 'integrate' racially and culturally distinct 'others', who have pushed the boundaries of what it means to be 'citizens' of the countries in which they have settled. Here I merely wanted to give one illustration of the limits of Western social explanation and

Introduction

social engineering. Seen from outside the country it might seem that the French have been particularly inept in dealing with the question of immigration and integration. There is much discussion in Britain and the United States of the rigid, if not blinkered, way in which France tackles this issue – particularly in view of the decision to ban the veil in secondary schools and to make the public wearing of the *burqa* illegal.[15] Indeed, there is much to criticise in the French attitude but that is not the point. Seen from the other side of the border, one's approach always seems more sensible – dare I say more rational?

And that is the crux of the matter: each society is now quick to expose the limits of the others' rationale and of their form of social engineering. But what I want to suggest here is that it is the whole notion of social engineering itself that is at stake. Unfortunately, this is not a discussion that is yet taking place in our countries. On the contrary, both in the academy and in the corridors of power, analysts and policymakers continue to approach these issues in the same old way. In effect, as I shall show in the book, what is taking place is a continuation of the form of thinking that has brought about the failure to deal with the problems in the first place. But, as I argue later, it is the process of *thinking* itself which makes it difficult to question the type of rationality that is the foundation of Western practical thought. In some crucial ways, there are aspects of Western rationality that seem to have reached the limits of their instrumental value.

Rationality, theory and thinking

So what has rationality got to do with all this? And what is the connection with the non-West anyway? Let me conclude this

---

15. On the wearing of the *burqa* in Europe, see Silvestri, 2011.

Introduction with a brief discussion of some of the key terms used in the book: *rationality*, *theory* and *thinking*.

On the face of it, these appear to be very abstract notions, with little connection to some of the concrete problems I have been discussing so far. Nor is it clear how a better understanding of these concepts would help make sense of what is happening in Western societies or how to deal with the issues that are now at the top of the agenda. This is true as far as it goes: there is no mileage in using abstract terms unless they can help explain the practical questions we are confronted with on a daily basis.

But the claim of this book is that it is precisely because we are failing to understand, much less to address fruitfully, some of the critical issues of our time that we need to re-examine the concepts that underlie our everyday assumptions. And as I will show in Part I of the book, there are in fact many issues that puzzle and challenge us today in the West. How we think through them and what sort of answers we come up with is, I would argue, directly connected to the way we are able to rethink what we normally take for granted – that is, effectively, rethink the *rationality* of what we do.

What do I mean when I speak of rationality? There are two parts to this question. One is simple: it is the fact that we *believe* that what we do is judicious. The other is that we assume there is basically *one* logical way of understanding and addressing a problem.[16] These are assumptions that we all share as human beings. But what is different in the West is the widespread notion that its historical and economic achievements are solely the result of *its* modern rationality. Or, to put it another way, we believe that rationality is improved over time by means of theoretical

---

16. Another definition of 'rationality' is the adaptation of the means to the end. So what may appear to us as irrational – say suicide bombing – is in fact wholly rational from the perspective of the suicide bomber.

refinement, and that in this respect the West is most advanced. The claim, even if implicit, is that the West has combined the highest degree of scientific and technological achievements with the clearest vision yet of how societies function and humans interact. This, it is argued, is the result of two different processes, which have combined to make the West dominant.

The first is the historical record since the Renaissance: it is after all the West that first accomplished and consolidated the Industrial Revolution, making possible modern economic development. It is also the West that went on to assert imperial control over virtually the whole world, thus demonstrating its domination. The second is that it is the intellectual, scholarly and scientific revolution made possible by Western Enlightenment which has laid the basis for the most advanced form of scientific knowledge the world has ever seen. And it is this science that has enabled the astonishing technological advances that have so transformed the world. Indeed, this is an impressive basis for the West's belief in the superiority of its rationality. But there are two aspects of the question that we often neglect to consider.

One should be obvious: in the course of human existence, the West's achievements are recent, building on the achievements of the non-West, and they are due to very specific (possibly unique) historical circumstances that have favoured its progress. So what we call rationality is not fixed and timeless: it *is* of its time. Our form of rationality, which we believe to be the pinnacle, is also necessarily of its time. Ours is obviously *not* the end of history, so we have no way of knowing how rationality will need to change in order to meet the challenges of the future. Nor can we be sure that these future forms of rationality will simply be refinements of the present ones or different species altogether.

The other is that we have been most successful in applying our thinking to scientific and technological innovation. But the assumption that this has resulted in more advanced understanding of our social, economic and political lives is not so clear cut. In other words, there is no way of being sure that our human and social 'sciences' are as obviously the best as we can claim our sciences of the physical world undoubtedly are. And this leads to another illusion, which consists in believing that, because the whole world is emulating the West's science and technology, it is equally likely to adhere to its human and social vision of modernity.

However, despite the assumptions made in the West, the one does not follow from the other – as is, for instance, obvious in the case of the French social engineering of its *banlieues*. So, one of the main weaknesses of Western rationality is precisely the belief that it *is* possible to develop human and social 'sciences' that can enable us to emulate the progress made in the understanding and harnessing of the physical, chemical and biological world. It is a profoundly engrained belief, if not an article of faith. Both the West's approach to personal and societal problems and the solutions Western societies devise to address them are rooted in the model of the physical (or hard) sciences. They rest on the assumption that, if we apply ourselves sufficiently, we can crack society's ills just as we have domesticated the atom.

But the results have not been up to expectations, as is perhaps best illustrated by economics, where the apparently scientific basis of the discipline has repeatedly failed to provide systematically solid knowledge, much less uncontested solutions. Although we have accumulated vast amounts of economic data, much of it very useful, we are still unable to provide a 'science' that would generate incontrovertibly 'rational' policies based on cast-iron prediction. Economics is in fact a very imprecise *art*, in which the number of (hard and soft) relevant variables is far too immense to allow any sort of firm quantitative calculations. And yet we tend to persist in the belief that such scientific rationality will one day be acquired and that when it is we shall know once and for all how best to manage the economy.

Yet, there is change in the wind. A number of recent books have offered economic insights that are based on the acceptance that human beings do *not* behave according to the 'rationality' assumed by economic theory.[17] Much of that work is derived from psychology, a field in which it is more readily tolerable to accept that 'science' cannot ultimately provide the answers to explain man's behaviour, and in which there is more space allowed for the study of what is still called the irrational.[18] In fact, it is clear that there has been a step back from the attempts in the mid-twentieth century to devise a wholly scientific enterprise under the guise of behavioural psychology. Indeed, there is more to the human psyche than what we have been conditioned to believe.

What this book will show is that there is a need to rethink the whole basis of our 'rationality' if we are to develop new insights in our approach to the problems (discussed in Chapter 1), which have become intractable and often seem to threaten the well-being of our societies. I say insight rather than solution precisely because it is clear that what we need is a new way of asking questions rather than simply a different set of recipes, and even less a list of concrete answers. A step in that direction will be to let go of the assumption that there is only one 'approach' to a question. Another will be to abandon the belief that we can apply to the human and social fields the scientific tools of the physical world. That will be difficult because we will come up against a way of thinking that has been refined in the past few centuries, which rests on the notion that what is rational is what can be tested by theory, as defined by the 'hard' sciences.

---

17. See for instance, Gladwell, 2006; Thaler and Sunstein, 2008.
18. For one relevant example, see Ariely, 2008

So the next step on this journey is to revisit the notion of *theory*, or rather the relationship between theory and thinking, which forms the nub of the book.

Although the idea of *theory* can be either vague or off-putting, it is in fact a very simple one. In the first place, it simply means the systematic organisation, or ordering, of our knowledge. So, for example, if we put together what we know about how plants grow in our gardens, we come up with a theory to explain their development and how best to care for them. In the process, we make connections between what is more or less important, what is cause and what is effect. This knowledge may be empirical or based on what we have read but it could equally, and more likely, come from what we've heard or been told. This is what we mean when we say that 'in theory, X should give flowers in early May'. There is nothing magic about it: it is simply the outcome of observation, knowledge and experience.

The very process of ordering our thoughts in this way, rather than looking for a religious or metaphysical explanation, is one of the legacies of the Enlightenment, when the West began to try to understand how the world worked rather than merely see it as 'God-given'. This is in fact what is meant by modern rationality: the use of reason rather than faith to explain what we experience. So, in part theory is the move away from attributing causes to unknowable forces – a move that is unlikely to be reversed unless mankind were to destroy itself and be reborn as something different! That is not what is at issue today. This book will not take you down the road of born-again mysticism – which in our societies is most often nothing other than the flip side of rigid scientific rationality.

But the other aspect of theory that is equally important is the systematic extension of the 'scientific' approach to the very process of *thinking*. A scientific approach means that the way we go about trying to understand, and solve, any problem is organised in a particular fashion. First, there is observation. Then, based on existing knowledge, we construct hypotheses – that is, we speculate on possible explanations. Finally, we test to find out whether these hypotheses make sense. A theory is confirmed if (a) it explains particular events and (b) it makes it possible to predict that, given the same conditions or causes, these events will always take place. One simple example is the transformation of water into ice. Our theory tells us that below a temperature of 0°C water will freeze and that when it does it will occupy more space. We can predict that this will happen, and indeed this is what does happen (except, and there is often an exception, in the case of supercool[19] water, for example).

Theory in that scientific sense, which is at the core of the Western way of *thinking*, means the ability to put together a model of what causes will always result in what effects. This is what we mean when we say that science helps us understand and resolve problems. For instance, the science of weather forecasting is being refined all the time. As we test whether some hypotheses are better at finding an answer about the changes in weather, we devise the means to test for these factors (known as variables). A hunch that the *El Niño/La Niña* phenomenon (that is, the warming or cooling of the surface water of the southern Pacific) has a direct impact on weather patterns in Europe, America and Australia has now been confirmed by the increasingly sophisticated testing of newly understood causal relations.

This is the undoubted strength of the science of the physical world, but the question here is the extent to which it applies, or even *can* apply, to the human and social fields. Or, to raise an even more arresting possibility, can one be theoretical and not

---

19. Supercool refers to the rare condition under which water remains liquid below its normal freezing point of 0°C.

scientific in the Western sense defined above – that is, can one organise one's thinking differently? These questions suggest at least two problems.

The first is that in the human and social arenas the number of factors and possible causal dynamics is so large that it is not really possible to devise, much less test, any model of human behaviour or social phenomena. Above and beyond very crude models – such as the theory that when people are frightened to the core they will either run or freeze – we can never put together a model that will enable us to predict behaviour with much certainty. This is obvious in economic forecasting. Who can today predict what the level of savings in the UK or the USA will be in three years' time with the degree of certainty that would allow precise planning? Indeed, do people save according to economically rational criteria? Despite the incredibly refined statistical instruments in both countries and a long experience of forecasting, this is still largely (informed) guesswork.

But the second is more important. The extraordinary power of theory in the understanding and taming of the physical world is so compelling that it has conditioned our very way of *thinking*. Not only do we in the West believe firmly in the idea that the application of theory will enable us to understand human and social behaviour, but we have also come to expect that it will afford us the required remedies to the problems at hand. We are led to believe that rationality equates with solutions.[20] The more 'rational' we are in our thinking, the more likely it is that we will devise the right answers. But is this necessarily the case? Is there only one rationality? Is 'rational' the same as 'logical'? Could it be that other forms of thinking are required?

---

20. The notion of 'solutions' is a reminder of the 'counter-Enlightenment' tradition, well represented by Isaiah Berlin, who rejects the idea of definitive 'solutions' in human affairs.

This is the dilemma of modern medicine. Conditioned as we are to think that medical science can deliver answers and cures, we find it difficult to accept that medicine is also part guesswork and part mindset. It is a mixture of hard science and more psychological approaches to managing ill- and well-being; as much conjecture as it is science. In the West doctors as well as patients are more comfortable with the 'hard' part of medicine, where diagnosis is simple and treatment straightforward: for example, bacterial infections require antibiotics. But ailments such as depression are not always so clear cut. Taking pills is not necessarily going to work. And this is where our modern medicine is found wanting. Yet, as we know from different medical traditions, particularly the Chinese, there are other, more holistic, ways of understanding and treating illnesses, which combine hard science and psychology.

However, the problem extends well beyond medicine. This mode of *thinking*, which draws a firm line between theory (science) and belief (superstition) – that is, in effect, rational and irrational – has brought about an utterly dichotomised approach to the world, of which we are now scarcely aware. The whole purpose of our education system, from the beginning, is to train us to 'think rationally', which means to learn from observation (science) and experience (history). And these are presented to us as though they were the simple result of the straightforward development of the application of a 'modern' form of *thinking* to our environment. As though there were straight lines in progress and development. *Thinking* means applying the lessons learnt and ordering our brain power around the trusted principles of the advancement of knowledge and science by means of the application of well-conceived theory. But there are two problems here.

The first is that this type of reasoning sets a firm dichotomy between *knowledge* on the one hand and *creativity* on the other. The Western form of education makes a clear distinction in this respect.

It encourages creativity in what are considered the arts – drawing, writing, painting, music, and so on – but it makes obvious that this area of human expression is both distinct from the scientific mind and inappropriate as a basis for tackling human and social issues. Yes, music might help recover after a traumatic incident. But, no, music cannot be used as a means of reducing unemployment. By implication, therefore, what is creative, however worthy or enticing, is not 'rational', at least in the sense that is normally given to the concept in Western societies. But in which ways is creativity 'irrational'? And is creativity not necessary to science?

The second problem is that in the West what is considered to be rational is wholly secular, meaning that rational *thinking* is considered separate from belief, which is seen as private and a matter of faith – religious or otherwise. This divide has become both ingrained in our approach to the world and wholly unimpeachable: there is rationality and then there is faith; never the twain shall meet – even if, as we shall see, the Americans tackle the question of secularism differently from the Western Europeans. This has created many difficulties in the way in which we actually live, which I shall discuss in the book. Here I want to stress how central this divide has become in our lives. And it raises a couple of difficult points, which will require attention. One, again, is the assumption that religious belief is 'irrational'. The other is that religious faith is in fact by definition not open to 'rational thinking'. So it may well be that the secular nature of the West's rationality is in fact a hindrance in the understanding of a range of human and social issues for which matters of belief and faith are central. By considering those as 'irrational' we constrain our ability to think. And this has fateful consequences, which are at the heart of what might be considered the present threat to our rationality. Of these, two may turn out to be more ominous than the others.

Introduction

The first consequence is that this extreme divide in our thinking between rational and irrational makes us, individually and collectively, schizophrenic. We cannot entertain the possibility that in point of fact we might be both – at least not when it comes to the diagnosis of our ills and the remedies we propose. For instance, it is often argued that racism is 'irrational' because there is no scientific basis to racial differences. However, people's reactions to racial difference may mean that some of them want to put distance between themselves and the racially distinct 'other'. But since society considers such attitudes 'irrational', some of these people might be driven to embrace more extreme ideologies that accommodate their fears. For example, we know that dubbing 'irrational' the political support garnered by xenophobic parties is in large part due to the refusal of mainstream parties to pander to what they see as racist prejudices. However, as a society, it would be more 'rational' to accept that human beings are in fact sensitive to racial differences and to think how to improve race relations from that starting point – rather than to banish such positions on the grounds that they are 'irrational'.[21]

The second consequence is that this conception of the rational and this form of *thinking* may well reduce considerably the scope of our search for explanation and solution. This is particularly true when it comes to the West's approach to the rest of the world. An inability to conceive of other beliefs, other rationalities, confines our ability to make sense of what we observe. It restricts our capacity for thinking through the nature of the issues and the range of solutions to which they might be amenable. For example, there are many in the West who think that the only key to the alleviation of poverty in Africa is radically to increase foreign aid, on the assumption that more aid will mean more resources

---

21. Here see Amselle, 1990.

for people to improve their lives. However, this approach may well come up against different types of rationality in which the more aid is given the less the incentive there is to generate wealth internally. If this is true, then it is unlikely that more aid would result in less poverty.

What this book aims to do, therefore, is to try to explain why our present mode of thinking is a threat to our own rationality, which is the foundation of our Western societies. The reluctance to accept that our inability to 'resolve' certain kinds of human and social problems is due to the way we approach them represents certain danger for the future of our societies. What is required is the willingness to reconsider what it is that we do when we *think* about the evolution of the world and our place in it.

The realisation that resources are finite, that growth cannot continue to be the sole basis of development, and the necessary acceptance that ecological constraints are reducing our options are already forcing a rethink. But it will take more than the mere refinement of our existing theories to revise our way of thinking. One necessary first step is to open the discussion with our eyes wide open and to apply our minds to different forms of thinking. If we conceived health not as the absence of illness but as the management of constant physiological and biological mutations, including illness, our whole outlook on medicine might change.

Although the West may think it is special, Westerners need to accept that they are but humans. Our theories should be set in their appropriate historical and conceptual framework. And we Westerners need to accept that such theories might have reached their limits, and for this reason have now become so many obstacles to *thinking* – as the rest of the book will attempt to show.

ONE

The problem

ALTHOUGH MY CONCERN is with the way in which our theoretical presuppositions affect our thinking, my interest is not primarily theoretical. If this concern matters, it is because our contemporary societies face problems they seem increasingly at a loss to manage. Under a veneer of (sometimes brash) self-confidence, there is fear among the political class, whose tried and trusted methods of government are being severely tested. Recent elections in the West have shown that the electorate is increasingly disenchanted with politicians *but* that at the same time they are groping for 'solutions' to the problems they face. For all the magic woven by Barack Obama, the more prosaic reality of the American political scene is the resort to an extreme form of conservatism that seeks in the past a key to its present predicament. Similarly, the excitement generated by the Sarkozy campaigns in France was extinguished by aggressive hyperactivity and an obsession about national 'identity'. But if democratic politics is unable to offer 'solutions' to Western citizens, there is real and present danger for the running of our affairs.[1]

---

1. By 'democracy', I refer to the cluster of institutions and the electoral practices of Western countries as codified in their respective constitutions.

Of course, this political disenchantment is nothing new. Neither is the danger of the turn to the extremes. Fascism blighted Western Europe for a generation. But the fascist turn was but the flipside of the communist threat – the obverse ideology of those who hated what the left revolution entailed. Whilst violently opposed to each other, they shared an ideological approach, one that enabled them to justify the taming of the masses in the name of a better future. Fascism was also revolutionary.[2] And that understanding of revolutionary politics was built upon the theoretical, intellectual and historical foundations of the post-Enlightenment's conceptualisation of the world. Both ideologies were rational, possessed of a 'reason' that was supposed to provide politicians with the keys to a superior organisation of our social and economic lives. In that way they can be seen as the political culmination of the exercise of 'pure reason'.

What is new today is that our response to the main political and social dilemmas of the present age point to cracks in our very notion of rationality. Again, this does not mean that the 'irrational' is any more palpable now than it was a century or two ago. The turn to the 'irrational' has been part of our response to the place of modern man in modern society since the 'age of reason' descended upon us. It is true that the romantic backdrop to the Nazi project was partly rooted in an 'irrational' attachment to a powerfully reinvented past. Nevertheless, that vision was ruthlessly rational in the deployment of scientific tools. More importantly, however romantic the ideology may have been, it rested on social, economic and racial theories grounded in well-established and, at the time, well-respected scientific theories. And these theories, abhorrent as they were, had entirely respectable genealogies.

---

2. See Paxton, 2005.

At present, there is a distinct retreat from the absolute belief in the deployment of scientific reason and a clear search for non- or para-scientific approaches to many of our problems. A simple explanation of this trend is to attribute it to the decline in religion in Western societies. As we have become more secular, the argument goes, we have lost that side of our personal and psychological make-up that answered to our spiritual needs. These needs, which cannot be satiated merely by the exercise of 'rational' thinking or the acquisition of material goods, can only be met by a form of spirituality that is incommensurate with the scientific world we now firmly inhabit. All this is true but it does not capture the complex texture of our current disenchantment. It is surely the case that much of the new 'religiosity' we witness today is due to the weariness with which the 'rationality' of the modern world structures our lives around increasingly material ambitions. But there is more.

There is now a discernible move in Western societies towards a form of understanding of the world that seeks to build on religious, spiritual, or at least non-scientific, foundations. The currently fierce debate between secularists like Richard Dawkins and those who wish to marry religious belief with scientific theory is one illustration of this tension.[3] Secularists would not worry so much if they did not feel that the 'new believers' threatened to undermine the rationality and the science that have created our modern lives. The debate is conducted in terms of science versus religion but it is far wider and more significant, going back to the origins of the Enlightenment. What the present dispute is about is not merely the place of religious belief in Western 'modernity'. Even if the protagonists do not see it that way, it is at heart a debate about the meaning of rationality.

---

3. See Dawkins, 2006.

The acuteness of this debate is in itself an indication of the limits of our scientific consensus. Although only a handful of extremists still dispute Darwin's findings, the present controversy over the relevance of evolutionary theory for social behaviour is proof that we are no closer to a theory of social behaviour than Darwin's contemporaries were. Do women prefer tall, dark and muscular men because they have been 'programmed' by evolution to maximise their chances of successful reproduction? By the same token, do men prefer buxom, nurturing women? We recoil at such scientific implications because we like to think we exercise free will. And, in any event, is that really what the theory tells us? Would Darwin himself recognise such usage of his insights? So, what this (perhaps futile) debate points to is a question about what it is 'rational' to believe in the circumstances.

My point is not so much that the argument about rationality is new, because it is not, but rather that its renewed vigour at a time when the West is apparently agreed on the superior virtues of its scientific, economic and political advances is a sign of deep unease. This unease has been made more manifest, although it has not been caused, by the West's need to rethink its relations with the non-West. Perhaps there is poetic justice in the fact that it is this constantly changing 'encounter' with the peoples the West claimed to want to civilise that is now crystallising most clearly the challenge to the imperial claim of rationality. Indeed, I believe this is no coincidence, for this encounter makes plain both that there are distinct rationalities at work in the world *and* that there is no necessary evolution from lower, non-Western, to higher, Western, forms of rationality.

Let me illustrate this argument with a discussion of a number of contemporary issues, and their attendant dilemmas, with which the West is doing battle. There is no pretension here to offer a systematic, even less a complete, list of present-day problems.

The problem 39

Nor is there any claim for the greater importance of the issues selected over others. This chapter is merely an attempt to bring into play some topical questions, all of which test the West's vision of itself and of what it would like to be and do, both domestically and in the wider world. Taken together they will hopefully make plain what I mean by the questioning of our present Western rationality.

At home

Current debates in much of Western Europe – at least if the arguments that have engulfed recent elections are any guide – centre on a cluster of issues that relate economic tensions to the social make-up of our societies. If unemployment and racism are perhaps the most emblematic of these questions, there are in fact a large number of related concerns that are in my view symptomatic of the current challenges faced by Western rationality. Both the perception of these problems and the approaches taken to attempt to tackle them are a good indication of the limits of our Western 'way of thinking'. My intention in what follows is not in any way to decry the attempts made by politicians, social engineers and international experts – which it would be all too easy to do – but instead to show why our apparently rational and 'scientific' minds are baffled by what the world is throwing at us.

Identity: is multiculturalism the solution?

Since the beginning of this century there has been an increasingly sharp concern about national identity, which has had serious political implications. Ranging from the French legislation banning the *burqa* (the *voile intégral*) to the spectacular success of Geert Wilders in the 2010 Dutch general election, this question of national distinctiveness has provoked greater and greater agitation.[4] Although the ostensible cause of such political gyrations is easy to identify – the number and social place of immigrants – the deep reasons are more revealing. After all, every Western society is made up of immigrants and notions of national identity are fairly recent inventions, as Benedict Anderson reminds us.[5] So what is happening today?

What is perceived by many to be an 'immigration crisis' is ostensibly due to three factors. The first is that Western economies are no longer in need of *large* numbers of unskilled immigrant workers. At best, they seek highly qualified foreigners who will contribute to technological development and managerial efficacy. The second is that there is a sense in most Western countries that there are now too many immigrants. Subjective as that perception might be, it is in part connected to the cost of social welfare and unemployment. All too often it is believed that immigrants make inordinate demands on social provisions and 'take away' jobs from those who are trying to find employment. The fact that these two claims are incompatible does not deter the anti-immigrant lobby. Finally, there is a relentless flow of what are called illegal immigrants, who appear to be flooding in and to flout all counter measures designed to keep them out.

But the fourth and probably most important factor is that the immense majority of these more recent (post-World War II) immigrants come from the non-West – that is, the former colonies, the so-called Third World or the South. The early (from the 1940s to the 1970s) such immigrants were able easily to find employment – indeed, many were recruited – and worked hard to integrate,

---

4. In the 2010 general election, Geert Wilders's Freedom Party won 24 out of 150 seats.

5. Anderson explains in his book *Imagined Communities* (Anderson, 2006) that the concept of nation is a recent 'invention' made possible by the expansion of the print medium that brought people together around the notion of a bounded community sharing a common language and a common 'invented' history.

facing years of racism with extraordinary fortitude. Today the situation is different. There is first the large number of second- and third-generation 'immigrant' populations, which continue to face problems of integration and racism *and* who are no longer willing to tolerate discrimination. They see themselves, and indeed they are, fully fledged citizens of the countries in which they live. Second, there is a perception that recent immigrants no longer care to integrate and that the descendants of the earlier immigrants do not want to feel part of the society in which they were born. Their sense of estrangement draws them to their 'imagined' homeland (by way of culture, religion, etc.) whence their parents came.

From the 1970s onwards, then, all Western societies were confronted with the problem of 'immigration'. In some countries, like the USA, the question of integration has been less salient because multiculturalism is at the heart of the country's identity. Not only is there nothing special about peoples of various origins continuing to live as discrete communities but the very principle of social distinction is based on 'ethnic' identity. Therefore the issue in North America, and the former dominions, is that of 'illegal' immigration. In Western Europe, however, the central issue is how different groupings live together – that is, how they blend into a supposed national mould. It is this process – known by a different name in every country, including *intégration* in France and 'multiculturalism' in the UK – that is at stake and on which there is little consensus.

Analysing the French and British approaches to this question is instructive because they are at the opposite end of the spectrum. The one rests on the 'republican' assumption that social equality depends on the forging of the individual into a French citizen, by which is meant a person who subscribes to the national myth of the republic. The other depends on the presumption that the best way of ensuring that different communities can live together is to acknowledge and respect their differences. So, the former seeks harmony in the dissolving of difference and the promotion of a single French individual. But it neglects to take into account that there can be no 'neutral' such citizen and that the model, as it were, is one derived from a distinct European and Christian past. The latter envisages a mosaic of distinct groupings who value each other's distinctiveness but come together to live under a common British umbrella. But it, in turn, fails to take into account that the emphasis on difference can all too easily accentuate social separateness.

Clearly, these approaches are not primarily based on theoretical considerations. They arise from the deep historical processes that have created the two countries. Therefore it is quite pointless to argue (as many commentators are prone to do) that one method is inherently superior to the other. Both have their merits, or rather both have had their merits. But both have their limitations, as present circumstances make clear. Although the problems of integration in these two countries are quite dissimilar, they have now become socially acute in both. The assumption that European societies were able to assimilate large number of (particularly) non-Western immigrants by means of distinct forms of social engineering has now been exposed as an illusion. The fact that those countries (such as Sweden or the Netherlands) that had the most flexible and tolerant attitudes to immigration are now prey to major social and political convulsions is an indication of the depth of the problem, at least in Western Europe. So what interests me here is not so much how 'successful' different approaches to integration have been but why they have all run into the sand.

It strikes us today in the UK and the USA that the thinking behind multiculturalism – that is, to allow each community to live as it chooses so long as each abides by the laws and social 'conventions' of the country – is both more sensible and more effective than the French *dirigiste* attempt to lay down the cast-iron requirements for citizenship. Interestingly, however, surveys show that immigrant communities in, respectively Britain and France, tend to agree with the existing national approach. So, the former favour multiculturalism while the latter adhere to the republican ideal of citizenship. This suggests, at the very least, that both communities are in some important ways already profoundly integrated into the culture of the countries from which many may otherwise feel alienated.[6] It also brings to the fore the conclusion that they do not object to the *aims* of integration but only to the poor results it has achieved, which points to the limits of the rationality of the two respective approaches.

However, what is common to both approaches (indeed to the whole of Western Europe) is fourfold. There is, first, a notion of national identity that appears clear but is in fact ambiguous. Second, there is a narrative of national construction that turns out to be but the latest incarnation of the historical interpretation of the national past. Third, the thinking about the question of integration rests on a body of assumptions about the nature of society and the role of social engineering. Finally, there is an inability to understand why ostensibly integrated minorities should want to defy national 'harmony' and hark back to what are seen as 'backward' beliefs or practices. These four issues raise the question of, respectively, history, culture and social theory. Let me consider them in turn.

The European vision of its *history* underwent several important turns after the Second World War. The first occurred in the late 1950s and early 1960s, when the colonial powers finally lost, or divested themselves from, their last colonies.[7] There thus emerged

---

6. See report on European survey of Muslim opinion about national integration: http://news.bbc.co.uk/1/hi/8038398.stm.
7. Britain, Belgium and France relinquished colonial control in Africa between 1957 and 1964.

a postcolonial narrative that stressed a new spirit of cooperation with the former colonies and gave the image of the metropolis as a 'mother' country, open to immigrants from the colonies prepared to work hard and integrate into the economically thriving Western economies.[8] This was couched in the terms of a benign paternalism: the formerly colonising West would now be godmother, promoting the development of the emerging non-West. And the West would welcome those who chose to settle in the West.

The second turn came as a result of the burgeoning economic crisis in the second half of the 1970s. Reduced economic growth and the rise in unemployment limited the scope for further immigration and focused attention on the competition for jobs, mostly at the lower end of the economic scale. Whereas before, the national narrative had made much of the melting-pot quality of Western societies, along with their ability to integrate those who came to settle, a new discourse on identity became more manifest. This drew on a different perception of the relations between the West and the non-West. As colonial guilt began to dissolve, new visions of colonial history now emphasised the benefits of colonial rule and the need for the former colonies to stand on their feet. The West would continue to assist the non-West but successful development, as was now taking place in East and Southeast Asia, should reduce the need for the peoples of the non-West to migrate to the West. The West had discharged its immediate postcolonial obligations and would now concentrate on the well-being of its own citizens.

The most recent turn might be termed the challenge to liberalism. Ranging from a more self-confident assertion of the benefits of globalisation to the militant assertion of a supposedly well-defined Christian European identity, this belief became politically stronger

---

8. This was a period of economic expansion, which is captured in the French expression *les trente glorieuses* – referring to the thirty years after the end of the Second World War.

in the last decade of the twentieth century. This latest historical narrative constructs, or better invents, a past of homogeneity and coherence that justifies an exclusive, reductive and intolerant vision of national distinctiveness. The argument (ideology?) now states that national identity is made up of clear personal, social, cultural and even religious characteristics which define citizenship and to which immigrants need to subscribe if they are to be integrated into society. Multiculturalism, in other words, had its limits.

This narrower and more exclusive historical narrative is contested, of course, but it is gaining ground under many guises. In France, neo-republicanism is now the dominant ideology and it supports the moves to legislate against religious or cultural behaviour that is deemed unacceptable. In the UK this has translated into an increasingly strident campaign to limit immigration and impose much sterner tests to the granting of citizenship. In the Netherlands, Wilders's movement has removed the stigma attached to an anti-immigration and anti-Islam discourse that would have been previously unthinkable. A similar evolution has taken place in Denmark. In short, history is now invoked more insistently in the debate about national identity and the search for solutions to the problems of integration. This has resulted in the perceived need to provide a more focused 'national' historical curriculum, which brings to light more clearly the supposed continuities of the country's history.

This historical revisionism ties in with a fierce debate about the role of *culture* in the definition of national identity.[9] As the West has felt increasingly challenged by the presence of non-Western immigrants in its midst, it has cast a new look at its supposed cultural roots. On the one hand it has tried to define more accurately what the cultural core of the nation is. On the other hand it has made an

---

9. I define 'culture' as a system of meanings shared by a particular group, here the nation, and not, as is more commonly the case, as 'values'. Here see Chabal and Daloz, 2006: 22.

attempt to make plain what is culturally unacceptable. Both have been fraught because there is little that can be identified objectively as 'national' culture and there is much that is contested. In the West, scholars, philosophers, religious leaders and policymakers are all involved in the search for the cultural matrix that forms the ostensible core of what we believe ourselves to be. What is it that we cherish and want to uphold? Are there *cultural* reasons why Turkey should not be in the EU?

As might be expected, the French efforts in that direction have been the more systematic. A near universal adherence to the legacy of the (myth of the) Revolution and a greater sense of what constitutes Frenchness have contributed to the emergence of a neo-republican definition of culture. This includes a commitment to the abstract citizen, who is deemed to enjoy total equality, and, therefore, a rejection of any communal identity. It involves a stringent notion of equality, which brooks no special dispensation on the grounds of ethnic or cultural difference. It is centred on an almost militant devotion to secularism that allows religious freedom in the private sphere but enforces a total separation between the public realm and religion. Finally, it implies a strong relationship between state and citizen, a relationship that fosters a political culture of dependence and revolt vis-à-vis the administrative authorities that embody the state throughout the land.

If it is easy to see how that conception of national culture might grate with many immigrant communities, the British (ostensibly more flexible) view of their own culture is no less problematic. The recent, faintly amusing, discussion about the appropriateness of displaying the flag of St George in support of the England football team has highlighted the complexities of British culture. In the first place it has shown that until the question of national identity had been made more acute by the issue of immigration, the English had never really felt the need explicitly to define who they were.

The Welsh, Scots and Irish, on the other hand, had a clear sense of who they were, which was largely a result of their not being English. Second, it raised the question of whether non-Western immigrants, most of whom were racially distinct, could claim to be English and fly the flag. Were the English (as the British National Party claims) the notional descendants of the earlier inhabitants of the land, many of them immigrants from other European regions, or were they those who now lived in England?

Therefore the cultural dimension of the debate on national identity has made obvious the fact that integration was not just a social and economic issue. It was not enough to assume that if immigrants found jobs and earned a decent living they would 'naturally' become integrated. It has now become apparent, and this in itself goes against the assumptions made about the process of integration, that the more intangible question of what immigrants (and their descendants) believed, valued and cherished mattered a great deal. Crucially, it seems to matter more, rather than less, as time passes. Or at least it seems to matter in certain ways that are a distinct challenge to the concept of 'national' identity. It may have come as a shock to the French that third-generation *beurs* flew the Algerian rather than the French flag at the last football World Cup, but the British are similarly puzzled that third-generation British Asian women should choose to wear the *burqa*, and prefer not to go to school rather than compromise on their attire.

Whether these are primarily cultural challenges or not, such behaviour flies in the face of those who believed that time would settle the integration of non-Western immigrants as it had those of previous generations of European immigrants. It disturbed the comfortable assumptions Europeans made about the nature of social developments and was a direct challenge to their presumed historical narratives. These cultural conundrums raise disturbing questions that the West is ill equipped to tackle. Is the unexpected behaviour of the locally born descendants of immigrants to be explained by their different cultural heritage or is it the result of a 'culture' of defiance on the part of those who feel discriminated against. If the latter, this is a problem since these more recent generations are seen to have benefited from the social, educational and economic advantages available in the countries in which they live. If the former, the conclusion is even more disturbing since it would appear that there is something intrinsically irreconcilable between Western and non-Western 'cultures'. And this interpretation can all too easily lead to the belief in the clash of civilisations and to theories of necessary 'separateness'.[10]

This cultural puzzle, which goes against received 'national' narratives, brings us to the question of *social theory* – that is, the analytical means by which we try to make sense of the social dimensions of our lives. It may well be that what we understand by 'national identity' is confusing because of the instruments we use to delineate the meaning of that concept. Although I will return to this issue later, I want here to highlight a few of the difficulties that arise from our conception of identity. There is, first, the assumption that there can be a recognisable single and consistent form of 'national' identity. This is clearly wrong, both in theory and in reality. We know, without having studied sociology, that all of us possess multiple identities – local, gender, social, ethnic, racial, educational, professional, political – that not only separate us but also keep us apart. But more importantly from my perspective is that when we think analytically about this question, we resort to a theory of identity missing the crucial point that our multiple identities are not necessarily compatible.

Second, we rely on accounts of the formation of 'national identity' that assume a linear, progressive, evolution from a situ-

---

10. *Apartheid* in Afrikaans.

ation in which the nation was consolidated out of a supposed gaggle of tribes into a single entity. Whilst this may, very roughly, reflect what happened in Europe between 1500 and 1900, it does not mean there is an iron law of development whereby the peoples brought together under one 'national' umbrella continue to dissolve themselves into the recently invented 'national identity'. There is no reason to suppose that identities will narrow and cohere in the modern setting. Nor is there good ground for thinking that the definition of the 'national' is now immutable.

Finally, therefore, it is questionable whether what we believe present 'national' identities to be will continue to be viewed in the same way in the future. The process (discussed in the Introduction) whereby globalisation is bringing about a renewal of the local perspective is likely to affect the way in which we think of the 'national' component of our individual and collective identities. It could be, as has been suggested, that the result will be a renewed bout of nationalism, or even jingoism. But it is equally possible that the 'national' element of the identity of modern men and women will become increasingly marginalised as other forms of identification become more relevant to contemporary living.

The point here is less to attempt to second-guess the future than to accept that the very theories we rely on to inform and explain the nature of our 'national' identity are themselves the product of a specific historical evolution. And it is the assumption that they are the result of reliable scientific advance in our knowledge that leads us to believe they are able ever more accurately to make sense of what is happening to our identities. But, clearly, the question of integration has now exposed the limits of these theories' capacity to provide the answers that are required if we are to rethink the problems in a more constructive way. To return to the original question: multiculturalism *per se* is obviously not 'the' answer. But perhaps a key aspect of the problem is that we are looking for 'one' answer – in part, no doubt, because our rationality commits us to think 'scientifically' in terms of a 'single' answer to every question.

Religion: should there be more mosques in Europe?

In November 2009 the Swiss held a referendum on whether to give permission for the construction of new mosque minarets. To the astonishment of the world and the great embarrassment of the mainstream Swiss political class, the vote confirmed the Swiss People's Party's and the Federal Democratic Union's populist campaign and went against further construction. The result triggered an avalanche of commentaries throughout Europe and the wider world, most of which deplored a provocative and xenophobic attitude that would inflame Muslim opinion. Rather fewer voices pointed out that the decision was the outcome of a democratic vote and the result of obvious disquiet among a majority of (admittedly inward-looking) Swiss citizens. But this vote triggered a debate that had not fully surfaced until then: how can Islam be practised in an ostensibly secular Europe?

The genuine shock that greeted the outcome of the referendum was in keeping with the view that integration is best achieved by allowing multicultural and multi-religious diversity to flourish. However, this is now clearly countered by a growing body of opinion in the West that Islam as it is increasingly being practised in what are believed to be Wahabi mosques is not compatible with European values. And here the confusion begins. On the one hand, all European countries stand constitutionally in support of religious freedom. Discrimination on grounds of religion is illegal and there is general support for the notion that each person is at liberty to live his/her particular faith to the full. On the other, there is growing unease at the realisation that some Muslims see it as their obligation to live a life that ill fits the European mould and to engage in a type of religious politics that is unacceptable to the West. The voice of the extremists, who claim to want to establish the Caliphate in Europe, is increasingly (and unfairly) seen by popular opinion to represent the views of Muslims settled in the West.

I do not want here to enter this increasingly sterile debate, which has evidently acquired the 'national' garb of the country in which it takes place. Rather, I want to try to tease out the assumptions that inform both sides of the argument. In so doing, I shall show that the discussion of the place of Islam in the West is vitiated by the way in which we think through this issue. And the debate about Islam is opening up the whole question of the place of religion in our societies. Thus, the matter of whether to allow the construction of more mosques, or even minarets, is really a question about how we conceive of the role of religion in our own countries. And this in turn brings out the issue of the West's reaction to the non-West's attitude to religion, religiosity and secularism. So, the question is not only that which is commonly asked – can there be a European form of Islam? – but also whether the way we conceptualise religion is fit for present purposes.

As is my wont, I engage this question by way of three distinct angles of attack. The first is a brief discussion of how historically Islam has been regarded in Europe. The second is a round-up of the assumptions underlying that discussion. The third is an attempt to show why it is that our approach to the question of religion sets limits to the reach of our analysis.

The history of the relations between the West and Islam is a long and fraught one, which is not my subject here. Rather, I should like to show which aspects of its legacy are relevant to the present situation. The nineteenth century, and the onset of colonial rule, presented a dual image of that religion. On the one hand, Orientalist scholarship often painted a picture of Islam that combined a mix of shrewd and romantic appreciation, which was generally positive.[11] On the other hand, the historical memory of the long-standing clashes between Christian West and Muslim East going back to the Crusades informed a colonial view of Islam as dangerous and violent. The travails of the end of the Ottoman Empire, the 1857 Rebellion in India and the encounter between the French and the Arabs in the Maghreb resulted in a fair degree of hostility. The French, like the British, tended to consider the Muslim 'tribes' in their colonies as possessed of special toughness and warrior-like qualities. There was thus a degree of respect for kingdoms and empires ruled by Muslim autocracies. And the realities of indirect rule in Africa showed that the colonial powers preferred to find accommodation with, rather than fight, Muslim rulers.

However, the West also came to admire the Sufi tradition in Islam, which it duly exoticised, and it was impressed by the attempts of Muslim thinkers and politicians to find ways of 'modernising' Islamic political theory and practice. The forward-looking and accommodating teachings of Muslims as far apart as Sir Syed Khan, the father of modern Islamic education in India, and Amadou Bamba, the founder of the Mouride Brotherhood in Senegal, seemed to indicate ways in which West and Islam might work together. And Atatürk's radical revolution in Turkey gave the impression that the political 'modernisation' of Islam would entail the 'Westernisation' of its political system. The non-West could become the West. If nationalism gave warning to the colonial powers that Islam could also be mobilised to claim independence, the leftist leanings of most anti-colonial rebels alarmed them because of the danger of communism, not Islam. Indeed, the colonial rulers often found allies in the more conservative Muslim

---

11. For a critique of this notion of 'orientalism', see Said, 1978.

elites who feared godless Marxism more than they resented the often comfortable relationship they entertained with a relatively respectful colonial master.

The move in the Arab world, except in the Gulf States, towards secular (often socialist) politics, as embodied by Nasser and displayed violently in Algeria, confirmed the West's impression that Islam was progressively being 'modernised'. Therefore the large-scale immigration of Algerians to France, Turks to Germany and Asian Muslims to Britain was not believed to raise any particularly serious *religious* problems by the Europeans. These Muslim immigrants would be free to worship and practise their religion whilst they adapted to the strictures of life and work in the West. The discreet and pliable attitude ostensibly exhibited by the early immigrants seemed to indicate that religion would not be an issue. No particular attention was paid to the provision of appropriate places of worship since, especially in the early days, Muslim immigrants made no pressing demand for the construction of mosques, being content with the allocation of locales for prayer in ordinary buildings. Such an attitude was in keeping with the West's expectations of religion as belonging to the private sphere within a secular society.

This vision of Islam as a 'secular religion' in the making began to change in the West with the realisation that secular politics in the Middle East was increasingly challenged by reformist movements, of which the epitome was the Muslim Brotherhood in Egypt. Furthermore, it became clear in the 1970s that the religious dispensation of the oil-producing Gulf States, particularly Saudi Arabia, now began to exercise greater influence throughout the Muslim world. The financial clout generated by petroleum export was increasingly being used to sponsor the spread of Wahabi Islam beyond Islamic countries. Although the West did not at first worry unduly about these developments, they were obviously caught unawares when they realised that the funding of that conservative form of Islam now extended to Europe.

However, it was the rise of al-Qaeda and the anti-Western terrorist campaign it helped to unleash that transformed the vision of Islam in the West and changed radically the Westerners' perception of European Muslims. The savagery of these attacks and the realisation that many of them were hatched by Muslims living in the West was a shock. The fact that these attacks were justified by a type of Islamic thinking which received some (if very limited) support among a few Muslim immigrants in the West was traumatic to Westerners. Almost overnight, Islam came to be viewed not as one of many faiths, but as a religion that was both incompatible with and hostile to Western values. The volte-face was as extreme as the belief that Islam could not be but an extremist religion. Suddenly, the West re-examined Islam and many began to argue that it was a faith incapable of being modernised and thus irredeemably alien to contemporary Western societies.

This brutal reversal of a long tradition of benign paternalism towards Islam exposes the assumptions made by the West in regard to that religion – and by implication all religions. It was less the resort to terrorism by militants using Islam as a weapon of war than the acknowledgement of a 'new' face of Islam in Europe that revealed the limits of the West's understanding of that religion. After all, terrorists who happened to be Muslim (like the Palestinians in the 1970s and 1980s) had already used terrorism in the pursuit of clearly asserted political objectives. But the argument that terrorism was now to be used in aid of a Muslim 'religious' revolution (aiming ultimately at establishing the Caliphate in the West) seemed to be beyond the comprehension of a Western world that had long taken for granted that religion belonged to the private sphere and that faith was not a matter of politics. It now found that the theoretical and analytical instruments it used to conceptualise religion were unable to make sense of what appeared to be a new, *modern*, trend in contemporary Islam. The difficulties for the West were twofold: one concerned the meaning of secularism; the other had to do with the common assumptions about the development of the social 'individual' in the West.[12]

Secularism as it has arisen in Europe is the outcome of a long and violent evolution leading eventually to the separation of State and Church. This process, perhaps most fully applied in post-Revolution France and least fully in post-Restoration Britain, constitutionally removed all political power from the Church. Furthermore, it established rules (albeit unwritten in the case of Britain) for the exercise of religion, now confined to a spiritual or ceremonial role. Simultaneously, there emerged an understanding (if not always a consensus) that religion belonged to the private realm and ought not to have particular purchase in the organisation and operation of political, social or economic institutions. This may have been an illusion, but favour or discrimination on account of religious belief was outlawed, even if in practice matters of faith (or Freemasonry) continued to exercise strong influence.

Whatever the concrete legal framework that enshrined secularism in the different countries, the net effect of these developments was to consolidate the assumption that religion is to be confined to the modern citizen's personal spiritual space. A consequence of that presumption is that secularism has become a foundational ideological plank of the 'modern' way of thinking. This implies not just that it is taken for granted but also that it embodies a sense of superiority over those societies where it does not prevail. In other words, secularism has become equated with 'modernity'. It is partly for this reason that the West finds it well-nigh impossible to fathom why Western-born individuals should want to 'revert' to a

---

12. Here see, among many, Kepel, 2004.

non-secular way of life. It is also partly for that reason that Western governments view with great alarm the policies of the Turkish government – whose religious inclinations are adduced as further argument why the country should not be admitted into the EU.

Returning to the question of the individual, both the lessons of the evolution of Western societies since the Enlightenment and the theories evolved to account for the social transformation of the West stress the emergence of the discrete individual possessed of free will as the centrepiece of 'modern' society. The consequence is that it is also assumed that religion is entirely a matter of *personal* faith. The individual receives and practises his/her religion in a private space, into which others only enter by invitation. Furthermore, it is also assumed that this *is* the 'modern' way of living one's religion, so that by implication any other form of worship is *ipso facto* seen to be 'traditional', when not backward. There is thus a normative judgement attached to the religious life of the individual. And it is this assumption about the 'modernisation' of the process of individualisation in our societies that has become equated with the superior virtues of Westernisation.

Now, there may well be merit in the preference for this form of individual secularism over what is on offer in Wahabi Saudi Arabia, and countless Muslims, in and outside the West, also subscribe to the ideal of secularism. But this is not my argument. My point is simply that the assumptions underlying our understanding of religion in the West makes it virtually impossible to conceptualise other forms of religious practice. This matters, since there are now in our countries a number of Muslim citizens who do not accept these premises and challenge society to accept their distinct standpoint. Their numbers are small and their claims largely unsupported by the majority of Muslim Europeans, but their defiance of Western political, social and constitutional norms has provoked inordinate and sometimes inconsiderate reactions.

As a result, Western governments have been at a loss how to react. The responses have ranged from benign neglect to drastic legislation, with much hand-wringing in between. But whichever the reaction, the common denominator has been the failure to conceive of the issue other than in strictly conventional Western terms.

The present move in Western Europe to ban the *burqa* is a good example of the limitation of our thinking.[13] Whilst the arguments for and against the ban are perfectly consistent with the two strands of secular Europe – the unacceptability of the social constriction of women and the freedom to choose one's attire unimpeded – the ground upon which the disagreements occur is shared. The arguments take it for granted that the wearing of the *burqa* is primarily to be analysed both within the parameters of the individual's place in 'modern' society and on the assumption that religion is a private act. The further dilemma for social theory is that those who choose to wear the covering robe and scarf are usually Western-born and -educated, when not converts – thus making it plain that they are 'modern' rather than foreign and 'backward'. And there is simply no good theory to account for such behaviour in our own Western societies. The wearing of the *burqa* is conceptualised as either a sign of 'backwardness' or as incomprehensible – at best to be explained in psychological terms. It is, on the face of our social theory, not 'rational'.

Like the construction of minarets, the wearing of the *burqa* induces a response in our own societies which goes against the principles enshrined in our constitutions and which is ultimately counterproductive. Indeed, this overreaction is proof that the assessment of the vastly exaggerated potential 'danger' of these symbolic acts is a measure of the fear induced among apparently

---

13. See Silvestri, 2011.

rational societies that pride themselves in their scientific reasoning. My point here is not to debate whether any of these decisions makes sense – they obviously do make sense in their own, limited, terms – but to suggest that the overreaction is a consequence of the inability to step out of the constrained rationality of our social science form of thinking. A reconsideration of whether we are *only* discrete individuals and whether religious secularism is *always* incompatible with those who choose to see themselves primarily in religious terms would obviously lead us in other analytical directions, which I explore later in the book.

Culture: is Beckham the new black icon?

In 2003 the British independent television company Channel 4 made a programme in which it suggested that the (white) footballer David Beckham was now a 'black icon'. The show cited his taste in clothes, cars and music as effectively making him an honorary black man. The programme makers held they had a point to make in that the meaning of race was now no longer confined to skin colour but involved a style and way of life. Since Beckham was thought to have borrowed so much from black culture, it was now fair game – and amusingly provocative – to set him as a black icon. Executive producer Bruce Hepton said:

> We are being light-hearted by calling Beckham Britain's most famous black man, but he really does behave like he's black. On a superficial level, he looks like he's stepped out of a P Diddy video. He wears the bling bling jewellery and the clothes, he drives a Bentley convertible – he even called his dogs Puffy and Snoop.

The presenter, broadcaster Paul McKenzie, observed: 'He's a sex god, he's a ghetto superstar. He's got black style and he's accepted by black people as a hero.'[14]

---

14. www.dailymail.co.uk/tvshowbiz/article-172057/Beckham-new-black.html.

Although the programme was castigated by a large number of black Britons, who claimed that it had peddled the worst type of clichés about black people, it resonated with many, including white admirers of the footballer.[15] Clearly, the suggestion that Beckham was a black icon chimed with the times and with a widespread (though not universal) notion that the term 'culture' could be applied to lifestyle and tastes. It also brought to the fore the idea that culture now trumped race in contemporary Britain. Indeed, the fact that the programme had such an impact suggests that the perception of identity and image (and even gender) had been so thoroughly transformed that they could subvert such an apparently non-negotiable characteristic as race. What could it all mean?

In the first instance, the affair implied that the marker 'black' now transcended race. Although this epithet has long been adopted by other minorities to infer that they felt discriminated against, it had hitherto mostly concerned racially distinct peoples such as South Asians.[16] But it was now extended to whites, and not on account of discrimination – thus apparently dissolving the red line that separates ('Caucasian') locals from people of African or Afro-Caribbean origin in contemporary Britain. This is a significant change, not just because that racial divide is rightly taken to be the widest in social terms but also because it is clearly the case that blacks have suffered most from racism in the West. For a mainstream television programme to step onto such delicate territory meant it believed there had been sufficient change in society.

Second, the debate brought to the fore the undeniable fact that black culture (as understood in the programme) had an increasingly powerful hold over taste and identity in Western society. It was now no longer just black music, which proved influential, but a whole way of life. Admittedly, the black celebrities still appeared

---

15. A similar controversy has raged in the USA over Eminem as a white rapper.
16. Salman Rushdie once claimed he was 'black'.

to come from the musical world (primarily that of the rappers) but this was still a significant move. All the more so since these supposed icons have long been rebuked, even within the black community, for peddling violence, misogyny and crudeness. That such inadequate role models should now appear to be associated with someone like Beckham, who has cultivated the opposite image, was nothing short of astonishing. Tongue-in-cheek the programme may have been but it certainly touched on very sensitive issues indeed.

Third, and perhaps most importantly, this affair revealed an interesting shift in the understanding of what constitutes Western popular culture. That shift reflects a genuine trend in Western societies: namely, the growing influence of both 'lower class' and non-Western characteristics upon conventional lifestyle. The former is not new, of course: ever since the 1950s there has been in the West a strong component of 'working-class' manners in the demeanour of the middle classes. And films like *Room at the Top* and *This Sporting Life* were instrumental in giving glamour to the working-class hero. However, the present influence of non-Western, or black, culture on ordinary European youth is a decidedly new phenomenon, which deserves attention. Much as the programme irritated black activists, it nevertheless pointed to what might be seen as a positive change: 'black style' now permeated popular culture. Or, to put it another way, the accoutrement and tastes of that perennially discriminated section of the population could be seen as the harbinger of a change towards a less racist society.

Thus the question of whether Beckham was, is or ever could be a 'black icon' goes well beyond the controversy generated by the television programme. It raises a number of issues that are at the heart of any discussion of Western values, ideals and even rationality. Of these, I should like to take up two: how significant is it that such changes are taking place in popular culture; and in which ways do these changes in culture reflect a more profound shift in the West's sensitivity to the non-West – changes that may affect its self-perception?

The significant aspect of the Beckham story is that it breaks the race taboo. But its more relevant meaning is that it makes manifest a change that has been taking place whereby young people in the West associate themselves with the popular culture of the racial 'other'. This obviously includes musical taste: everyone now listens to rap. It also extends to clothing style: the falling, baggy jeans have become the sartorial signature of many young males. And it has now permeated the very language and accent used by Western youth, as is blindingly obvious in France where *beur* and black mannerisms, twang and vocabulary are now ubiquitous. It is a great paradox, and certainly poetic justice, that middle-class white French teenagers should now speak like the North Africans so despised by society at large. A similar process is under way in the USA, where black influence on language, style and deportment is profound.[17]

Indeed, of all the changes currently taking place, language is probably the most momentous since it demonstrates the power of popular culture on one of the key markers of identity. Educational institutions are on the front line of such linguistic tensions. On the one hand, they are expected to teach the basics of 'proper' or received language and to expose pupils to the canons of Western literature. On the other hand, they are under increasing pressure to recognise the changes taking place in society and thus to give more prominence to 'popular' forms of expression. Does this mean that, if Shakespeare and Dickens no longer matter much, rap music and Caribbean storytelling should become the more relevant linguistic models? Perhaps not, but the question of which form of

---

17. See, as one example, the American television series *The Wire*, in which black parlance is dominant.

'literature' will serve to improve linguistic expression in today's Britain is one that it is difficult to avoid. The same goes for most other Western countries.

What appears a mutation in apparently fairly innocuous aspects of youth lifestyle, such as slang and clothing, represents in fact a deeper transformation of society than may at first be apparent. Popular culture is in this way merely the portent of changes that reflect more profound, if perhaps more subterranean, social movements. Of course, it may well be argued that these are but superficial indicators. The fact that affluent 18-year-olds in France or Britain should unthinkingly inflect their speech patterns to mimic those of the 'underclass' will not deprive them of the privileges their parents have secured for them. Even if Prince Harry should like rap talk, it does not mean he will be any less a member of his upper class. This is true as far as it goes but it does not gainsay the argument that such influences may in due course affect mainstream ways of seeing, and thinking about, the world. Could it be that in years to come one of the European royals will marry someone from a different ethnic or racial background – as they now routinely cast their lot with partners from 'lower' classes? Will there one day be a black royal consort?

What even a cursory examination of contemporary popular culture in the West shows is that the most potent and dynamic sources of change now tend to come from diverse ethnic/racial inspiration. This is reminiscent of the effect the new generation of 'working class' writers, singers and moviemakers had in the late 1950s and early 1960s in Britain. The 'angry young men' and the Beatles brought about a cultural revolution, which marked literature and music for generations to come. If that parallel has any merit, then it would tend to suggest that the so-called black, or more generally non-Western, influence is not just meaningful but could in due course translate into other important social transformations. Returning to language, it is no coincidence that the BBC opened up both its recruitment and its speech patterns in the wake of the impact made by that fiercely bright generation of writers and academics who hailed from working-class backgrounds but benefited from grammar-school education. Will *beur* talk make its appearance on France Culture in the future?

Beyond these more obvious effects, mutations in popular culture also point to less visible changes in values. A renewal in style, taste and leisure allows a different vision of aesthetic norms. Just as the introduction of paid leave in the 1930s brought the masses to the beach and ultimately legitimised bronzing, today's ethnic/racial influences might herald a fresh look at the canon of beauty and attractiveness. There is a long way to go yet: many blacks and Asians still try to lighten their skin. But the gradual acceptance of sun-darkened skin and dreadlocks among whites may mark the beginning of a change that might in due course make black physiognomy more attractive to the majority of the white European population. Racism is deeply ingrained in all peoples, but the increasing frequency of mixed-race marriages in Western Europe is, among others, surely a sign that aesthetic racism is reducing. People from different races now increasingly find each other beautiful – not just interesting.

But in which ways are these changes affecting the West's self-perception and what consequences might this have on the foundations of its rationality? At a very basic level, it reveals an interesting normative inversion. In the course of a century the West has gone from the conviction that it must 'civilise' the lower, backward races, to the embracing within its own societies of some aspects of the culture of these so-called inferior peoples. Admittedly, a liking for rap or African highlife is not the same as the conversion of Britons to witchcraft, and there is still in the West widespread revulsion at some of the non-Western practices, such as genital mutilation. Nevertheless, both the notion that the non-West has a deep (rather than superficial) culture and that such culture might now permeate the former coloniser societies are significant facts. Fashion and taste are no longer the preserve of a European, or Western, aesthetic sensibility; they now range as wide as the mix of peoples who have settled in the West. We have not yet reached the stage when white women will prefer a 'black' braided hairstyle but it is no longer as outrageously inconceivable as it was, even twenty or thirty years ago.

A change in the aesthetic or musical taste is clearly a fairly shallow marker of the transformation of society. After all, a century ago the major European painters were deeply influenced by African art and that did not result in less racism. The difference, of course, is that today the West is home to millions of people of non-Western origin who, though thoroughly Westernised, still cherish, cultivate and celebrate some key aspects of the cultures of their forefathers. It took a long time before blues and jazz, the music of the former slaves, imposed themselves on the Western musical canon. The influences are now swifter and more permanent, since they are brought about via a population of younger native-born citizens who no longer simply aspire to the white, Western bourgeois normative universe. And this is more ominous for Western societies. The danger in the French *banlieues* is not the risk of violence but the abandonment of the 'republican' values that underpin French society. Are alienated *beurs* no longer French or are they changing the meaning of Frenchness?

The process by which foreign, exotic, non-Western taste and aesthetic norms influenced the West is not new: Chinese and Arab art brought sophistication to the West. But the imperial West asserted its values upon the world with little regard for other views and its (political and economic) might imposed a normative order that brooked little dissent. And today many believe that globalisation is the continuation of this cultural imperialism by another name. But this is a narrow instrumental view of what is going on. The more original and subversive impact of globalisation is precisely the reverse: the penetration of non-Western art, culture and taste into Western societies. The great museum exhibitions in the West today seek to place Western artistic evolution within the more global context of the reciprocal influences between different parts of the world.[18] Popular programmes on science and mathematics now show clearly that the present Western achievements are but the latest in a long chain of knowledge that came to us via the non-West.

Thus, the vision of the West as indissolubly related to, and legitimately reassessed by, the non-West is a recent development, which has been brought about and accelerated by the presence and influence of non-Westerners in our midst. But whilst Western societies may take pride in their 'rainbow' cultural mix, they still often baulk at the behaviour and values displayed by their non-Western population. Yes to Afro-Caribbean music and multicoloured fabric – and even to mixed marriages – but no to polygamy or to the *burqa* – not to mention female genital mutilation. These values strike at the core of the West's perception of itself. Again, it is not that these 'backward' practices still exist in our midst that is worrisome since there is near-universal consensus that they are objectionable. Rather, it is the fact that some locally born and educated citizens of the West should willingly support them, on the ground that they represent the values of the societies from which their forefathers came. What appears at first to be merely a rather jejune reaction to Western arrogance mutates into a spirited or militant defence of offensive, often abhorrent and increasingly illegal acts: a deliberate challenge to Western 'rationality'.

---

18. Witness the 2010 West Africa Sculpture Exhibition at the British Museum, which made every effort to present the African material in an international context.

Whilst Western governments have remained firm on the banning of practices they (and the majority of the electorate) consider to be objectionable, or non-negotiable, there has been a notable breach in the Western cultural consensus. Of course, no-one in the West, least of all women, would support female genital mutilation. But there has been a remarkable evolution in respect of the covering of women, even among Western feminists. And here there is a most interesting dissonance between women in France and in the USA. In the former, there is near-universal agreement among women, including Muslim, that the banning of the scarf in schools and of the *burqa* in public places is desirable.[19] The reasoning is simple: republican values, of which the equality of all citizens is the key, cannot tolerate practices that challenge secularism and seemingly validate the oppression of women. In the USA, individual freedom – including that of covering oneself – trumps the other constitutional principles of equality and non-discrimination on grounds of race, sex or religion. And this has resulted in the paradoxical situation whereby some American feminists support the wearing of the veil and the home confinement of Muslim women who so choose. In other words, restrictive piety can override secularism if it is freely willed.[20]

This surprising position raises the issue of what is often called cultural relativism – that is, the view in the West that non-Western values, norms or practices that go against the grain ought to be accepted because we owe due respect to those non-Western 'traditions'. There are two aspects to this question that are relevant here. One is the claim that it has now become part of the Western normative armoury to give equal respect to other 'traditions', no matter how different or alien they may be. This

---

19. The 2003 Stasi Commission in France, set up to assess the relevance of *laïcité* to the wearing of the scarf in schools, included Muslim members who agreed with the recommendation to ban the garment from state schools.
20. See Scott, 2007; Mahmood, 2005.

implies a transposition of the principle of equality from individuals to wholesale 'cultures' – as though these were well defined and clearly delineated ensembles. The other is the deliberate subversion, or suppression, of some key Western moral principles on the grounds that the West cannot now stand in judgement of other peoples' norms and values. This entails the tacit acceptance of what is otherwise anathema – a strange ethical volte-face on the part of a West that has for so long stood firm in the belief of its moral and cultural superiority.

Unemployment: is globalisation to blame?

Of all the problems currently affecting the West, none, I would argue, is as pressing as that of unemployment. This is so for three reasons, which are related to the above discussion. One is that work (that is, paid employment) is at the core of individual identity in the West. People who do not work are often seen, and indeed may consider themselves, as inadequate since self-worth is now so intimately bound up with employment and the ability to consume. The second is that the cost of social security and pension provisions is now crippling Western economies. The greater unemployment is, the lesser tax receipts are and the higher workless benefits become. This economic shortfall, with its potential for stringent reform and swingeing cuts, threatens the welfare expectations of Western citizens. Finally, unemployment is often seen in the West as being the outcome of immigration, for it is believed that foreigners take away (usurp?) the jobs the locals believe they are entitled to have. Thus, high levels of unemployment tend to generate strong dissatisfaction, which focuses on the culpability of foreign immigrants settled in the West and frequently degenerates into racism and xenophobic politics.

Clearly, unemployment is not just an economic problem. It is also a social, cultural issue, which challenges the West's sense of itself and its conception of the good life. But first, what does the 2008–12 economic crisis tell us about the West? I shall leave aside here the technical arguments about the nature of the world economic system, except to say that present trends point to three clear conclusions.

The first is that, left to the devices invented by its most zealous financial practitioners, and contrary to standard economic theory, the world market is incapable of regulating itself. And its convulsions threaten the economies and well-being of all peoples, including in the West. We are now all at risk of an economic collapse that would have dire consequences for our way of life. Of all the hazards we face, unemployment would come first. Clearly, our fate is in the hands of government – however devoted we may be to the capitalist cause. Therefore the paradoxical lesson of the early part of the twenty-first century is that we are subject to a global economic system which only individual states can regulate; hence the need for international cooperation of some sort.

The second conclusion is that our understanding of climate change has for the first time checked the notion that growth will in and of itself resolve the economic problems faced by Western societies. Although there is still doubt about global warming in some quarters, the recognition of its consequences is slowly gaining ground. So is the realisation that, as resources are finite, the logic of our economic system cannot rest on the premiss of continued expansion. However, here the West is confronted with a difficult dilemma: the non-West wants to accelerate economic development and intends to do so by means that are likely to contribute greatly to climate change and the depletion of natural resources. So, the putative solutions to this double conundrum are largely out of the hands of the once dominant West, which will now have to pay an economic price for international cooperation. Although it is claimed that technological innovation will eventually devise the means to move to a 'greener' economy, that transition is likely to be disproportionately costly to the West.

The last conclusion is that, as presently devised, the economic system that sustains the West's way of life is more likely than not to lead to greater unemployment. The crisis that broke in 2008 shows clearly that one of the main policy options for Western governments is to cut back on state expenditures. But since so many are employed by the state, particularly in Western Europe, and so much economic activity depends on state investment, this has drastic consequences and results in large-scale job losses. And because of the welfare system, greater unemployment inevitably increases state expenditure. This can easily become a vicious circle, putting enormous pressure on governments to reform the welfare provisions by reducing social expenditures – and in particular unemployment benefits. Such policies inevitably impact strongly on the quality of life of those without employment and have serious political consequences, domestically and in the international arena.

The economic crisis and thus unemployment are commonly attributed (and not just in the West) to the effects of globalisation. Although the exact meaning of that term is often obscure, it is understood by popular opinion to refer to the myriad economic links that bind us to business worldwide, and to the financial flows and commercial exchanges over which no single country has control. It is assumed not just that we are now more dependent on a world economic system that is beyond our remit but also that we cannot devise any economic policy independently from what is happening elsewhere in the world. The fact that our governments claim their ability to address the consequences of the economic crisis is largely constrained by international factors serves to reinforce the message that it is the world market, or globalisation, which is to blame. Whilst the politicians' message is that we need to cooperate across borders to resolve these issues, the local reaction to the crisis is more focused on the damage this 'outside' globalisation is inflicting on people.

This perception of a 'hostile' world has had a strong influence on our views of the non-West and is having an impact on our sense of identity and our thinking. Whilst most economists stress the beneficial aspects of a globalised economic system – its flexibility and lower consumer prices – the reality of the crisis focused public attention on its dangers. The cry today in the West is about the looming economic dominance of China, and soon India, and the perception that unemployment is made worse by the unfair competition of immigrants willing to work for less. What is common to both is the fear of the outside and the realisation that the West is no longer 'secure'. This fear, to which Western politicians all too easily fall prey, is at odds with the vision of a dominant West, long held by Westerners and non-Westerners alike, which has sustained our system of beliefs and our identity.

The fear finds its most concrete expression in the obsession about the threat of unemployment that now stalks the West. Indeed, the problem with joblessness, particularly among young people, is that it implies a reversal of the expected social trajectory. It is not just that those who are not employed lose both purpose and morale in a society that values work and material possessions. It is also that the lack of job opportunities to match both skills and educational qualifications enforces a downward social trajectory, with its attendant disillusionment. This negative social mobility goes against the core expectation in the West that our economies are able to offer economic advancement for all those who work hard. In turn, this can lead to a belief that the ethos of capitalism is built on a lie and can result in (especially) young people opting out of the system, when not actively militating against it.

The erosion of the belief in the Western ideology of individual and collective progress is already beginning to affect the social fabric of our societies. There is, first, what might be called a loss of nerve. The prospect that our economic system might no longer manage either to provide employment or to offer social assistance to the jobless is unsettling. It has social and psychological effects, which are not yet clear, but which will undoubtedly change people's outlook on life, work and well-being. The effects of what psychologists term cognitive dissonance – that is, the perception of an excessive gap between expectation and reality – induce a sense of confusion that eats away at the foundations of self-worth. It is notable that in areas where there is a concentration of very high unemployment (sometimes over several generations) people's goals, values and identity have shifted markedly. In extreme cases, such as some French *banlieues*, there has developed a ghetto mentality that cuts off the local population from the rest of society – thus creating what has been referred to as a 'Fourth World', wholly disconnected from mainstream society. And it is argued by some that those who live there act as social 'parasites' – manipulating the social welfare system to their advantage whilst arguing that they have no need to put anything back into a society that has turned against them.

The flip side of this process is that a growing number of people in the West now consider this 'Fourth World' a hostile, largely non-Western, force within. Many of the unemployed blame 'foreign' immigrants for taking their jobs, even though studies have shown both that the majority of immigrants take jobs that the locals do not want and that they make a net positive contribution to the national economy.[21] The problem is not with current immigrants. It is that unemployment affects disproportionately the second- and third-generation descendants of earlier immigrants, who harbour great resentment at the blame attached to their communities. They

---

21. See, among many, 'Why Immigrants Aren't Taking British Jobs', *Telegraph*, 30 January 2012.

sometimes react with a rejection of the local values and ideals, turning instead to those of their forefathers' lands or religion, which they all too easily romanticise. In what turns out to be a self-fulfilling prophecy, this commitment to a non-Western view of politics or religion marks them out as a potential 'fifth column'. So, for instance, the fact that a tiny number of Western Muslims are willing to use terrorist methods to strike at their country of birth casts a dark shadow over all Western Muslims.

The net result is that there is now a potentially dangerous fault line appearing in Western societies, dividing those who feel they are the victims of unemployment and those who continue to believe in the benefits of globalisation. This fault line tends to pit the West against the non-West in two ways. There is, first, a perception that the economic future lies in the non-West, which is now an economic force threatening the West. And, second, there is a widespread belief that 'non-Western' immigrants are undermining the social fabric of Western societies. This has political consequences, as is being demonstrated by the shifting agendas of both fringe nationalist parties and mainstream formations – illustrated by electoral results in Western Europe in the last ten years.[22] Although environmental issues are slowly coming to the forefront, it is noticeable that this concern too is now also often being reinterpreted in terms of a clash between West and non-West. Both economy and ecology knock at the long-held Western sense of superiority and create an atmosphere that can, indeed has, become politically corrosive.

So, under the guise of unemployment, the present economic crisis brings to the fore a number of challenges to Western rationality. These fall into two distinct categories. One has to do with

---

22. Parties campaigning on an anti-immigrant platform have received a high, and rising, number of votes in countries like France, the Netherlands, Austria, Switzerland, Sweden, and so on.

the relationship between economy and politics; the other with the notion of progress. Since the two are central to our way of thinking, they combine to shake both the assumptions we make about modern society and the theories we deploy to explain the world in which we live. I examine each one in turn.

The emergence of successful capitalist economies in East and Southeast Asia has confounded the presumption, still widely circulated in development circles, that economic success is predicated on liberal democracy. The experience of Japan comforted the belief that its economic boom was triggered by the democratic new start after the Second World War. What has happened since in the rest of Asia has disproved such assumptions. It is now clear that in countries ranging from South Korea to Singapore, the process has been the reverse. It is economic growth that has spurred movements towards greater political freedom. And the experience of China and Vietnam does raise the hypothesis that successful capitalist development may not result in any recognisable form of liberal democracy – *pace* Fukuyama and his ilk. If that is the case – and there are good grounds for thinking that it might well be – then much of our political theory is at stake.

If liberal democracy turns out to be not the universal path to economic growth and technological progress, but merely one of the many possible routes, then our assumptions need revising. There may well be increasing divergence between the policies adopted by various Western countries. Under pressure, each will have to decide on its core values, norms and ambitions. Not only will 'old' and 'new' Europe move in different directions but those who favour social democracy above all may well have to make economic sacrifices in order to keep a lid on inequalities: the fight against unemployment and social distress will be at the cost of economic growth. Such tensions could, for instance, strain the European Union to breaking point. Conversely, the commitment to the free market *à outrance* could erode the welfare system to such an extent that it begins to threaten social peace. Here, governments might want to curtail democratic freedoms in order to maintain 'order'. This also would be deleterious to the survival of the European Union, as the 2012 euro crisis showed.

On the world scene, the obvious economic strides achieved by China reinforce the belief held by many in the Third World, or South, that capitalism can thrive without democracy. This comforts those non-Western politicians who wish to develop their countries but do not subscribe to the liberal democratic ethos. Or, rather, it gives succour to the numerous non-Western governments that assert their right to their own brand of democracy. Since the West's trump card in this ideological debate is its own economic superiority, the realisation that some countries like China can chart their own way would be a serious blow against the assumption that economic modernisation means political Westernisation. Although it may appear that we in the West are comfortable with such an idea, the ways in which we devise our relations with the non-West, which I explore in the next section, show that this is not the case. Our policies are based on the presumptions we hold about Westernisation.

Indeed, the need to accept that there might be non-Western forms of modernity that offer a different mix of economic and political dispensations would be momentous for the West.[23] It would recast our notion of progress. Of course the concept of progress is hazy but in the West it rests on deep-rooted and well-understood assumptions about evolution. And these in turn rest on our understanding of the scientific revolution and of the economic advances made possible by the advent of electoral democracy. To return to the question of unemployment, which concerns us here, it is

---

23. On different paths to modernity, see Ben-Rafael and Sternberg, 2005.

clear that our idea of progress makes assumptions about economic theory. Although it is generally accepted that modern economies cannot achieve *full* employment, it is assumed that the application of the appropriate fiscal and monetary policies can reduce unemployment to a minimum. This is because the economic system is flexible enough to respond not just to changing demand, but also to the application of appropriate fiscal policies. In any event, not all economists view unemployment as a 'curse'; many see it as a self-correcting market mechanism.

However, even within the framework of standard economic theory there is a wide gap between those who tend to believe that market forces will in due course correct the imbalances in the economy and those who hold that state intervention is necessary. Despite claims to the contrary, there is no 'objective' way of proving that one is superior to the other. As a result, the influence of, respectively, Keynesian and neoclassical policy waxes and wanes according to economic and political circumstances. Nevertheless, both sides make similar assumptions about growth and technology. That is, both take for granted that growth is the answer to unemployment *and* that technological advance will be brought to bear on the concrete impediments to growth. There is thus an unstated belief in the permanent and linear improvement of our scientific knowledge and our technological innovations. That assumption is now being tested seriously for the first time, as the West is forced to adapt to the realities of global warming and the rapid depletion of oil and other natural resources.

The revision of economic theory that will likely emerge as a result of the need to price environmental and resources differently will probably have severe consequences on our policies, and our politics. In point of fact, there is already a movement in Western Europe based on what the French call *décroissance* (that is, 'degrowth') – the very idea of which implies the obsolesence of present economic theories.[24] At this stage, *décroissance* is only possible, indeed conceivable, within the context of an economy that continues to grow. Those who downsize remain utterly dependent on the economic and social opportunities the world outside their front door continues to offer. However, if growth should no longer be the mainstay of our economies, then it is clear that apparently cast-iron assumptions will be blown away and new theories will emerge. Perhaps the notions of employment and unemployment will disappear, to be replaced by a yet-to-be-invented concept of paid/unpaid occupation.

Whatever happens, we are now certainly nearing the end of the monopoly of a type of Western economic rationality and of its corollary political economy. That economic theory should have to evolve is, or should be, par for the course – as the model of the physical sciences shows. But having to accept that economics is not a science may turn out to be more consequential, since it would then mean that we would have to reconsider our assumptions about the social sciences as a whole. I return to these questions in the second half of the book. For now, I turn to a number of international issues that cause the West concern today.

Abroad

If our domestic problems reveal clearly the limits of our understanding of these important social and economic issues, the relations we in the West entertain with the rest of the world are even more pregnant with meaning. Here, we come face to face with the full realities of the confrontation between West and non-West. Not only are we engaged in the continual reappraisal of our links with the former colonies and in the management of a post-Cold

---

24. See Latouche, 2006. The French term *décroissance* means 'degrowth' – that is, the opposite of growth. It is usually referred to as 'downsizing' in English.

War world but we are now in the throes of the so-called war on terror – the new cold war is against the Muslim non-West! And it is all taking place within the context of the widespread, though confused, effects of accelerated globalisation. All these problems raise fundamental questions about how we relate to the rest of the world. It is, of course, impossible plausibly to address them properly in this short chapter. Instead, my aim will be to look at a few key areas of our international relations, in order to examine both how we frame them and how we try to tackle them. Again, this is a very small selection, which does not attempt to cover what might be of greatest importance in foreign policy terms today. It is merely one possible way to approach the study of the relevance, and impact, of the non-West on our way of thinking, and on our rationality.

Human rights: are values universal?

Of all the issues that impinge on the West's relation with the rest of the world, that of human rights is critical. Not only does it inform a great deal of what the West says about, and does in, other countries, but it is deemed to be fundamental to the conduct of international relations. Now enshrined in the Universal Declaration of Human Rights, endorsed by the United Nations and all other international organisations, this code of conduct is usually the bedrock of written constitutions throughout the world. On the face of it, therefore, there is little to disagree about, even internationally. Indeed, it is one of the few areas of human affairs that appear to be universally recognised, if not always acknowledged, even by countries with an ostensibly poor record in the matter. And yet there are constant disagreements when it comes to the practical application of these lofty principles – disagreements that are at the root of a vast array of contentious issues between West and non-West.

The problems here are many, but they can be aggregated into the following categories: historical, moral and political. So, one of the very first causes of misunderstanding and tension is the confusion between the three when using the concept of human rights. To return to an earlier example, female genital mutilation is deemed illegal in Western countries because it is said to violate women's human rights. Yet the reason it is abhorrent is primarily moral, in that most people in Western societies consider mutilation of this kind to be repulsive, inhuman or entirely 'barbaric'. They would oppose it whether or not it was technically illegal. However, they rarely ask themselves why they are against it, and thus find it virtually impossible to entertain the argument offered by some, including women, who explain that, in some societies, it is an integral part of a woman's 'identity'. I will return to this later.

At the same time, as we have seen, many in the West (including feminists) look favourably upon the wearing of the *hijab* on the grounds that it must be seen as the freely informed decision of individual women who want to reconcile their attire with their vision of piety. In effect, it is viewed as the 'human right' of these women to dress as they please. Yet female genital mutilation could never be seen in the West as the 'human right' of those women who choose to undergo genital excision. Of course there seems to be a good enough common-sense ground for distinguishing between the two, since in one case there is actual violence committed on the woman. Nevertheless, circumcision for men is also technically an act of violence, even if it is required by two major world religions and is far less intrusive and dangerous. And comparing the degree of violence committed on men and women is surely not a very secure basis for making a moral decision.

If the above example is both extreme and to some extent simplistic, it shows clearly why the question of human rights is not so easily settled. A similar conundrum arises when trying to ascertain whether freedom from want is a human right – and, if it is, what would be the definition of 'want'. Many in Western Europe would argue that extending the reach of human right to the relief of want is indeed the mark of a 'civilised' society. But should it be included as a constitutional right? More pragmatic arguments hold that it is impossible to define 'want' since this is very largely a relative, rather than absolute, measure. Should it include a flat-screen television, or a car, or enough money to buy cigarettes? Even more controversially, should it apply to health? Should free health care be denied to those who insist on smoking or eating too much, or is that a violation of their human rights? Is the desire to have a child a human right, which ought to be subsidised by health-care provisions?

If we cannot agree what constitutes human rights in our own countries, how can we assess the situation in the rest of the world? Perhaps we might agree that each society holds its own version of what human rights are. But in fact this will not work out, and for two reasons. First, there is an agreed universal code of human rights, which is supposed to apply everywhere. Second, the question of what human rights means has strong influence on the way the West conducts its foreign affairs. And since the definitions enshrined in the Universal Declaration of Human Rights are effectively those of the West, the two are intimately connected. In international affairs, there is ostensibly no place for a 'relative' understanding of what human rights entail. West is best. So, in order to try to clarify matters, let us return to a discussion of the three aspects of the question mentioned above – namely, the historical, moral and political.

Looking at the question of human rights from a *historical* point of view, what is striking is how the definition adopted in both the Universal Declaration and all ancillary international agreements derives from the Western model. That conception of human rights is one that has evolved slowly over the centuries since the Enlightenment. But, to be even more specific, the actual provisions of such declarations are the direct descendants of those made following the American and French revolutions, which now stand as the two main pillars of the entire edifice. If it is understandable why this is the case in the West, it is nevertheless important to stress the historical circumstances that presided over this state of affairs. It is only after the Second World War, at the time of the creation of the United Nations, that these principles were laid down.[25]

Although the Soviet Union's vision of human rights was obviously at odds with those of the other victors in the Second World War, it suited them politically to subscribe to the aims of the United Nations. So long as they had a veto power, it made good diplomatic sense to show that the Communist understanding of human rights was fully compatible with those professed in the West. And it suited the West to pretend that the abominations perpetrated by the state in the Soviet Union were merely a domestic matter. No doubt this sleight of hand was justified on either side of the divide by the belief that they would ultimately prevail over the other – at which point the debate about the meaning of human rights would become redundant. Be that as it may, the net effect of this arrangement was to enshrine a code that was essentially Western. And the fact that Soviet Communism has collapsed and that many in the USA believe that their political system and way of life have indeed prevailed will add support for the Western view.[26]

Paradoxically, however, it is the end of colonial rule and the rising influence of East Asian countries that have raised more insistently the question of human rights. Because it is in these countries, rather than in Communist Europe, that the universal validity of Western notions was first challenged with any vigour.

---

25. See Moyn, 2010.
26. See Fukuyama, 2011.

In retrospect, this is not surprising. The idea that decolonisation would lead seamlessly to the adoption of Western models of human rights was comforted by what happened in India, which adhered to a Western-style democratic constitution. And Congress's early commitment to a secular and socialist agenda strengthened the view that local 'tradition' would not be allowed to stand in the way of universal human rights. Yet, India, which was soon confronted with major issues in this domain (such as the continued import of caste), turned out to be the exception rather than the rule.

In the rest of the colonial world, the ostensible espousal of Western (liberal or socialist) constitutional norms was illusory as the commitment to universal human rights was rapidly trampled underfoot. But whereas Communist Europe held that *its* constitutional provisions guaranteed human rights, the formerly colonised world has frequently argued that Western human rights were not compatible with local history, norms and culture. Since then, the booming states of East and Southeast Asia, such as Singapore and China, have added their voice to the notion that the so-called universal human rights actually embody Western values. Therefore each country ought to be left free to decide for itself the meanings and scope of its own human rights without interference from outside. Whilst this position is widely seen in the West as a smokescreen for the abuse of such rights, the argument does raise the question: are there, or can there be, such things as 'universal' human rights?[27]

Those who answer yes to that question often defend their stance on *moral* grounds. Here the contest is between the universalists and the relativists. The former believe that, however differently human beings may live, there is in today's modern world a range of fundamental human rights to which they are entitled. The progress made in the West with regard to the development and protection of

---

27. See Donnelly, 1989; Griffin, 2008.

these rights must be applied to the whole of humankind. Western 'imposition' in this regard is to the benefit of non-Western peoples. The argument rests on an analogy with medicine. Just as everyone ought to be entitled to the advances made by medical science, so everyone should enjoy the protection of human rights, which are worthy in and of themselves – even if such medicine and such rights are the products of the 'imperialist' West. This notion thus rests on the assumption that there is an identifiable path to the improvement of human rights, as there is for medicine, and that it ought to be open to everyone, regardless of origin. It is our collective duty to improve these rights.

The relativists are much more cautious. Whilst usually (at least in the West) acknowledging the intrinsic merit of the Universal Declaration of Human Rights, they are concerned with the imposition of these rights to the whole world, regardless of local specificities. A few believe that the West itself has no ground on which to require non-Western countries to comply with their moral injunctions since the West's history is replete with human rights abuse. In this respect, present Western conditionalities are nothing but a continuation of its imperialist mindset. Most, however, are not comfortable with the extension of Western morality to other settings. They would condemn practices that are at odds with their (Western) beliefs but allow for others to follow them on the grounds that it was part of their 'culture'. For the relativists, then, the change to a more 'moral' stance should be self-generated and not imposed from the outside. This perspective is shared by the realists, who profess the adaptation of one's moral stance to local circumstances, whatever one's personal standpoint.[28]

This more pragmatic approach takes us to the *political* aspect of the question. The debate here is about what should be done to

---

28. Vincent, 1986 remains the best introduction to this question.

ensure that human rights are upheld in the international arena. The present configuration of world politics presents us with a dichotomised situation, which turns around the issue of how powerful individual nations are. There is an all too neat division between those countries, largely Western, which comply, or seek to comply, with international legislation and those, largely non-Western, which do not. And there is growing pressure in the West to enforce a regime of implementable measures to sanction the abuse of human rights. Of these, two are becoming increasingly important: the growing support in favour of disregarding national sovereignty when crimes against humanity or genocide take place, and the resort to juridical sanction to bring the perpetrators of the worst human rights crimes to justice.

The first implies a fundamental change in the conduct of international relations, overturning the Westphalian principles that have hitherto underpinned the conduct of interstate affairs.[29] This consists in the absolute respect for the sovereignty of internationally recognised states unless a declaration of war has been made or, nowadays, unless action is approved by the UN. But the new model, for which a large number of NGOs have been lobbying, would make it incumbent on states, with or even without UN approval, to intervene militarily in cases where there were gross violations of human rights. If present thinking focuses primarily on genocide or ethnic cleansing, it is already being envisaged that it would cover an even wider variety of 'crimes', including perhaps criminal neglect resulting in famine. Now, this new right of intervention would obviously reshape international relations. And this approach, although it may appear both commonsensical and in keeping with the growing importance of human rights, raises

---

29. Westphalia refers to the treaties signed in 1648 to mark the end of the Thirty Years War. The Westphalian principles refer to the system of international relations built on the sovereignty of individual states and a system of diplomacy that only recognised state actors.

a host of difficult questions, which are at the heart of the relations between West and non-West, and which I discuss later.

The same goes for the operation of the various international tribunals, whether ad hoc or permanent, which are now supposed to sanction the abuse of human rights and make it impossible for political leaders to escape justice. Here again there seem to be unimpeachable moral grounds for ensuring that criminal politicians should be brought to book. But the (largely Western) good intentions run against what is often perceived as the outside imposition of justice by the powerful. In the first place, as in Nuremberg, it is the victors who enforce sanctions. If Milosevic had triumphed it is doubtful he would have been indicted. Today, Omar al-Bashir remains in power in Sudan and he receives plenty of (African and other) support in defiance of the International Court of Justice (ICJ), precisely on the grounds that the ICJ is biased against Africans. Furthermore, it is clear that this new principle will not be applied to strong states like China, regardless of the West's view about that country's political repression and violations of human rights. Who would sanction China?

Those who argue for the right of intervention and the extension of the international tribunals to all do so on the grounds of the universal validity of human rights and the moral obligation to protect them throughout the world. However, they fail to consider that, whatever the merit of this position, it can only be exercised fitfully. To begin with, the West applies double standards since countries like the USA have refused to sign up to international obligations that would make it possible to indict its military or political personnel. Nor do most Western countries comply with the possible use of existing legislation to make possible the arrest of (for example, Israeli) politicians or military officers for alleged crimes against civilians. On the whole, the West holds to the position that the 'impartial' application of its internal legislation is sufficient to sanction the putative crimes of its own politicians or military. So, rogue British officers who disregard the military code are prosecuted in the UK but, on the other hand, it is unlikely that Tony Blair will be put on trial for the Iraq War, regardless of the argument that the war was illegal.

The case of Rwanda is emblematic in this respect. Although this was probably the clearest instance of genocide since the Second World War, neither the UN nor the international community could bring itself to intervene. The issue could not have been more clearcut and there was evidence in real time of what was happening on the ground. Yet individual countries stuck to their own self-interests and the lack of consensus paralysed the UN, despite the desperate pleas of its own personnel in Kigali. France is even charged with either having turned a deliberate blind eye to the events or to have been complicit in training some of the troops that were guilty of the slaughter. Whatever the case, the operation of the International Criminal Tribunal for Rwanda (in Arusha) has not offered much confidence that the perpetrators of the genocide will face justice. Too few alleged criminals are caught and the tribunal is too cumbersome, too slow and too procedural.[30] The results achieved so long after the event are pitiful and will not unduly worry those who might be minded to indulge in similar violence in the future.

Although the importance of human rights is increasing all the time, the (largely) Western attempt to implement an international agenda raises issues that have not been thought through. If most agree that it is in principle desirable to improve human rights, many non-Westerners remain convinced that this campaign is yet another way of ensuring Western supremacy. Furthermore, significant numbers of Westerners (of non-Western origin) appear to reject the West's definition of human rights and oppose their imposition

---

30. For details on the Tribunal, see its official website: www.unictr.org/Home/tabid/36/Default.aspx; accessed 30 January 2012.

on other countries.[31] This is true, for example, of those who believe that there is in European countries like France an extreme brand of secularism, which is actively hostile to citizens who believe in the relevance of religion to everyday social and political life. Indeed, there is total incomprehension between them and mainstream political opinion, which is at a loss to understand how such views can be held. This has a direct bearing on the question of human rights within Western societies. But in the next three sections I want to look more closely at how this question impinges on other important aspects of the relations between West and non-West.

Policing the world: how to keep the peace

This new vision of human rights and the recognition of their growing importance in the conduct of international affairs have led the West to reconsider the question of how best to keep the peace. The four main factors that affect present theories on peacekeeping are the role of the UN, the end of the Cold War, the evolving perspectives on underdevelopment, and the growing importance of non-state actors. All of these are intimately connected with the interaction between West and non-West, the nature of which has been changing over time. This has brought about confusion, which leads to inconsistent foreign policy on the part of Western countries. So, I shall briefly examine these four factors before discussing why the question of keeping the peace has become more complex today than it ever was.

The UN was set up after the Second War World largely in order to keep the peace. To that end it outlined clear guidelines for military intervention and ensured that approval for any operation would have to be sanctioned by the Security Council. From the start, however, the fact that the right of veto was given to the

---

31. See Mamdani, 2009 for an attack on Western NGOs.

The problem

victors (and later to China) created a situation in which the West's influence was disproportionate and, because of the Cold War, it became difficult to reach a consensus. With few exceptions – such as the operation in the former Belgian Congo – UN peacekeeping was confined to conflicts where the superpowers could come to some agreement, as in Cyprus or Lebanon. Moreover, the UN stuck rigidly to a Westphalian conception of national sovereignty, which ruled out any intervention in (domestic) civil conflicts.

The limits of the UN peacekeeping mandate were cruelly exposed from very early on when it proved powerless to do anything meaningful about Western interventions in Suez, the Soviet incursions into Hungary and Czechoslovakia, or the Chinese takeover of Tibet. Clearly the violence committed by the permanent members of the UN would escape sanction and, more importantly, any hint of UN involvement on the ground. More recent events have tested further the relevance of the UN to the maintenance of peace. NATO's attack on Serbia and the invasion of Iraq by a far from unanimous 'coalition of the willing' demonstrated plainly that the West was prepared to act without UN sanction. And the terrible events in Rwanda, as noted above, exposed the impotence of the international organisation when its major players refused to take the risk of a potentially dangerous military involvement in a volatile African country. That event also demonstrated the inability of these major players to understand the causes of the genocide and revealed the lack of adequate analytical tools to make sense of internal conflicts in areas of the Third World like Africa.

The experience of UN peacekeeping operations in the last two decades shows clearly that it can only serve a useful purpose where the combatants want peace and where there is a process of conflict resolution in train.[32] Otherwise, the mere fact of inserting blue

---

32. Compare the failure of the UN in Angola, where UNITA and the MPLA government

berets to man a ceasefire line does not usually result in peace. The UN can do peacekeeping but it cannot do peacemaking. Indeed, the failure of peacekeeping operations in areas like Africa makes plain that there is an acute need for rethinking the whole issue of violence.[33] The international security system, of which the UN is the central pillar, rests on the assumption that peace is the 'natural' state of human affairs and that violence is always destructive. Yet, as has become more and more evident, such an understanding of the present situation is at variance with what many of the protagonists believe and with the ways in which they conduct politics. And history tells us that violence can be productive. The question is how and for whom.

The consequences of the end of the Cold War are many, and they are not all well understood. I shall restrict my remarks here to the impact it has had on peace. The collapse of Communism in the Soviet Union and the fall of the Berlin Wall marked the end of a system of international relations based on a hostile bipolar world. In the immediate aftermath of these momentous events, it was widely believed that the domination of a 'benign' democratic superpower (the USA) and the gradual, but inexorable, spread of market capitalism worldwide would ease tensions and favour peace. It was also presumed that the spread of democracy would reduce the risk of conflict, seeing that since the Second World War democratic nations have not waged war on each other. Furthermore, it was assumed, the exercise of democracy domestically would also allow for the peaceful, rather than violent, resolution of conflict.

Since then, most of these assumptions have been proved wrong. The world may no longer be strictly bipolar but it is not unipolar

---

did not seriously commit to peace, with the success in Mozambique, where RENAMO and the FRELIMO government did commit to peace.

33. The inability of the UN to keep the peace in Eastern DRC has exposed the impotence of the international body in the face of organisations and armies that refuse to abide by peace agreements.

either. Russia has remained a strong international actor and China is rapidly becoming one. The USA cannot disregard either, not primarily because of any military threat, but because both exercise strong influence on the politics of their region, the behaviour of their allies and the world market. Russia controls much of Europe's energy resources, which gives it powerful leverage. China is key to the successful operation of the international economy and its financial clout is a trump card. The European Union, though politically divided, still has strong political and economic sway in international affairs. It does not behave like a superpower but, individually and collectively, it is a major player when it comes to policing the world.

At the same time, the sole superpower has been at a loss to define for itself the most constructive role. It has swung from the blundering assertion of its power under G.W. Bush, culminating in the Iraq invasion, to the more thoughtful international partnership President Obama wanted. This is not new: the USA has often oscillated between inward-looking and belligerent foreign policy postures. But what *is* new is that it has exchanged an ideological foe – communist Soviet Union, threatening (conventional or) nuclear war – for an ill-defined religious enemy, engaging in indiscriminate terrorism, particularly in the West. And this 'war on terror' has implied a fight against the enemy within, since the most dangerous terrorists turn out to be Western Muslims. This new situation has propelled the USA onto far from propitious terrain, ranging from Iraq to Afghanistan, in which it has led a Western coalition, which is neither united nor full square behind the American political agenda. It has also led to widespread legal abuse, the torture of detainees, and, as in Guantánamo, the detention of alleged terrorists to whom justice is denied.

Indeed, Guantánamo stands as the symbol of the failure to come to terms with the nature of this new type of 'combatant' and of the inability to think through the best way to deal with captured 'terrorists'. Although many Western governments, not least the UK, were complicit in the torture of alleged terrorists held by others, they maintained that Guantánamo's existence and procedures could not be justified in law. However, the USA under the influence of the Bush administration stretched the meaning of the law and overrode legal and human rights protection – some zealous academics even proposed a 'moral' justification for torture.[34] Above and beyond the clearly illegal nature and counterproductive effects of these actions, what is significant here is the difficulty faced by American policymakers in thinking outside the box. The fact that the current Muslim terrorists do not fit either the model of conventional soldiers or that of political nationalist fighters in the mould of the Irgun, Fatah, the IRA or ETA has not yet generated new forms of thinking about security among those charged with protecting Western societies.

This is illustrated by the fact that the fear of terrorism has now been associated with poverty and the lack of development in the Third World. The theory is that underdevelopment is fertile recruiting ground for terrorists seeking new bases of operation or Western targets. The evidence for this is said to lie in what is happening in Africa, where Muslim radicals seem to make headway in a large number of countries (such as Nigeria) and not just in the Maghreb. So the danger of underdevelopment is not only that people will try to migrate to the West in search of a better life but that this lack of economic opportunity will turn ordinary people into terrorist fodder. This outlook, which has served to justify increasing 'security aid' to many of these African countries, is a curious misreading both of what current political Islam is and of the consequences of underdevelopment.

---

34. Most notably the Harvard law professor Alan Dershowitz. For a summary of the debate on torture after 9/11, see http://dissentmagazine.org/democratiya/article_pdfs/d7wijze.pdf.

The problem

The risk of Islamic terrorism is spreading in Africa not because these countries have suddenly become poorer but because of the apparent attraction of militant Islam to a small number of Muslims. As elsewhere in the world, the most dangerous and effective of these militants are not distinguished by a life of poverty but by a religious zeal drawn most frequently from a hatred of what the West has done or stands for.[35] Many of them are educated and not a few have experience of living in the West. Nor do they succeed in recruiting followers primarily because of poverty: their footsoldiers are mobilised either on a clan basis, as in Somalia, or because of their links to Islam. And many are paid for their services. In some strange way, militant Islam in Africa is also a business since it serves to acquire power and the economic benefits that may accrue from that. And in that sense it should be understood in terms of the role of violence on the continent. But the hatred of the West is in large measure the result of Western, particularly US, policies in the past decade. The 'war on terror' has served to create its own nemesis: a self-styled army of militant Muslims bent on wreaking havoc.

The question of the relation between underdevelopment and peace is perhaps more significant in the long run. It is a long-standing and well-established principle within the aid industry that poverty is a breeding ground for violence and conflict. Only development, it is said, can secure a more peaceful prospect for the Third World. And without peace there is little possibility of development. This theory, which is universally taken for granted, raises some difficult issues that mar our understanding of underdevelopment and deflect well-meaning aid policies from their original aims. What is the West to do? Is it first to achieve peace so that there can be development? Or is development needed before

---

35. In Nigeria the most active group calls itself Boko Haram, which loosely translates as 'Western education is a sin'.

peace can be consolidated? And is peace what is wanted locally? And how is peace achieved?

The problems are both conceptual and historical. Conceptually, there is great confusion about the meaning of both peace and development. Is peace to be defined negatively – that is, as the absence of violence or conflict? Or is it to be understood as a political and social dispensation in which people can work together towards agreed objectives? Similarly, there is little consensus about development. Is it economic growth, and if so how is it best measured – by GDP or according to how much poverty is reduced? Or is it the country's potential for sustained economic activities, which will lead in due course to self-propelled development? And what is the role of aid in all this? Is it intended to alleviate poverty, to buttress the state so it does not fail, or to help develop the infrastructure that is needed? Self-evident as these concepts may at first appear to be, an analysis of the development literature shows clearly that there is confusion.

Historically, there is scant basis for current theories on peace and development.[36] The consolidation of Western countries into nation-states was a very violent affair. Accountability was imposed on rulers by force, and conflict between emerging states was the main incentive in the development of more representative political institutions. War was at the root of the development of the modern nation-state, in Europe as elsewhere. Moreover, the Industrial Revolution, which was the foundation of economic development, was predicated on greater, rather than less, poverty. Indeed, it was the scourge of want that forced people to work in industry. And poverty was not alleviated merely by economic growth. It was achieved by the emergence of a state that would compel employers to improve pay and working conditions and

---

36. These theories share the assumption that peace is the natural order of society and that war is always noxious.

by the labour movements, which ultimately forced that state to protect better the conditions of workers and, ultimately, of the unemployed.[37]

So, the present conundrum of underdevelopment remains a constant factor in the approach to the question of peace, peacemaking and peacekeeping. The limits of Western thinking on this issue are, again, largely rooted in the inability to conceive that the reasons for the absence of peace in the Third World are more complex than allowed for by these current theories. Part of the difficulty has to do with a much larger problem, which I will pick up again later, arising from the Western assumption that modernisation is akin to Westernisation. As I suggested, the first flaw in our thinking is in forgetting that the development of the West was built on a history of violence, which ultimately turned out to be economically and politically productive. Peace was the result of, not the precondition for, development. And this flaw is compounded by the deeply ahistorical theoretical perspective, which consists in presuming that peace, or rather the absence of conflict, is what would make development in the Third World possible. But the really important question is why violence and conflict in the Third World are not more productive – that is why they do not lead either to more secure political institutionalisation or to sustained economic growth.

In the case of Africa, for instance, it appears that we may have a situation of what I call modernisation without development – a notion that appears nonsensical to most Western thinking. Here I mean that violence and conflict, among other factors, are used as economic tools to accumulate resources, not with a view to invest in development but in order to sustain the political (dis)order that makes such a state of affairs possible. If that is the case, then we

---

37. On the 'positive' consequences of violence, see Cramer, 2006.

would have to recognise that there is no peace because peace would not be productive in the way that some political elites would wish. Equally, violence cannot be conducive to the institutional progress that would reduce the occurrence of future violence. Indeed, in such circumstances violence can be a very lucrative business and consequently peace is simply not interesting.

Moreover, the growing importance of non-state actors in current conflicts has confused the nature of international politics even further. As is perhaps best illustrated by the 'war on terror', many of today's security issues, and therefore the prospects for peace, are conditional on the actions of informal and transnational groupings that use or threaten violence. Theories of international relations are still largely based on a conceptualisation of world politics that takes the nation-state as the prime building block. And they view other more informal actors as the emanation, or instrument, of individual countries or of nationalist movements seeking statehood. But what is new, and is yet poorly integrated into our notions of international relations, is the increasing significance of deterritorialised and transnational outfits, which do *not* pursue nationalist agendas.

Indeed, what is most relevant about al-Qaeda is not that it is a terrorist outfit targeting the West. It is that it is an organisation that is religious in outlook and conceives of violence – in the guise of *jihad* – as a worthy end in itself.[38] Its ambition is not primarily to 'overthrow' the West – although there is the important subtext of the establishment of a universal Caliphate – since it is equally contemptuous of all existing Muslim governments. It is rather to legitimise a form of self-validating violence: to kill in the name of Allah is *ispso facto* redemptive. And that philosophy is symbolised by the glorification of the suicide bomber, whose mission – indiscriminate

---

38. See Devji, 2005 for an intriguing discussion of al-Qaeda.

murder – cannot achieve any identifiably specific political objective but aims instead at creating a 'state of alarm'. Whilst this attitude is somewhat reminiscent of the nineteenth-century Russian nihilist terrorists, the difference lies in that those bombers did not seek to commit suicide and operated on the basis of clearly formulated social and political goals. On the other hand, the London 7/7 operatives had little notion of what it was they concretely wanted to achieve, beyond endorsing the mantle of martyr.[39]

The fact that religious zealots should turn out to be such an issue in international affairs at the turn of the twenty-first century baffles Western understanding and casts asunder most theories of development. As does the reality that many political actors today do *not* seek peace. In both instances, what is at stake is a kind of behaviour that appears to be irrational. But since it is clearly rational for those who act in that way, it is the nature of Western assumptions (as well as a failure of imagination) that makes it so difficult to make sense of such unexpected behaviour. All theories of international relations rest on some basic premises, the two pillars of which are that the relevant actors are states and that they act according to their national self-interests. There is no place here for either non-state actors or for actors whose sense of self-interest defies Western logic, or at least any logic that the West can conceptualise.

Try as we may, and there is now a thriving literature on non-state actors, we still find it difficult to agree on what these developments in world affairs actually mean.[40] Our mindsets are still conditioned to think in terms of social actors like classes, clans or tribes and national or would-be national actors like the Palestinians or the Kurds. So our conception of peace and of the means to maintain it are bound by theories of conflict and conflict resolution which

---

39. On the issues discussed in this paragraph, see Volpi, 2010; Roy, 2004.
40. For an overview of the literature on non-state actors, see Reinalda, 2011.

are built upon these assumed social and political dynamics. We still cannot fathom, let alone deal with, those who instruct suicide bombers or warlords, whose sole aim is to use, and keep using, violence instrumentally. Therefore, the contradiction between the morally worthy aim of ensuring peace and the means we deploy to police the world continues to provoke tensions or even violence, which makes peace impossible. Here too we are tested by the limits of our thinking.

Making poverty history: how to make people better

The Conservative/Liberal Democrat British government that took office in May 2010 announced swingeing cuts aimed at reducing the country's very large deficit (arising from the 2008–09 economic crisis). Interestingly, however, it ring-fenced two areas to be protected from budgetary constraints: health and foreign aid. The first is not surprising since this is the public sector institution most prized by the British and one which no government, including Thatcher's, has ever dared to cut back. The second is more surprising and certainly marks out the British from other Western European governments. Indeed, to protect assistance to poor countries at a time when the citizens of one's own country face severe curbs in public expenditure (including social security protection) and an increased risk of unemployment is surprising. It is a brave government that favours the Third World over its domestic constituency, especially when the relevance of foreign aid to development is increasingly challenged.

Although part of the explanation for this startling policy choice can be explained by the fact that all three major parties agreed on this in their election manifestos, it is still intriguing. Why is Britain showing such strong devotion to foreign aid when other countries, including some previously generous donors (such as the Netherlands and the Scandinavian countries) have begun to reassess the impact of assistance to poor countries? There is clearly an element of national pride, since former prime minister Tony Blair pledged the UK to be a driving force behind the G8 undertaking (at the July 2005 Summit) to double aid to Africa. Thereafter the Labour government was very proactive, increasing aid and working to develop more effective aid policies. Indeed, the Department for International Development (DfID) has been at the forefront of European thinking on how best to improve the impact of aid in countries where the state is fragile and institutionalisation poor. However, in other ways the 2005 Gleneagles G8 pledge to increase aid is also representative of an approach to underdevelopment which assumes that well-targeted aid can work to 'make poverty history' – as the catchy slogan of the period put it. As such it is symbolic of present thinking in the West about how best to help the non-West.

Making poverty history is not just a good slogan; it is also a clear statement of intent. Implied is, first, the notion that it is *possible* to eradicate poverty and, second, that it can be done by dint of judicious and well-funded policies – in other words, through acts of *will*. This approach, it seems to me, captures the specificities of Western thinking about the under- or undeveloped South. As in the case of peace, it undoubtedly reveals an underlying moral basis to an ostensibly well-meaning course of action. But it also displays great self-assurance in the diagnosis of the ailment and the remedies required to treat it. Indeed underdevelopment, like violence, is viewed as a pathology – that is, something that is not 'normal'. And the approach to such pathologies, as in medicine, is to seek a cure. The Western mind believes, *in fine*, that there must be a rational way of combating the ills that beset the Third World. However, the failure of Africa to develop despite a massive influx of foreign assistance raises serious questions about the logic and effectiveness of aid in alleviating poverty.

I propose to approach this question by examining in turn the concepts of poverty, aid and development. I will then try to explain why the failure of the 'making poverty history' campaign is less the result of insufficient aid than of the inability to conceptualise the matter in other than these narrow Western terms.

The slogan 'Make Poverty History' is interesting in two ways. One is that it proposes a linear, or chronological, conception of the problem: poverty is a state of affairs that prevails at a particular time and that can then be overcome. But this is both historically false and highly misleading. Since poverty is a relative condition, it is obviously one that cannot be eliminated as such. Other than those people who are bereft of food, protection and shelter, it is very difficult to identify precisely what poverty is. There are few objective criteria marking people as poor which are not relational: the most that can be said is that some are poorer than others. Indeed, in Western countries poverty is defined as revenues below a certain percentage of median income, which by definition rises over time. This is why it is so difficult for governments actually to reduce the numbers who are classified as 'poor'. And to do so inevitably involves redistributing public resources from the richer to the poorer through taxation, subsidies and social transfers.

The same goes for non-Western countries, where there is in addition another important factor. Everyone agrees that those in the Third World who do not have the basic necessities of life – food, shelter and some income – are poor and no one disputes that they need help. However, beyond these general characteristics it becomes very difficult to define poverty. Poverty is not just a relative condition; it is also a subjective one. So that, in order to be poor, people have to believe they are poor. And whilst it is no doubt the case that those who live in so-called 'sink estates' are very well aware they are poor, this is not so straightforwardly true in the non-West. The case of nomadic peoples is very revealing in

The problem

this respect. Most Western aid experts, and not a few locals, think that nomads are poor and that in order to improve their lives they should become sedentary. But research shows, for example with the Maasai in Kenya, that not only do they not consider themselves poor so long as they possess cattle but also that they actually view a sedentary occupation like farming to be a sign of poverty.[41] Not surprisingly the moves to settle nomads have often resulted in the creation, not the alleviation, of poverty.

Thus, one of the paradoxes of the Western approach to poverty is, inadvertently, to create the conditions whereby people who do not consider themselves to be poor are defined as such, in part because their occupation is deemed to be a mark of poverty. The syndrome is not dissimilar to that of the aboriginals in the former dominions, where enforced settlement and the disconnection from their original culture and customs produced poverty and despair. This is not to say that the West should simply assume that non-Western traditions are a guarantee against poverty. Far from it. But it is to stress that the notion of poverty cannot be dissociated from the norms, values and beliefs that make up a people's identity and way of life – that is, their history and culture. In many instances, it would make more sense to offer people what they want, indeed ask for, rather than artificially to try to engineer a change so that they can fit an outsider's notion of what being non-poor ought to be like.

But there is more: poverty is not an illness to which there is a ready cure. Nor is poverty a feature of 'tradition'. All too often, aid policies are misguided because they make assumptions about people's way of life. But it is precisely those people who, because of changing economic circumstances, have had to abandon their rural way of life and migrate to the cities in order to survive who

---

41. See Anderson and Broch-Due, 2000.

are the most likely to be poor – in both objective and subjective ways. They become the victims of changing economic circumstances, which are conditioned by such factors as the expansion of mechanised agriculture, world trade, economic crises and globalisation. So, again, paradoxically, it is in fact 'modernisation' that has made them poor, rather than the way they used to live before they became destitute. And it is historically the case that economic development creates poverty as much as it contributes to alleviate it. Poverty is part of the process of development. That much is clear, but it should at least make us more realistic in wanting to abolish poverty among people who do *not* consider themselves poor.

The second aspect of the question of poverty is historical. The idea that poverty can be eradicated through the application of judicious foreign aid policies is at odds with what happened in the West. In the West too poverty increased as a result of (capitalist) economic development, of which the Industrial Revolution was the quintessence. Poverty, which forced people to seek employment in factories, was historically a precondition of the Industrial Revolution. Without workers there would have been no industry. The capitalist wheel was powered by the desperation of those who needed to work in order not to starve. These were the real poor. Furthermore, poverty in the West was not abolished by enlightened government policy. It was tackled when the working classes, supported by a handful of dedicated 'humanitarians', acquired sufficient political clout to force both better working conditions and the creation of poverty-alleviating schemes. In other words, it was the awareness of the economic causes of poverty that induced the 'poor' to take matters into their own hands. As Marxists would say, without the consciousness that the causes of exploitation, and poverty, *can* be addressed, there is very little chance that changes will be made. And one need not be a Marxist in order to see that this is pretty much what has happened in the West.

Therefore, when examined more closely the main plank of the most recent aid 'ideology' – that is, poverty reduction – turns out to be muddled. And that is because the Western notion of assistance has evolved. Whereas in the 1960s it was built around the belief that what was required was primarily to support economic 'take-off', current thinking is more concerned to address the manifest signs of increasing poverty. I will return to the question of development later. Here I want to tease out the reasons for and the consequences of these changes in aid policies. The turn towards poverty alleviation is in the first place the result of the awareness within Western aid circles that foreign assistance has largely failed to generate economic development. In other words, the assumption that the governments of 'developing' countries would automatically use aid to spur sustained economic growth proved simplistic.

The lesson from that experience is that aid worked out differently in different settings. East Asia seemed to evolve much like Europe: industry created growth; the working classes demanded better conditions and the middle classes more political accountability. But the scenario in Africa was entirely distinct: there was little industrial development and aid was siphoned off non-productively. The state appeared to be part of the problem, not the solution. So, Western aid policies changed in two fundamental ways. One was that assistance was now channelled more and more through non-governmental organisations (NGOs), so as to bypass the greedy and wasteful state. The other was that aid was targeted to help the poorest – that is, in aid parlance, to alleviate poverty. At least what the West gave would serve to assist those in greatest need. Or so it was in theory, but in practice it has not been straightforward. Among the many side effects of this supposedly rational approach, two are clearly counterproductive: one is that aid is still diverted by local politicians for clientelistic purposes; the other is that NGOs often impose their 'solutions' and compete both with other NGOs and with the local administration. And they are not accountable to those they aim to aid. This merely replicates the problems of aid found at the national level, as is potently illustrated by what has happened in Mozambique.[42]

The other paradox of the use of aid as a means to alleviate poverty is that it reflects a move away from the concern that assistance should serve to spur economic development. But since development is the only long-term sustainable answer to reducing poverty and improving the local conditions of life, the whole question of how to help people improve themselves is riddled with further contradictions. Western policy, based as it is on its own vision of what a rational course of action for aid should be, is confronted with a challenge that appears difficult to comprehend, let alone overcome. As is to be expected, there are two contradictory views here. One is that more aid will eventually do the trick, even if much of it is diverted to non-productive ends. More resources will eventually trickle down to those who want to invest productively.[43] The other is that aid distorts the local economy and creates the conditions for further dependence on foreign assistance, thereby undermining the very possibility of sustained growth.[44] Whatever the merit of these two positions, they both point to the confusion surrounding the causalities between aid and development.

This is not entirely surprising since here, too, current theories of development are generalisations based on the Western experience.[45] The most common understanding of the concept is economic: it is the onset of sustained growth that makes development possible – as the experience of the Western, Asian and Latin American countries shows. However, as the experience of the West makes

---

42. Aid is so important to the country's budget that any decrease in what is given has dramatic consequences. But this also means that the government is severely constrained by aid conditionalities. See Hanlon, 1991, 2009.
43. See Sachs, 2005.
44. See the argument on aid in Moyo, 2009.
45. For a critique of such generalisations, see Connell, 2007.

plain, economic growth also creates growing social inequalities that are only tackled by political change. For example, the recent rapid economic development in Brazil has not resulted in a market-led lessening of inequalities or the alleviation of poverty. These can only be addressed by a government that will make deliberate and consistent efforts to redress the economic and social balance in the country – as the Lula administration to some extent tried to do. So, the idea that development will in and of itself reduce poverty is one that is assumed rather than demonstrated. The Western mind focuses on what has happened in the West and presumes that similar processes are, or will be, at work elsewhere.

The next confusion is the assumption that aid will trigger economic development. But here, again, the West is projecting its own rationality upon the non-West. Some of the more recent work on the plight of what has been called 'the bottom billion' has shown that aid as it is presently conceived might in fact work to the detriment of development.[46] So long as the political elite in 'undeveloped' countries know that a significant proportion of the national budget will come from foreign assistance, from which they will personally benefit, it is unlikely that they will devote themselves to the difficult task of investing for the future. Their aim will be to continue to maximise foreign transfers and they will become more accountable to their foreign donors than to their local constituencies. If, as some have argued, foreign aid were cut, then these politicians would have to prioritise policies that would placate their own people and result in some developmental progress.

There is another aspect of the present condition of some parts of the non-West that baffles the West: that is, the apparent lack of commitment to development. Clearly, what is happening in much of Africa, many Central Asian countries and some areas

---

46. See Collier, 2008a.

in the Middle East goes against the expectation that politicians will necessarily engage in a form of development that is akin to what took place in the West. Furthermore, the Chinese (and now Vietnamese) experience suggests a type of development – capitalism without democracy – that is thought not to be viable by many Western theorists, who assume that capitalist advance and liberal democracy are two sides of the same coin; or, to put it another way, that modernisation is the same as Westernisation. However, that is questionable. Is it not at least conceivable that there will be various kinds of modernisation, several of which might be different from the Western? Might it be the case that the political evolution of countries like China will differ significantly from what took place in the West? And is it also not possible that there could continue to be, as in much of Africa, modernisation without development? We are not sure, but we presume to know.

Freeing the non-West: how to export democracy

The concern about the political future of the non-West thus easily morphs into a discussion of the spread of democracy.[47] From a Western point of view, making people more free is synonymous with ensuring that they live in ostensibly more democratic societies. The protection of human rights, the alleviation of poverty and economic prosperity in the end are all seen to depend on the development of the political system that seems to have benefited the West most profitably. In the mind of Western politicians and of the experts who advise them, there is no other route than the democratic one. Indeed, so strongly held is this view that the Bretton Woods Institutions – the World Bank and the IMF – effectively impose political conditionalities on the disbursement of aid and

---

47. For a discussion of the spread of democracy, see Burnell, 2011.

loans. Foreign assistance is now dependent on democratisation, or at least the organisation of regular multiparty elections.

For the West, the case for the establishment of (liberal) democracy is unimpeachable, and because this assumption is so deeply rooted in the Western outlook on the world it is worth revisiting the 'end of history' argument.[48] Fukuyama's thesis was not, as has been sometimes suggested, that there could be no further improvement in the way we organise ourselves politically. It was that the evolution of political systems had reached a point where it had become historically self-evident that liberal democracy was the most effective way of combining political freedom and economic prosperity. In what was undoubtedly a very Hegelian conception of progress, there was therefore no need to try to 'invent' any new political dispensation. The model had been found; it remained for us to refine it and share it with the rest of the world.

If the argument was primarily pragmatic, there was still a strong ethical basis to it. It was not just that liberal democracy was more effective than any other political system; it was also that it was more moral. The search for the good *polis*, which in our tradition was seen to have started with the Greek city-states and refined by the moral, philosophical and scientific revolution of the Enlightenment, had now come to fruition. Man had succeeded in devising a political arrangement that combined stringent accountability and the protection of the market economy, on which our material well-being depended. And, if anything, the totalitarian follies of the twentieth century had made clear that democracy was not only better but also ultimately more powerful. It was the system that channelled force most productively.[49]

Given that, however diverse their constitutional arrangements, Western countries are by and large democratic obviously lent

---

48. Fukuyama, 1992.
49. Fukuyama, 2011.

great force to the argument that democracy would also serve the non-West best. However, as we know, the desire in the West to 'export' democracy has been fraught with difficulty and has resulted in much (admittedly often unwanted) violence. So, it is important to reconsider the issue afresh and try to understand where the difficulties lie. Is there a problem with the argument itself – that is, is it wrong to assume that democracy is the best political arrangement man has devised? Is the problem with the complexities of implementing a democratic agenda? Is it that the Western version of liberal democracy is ill-suited to non-Western settings? Or is it perhaps that we are making the wrong assumptions, asking the wrong questions – or the right questions in the wrong way?[50]

I approach this debate from three different directions. One is to ask whether the interpretation of the historical record is accurate, or even plausible. The second is to review the evidence for or against the primacy of local cultural factors in the organisation of politics. The last is to discuss the theoretical underpinnings of the West's claim for the superiority of liberal democracy.

The view that Western forms of democracy are the political arrangements that best combine individual freedoms and economic progress is a recent one. For a long period during the twentieth century, there was widespread support (even in some sections of the West) for the belief that socialism would eventually become a better alternative. Where capitalism put profit above equality and humanity, socialism would offer a superior combination of economic advance and quality of life. Although it is hard today to accept that this was a widespread opinion, it is important to remember that such was the ideology not just of communist states, but also of a large number of Third World countries and former colonies. Even a stalwart of present-day free-market economics such as India

---

50. It is also well to remember that the Eastern Bloc countries advocated their own political systems, based on 'democratic socialism'.

started its independence committed to its own version of socialism, viewed at the time by Nehru as the most suitable system for a poor country bent on the improvement of *all* its people.

It is the collapse of Communism in the Soviet Union and Eastern Europe, as well as the manifest failure of socialist Third World countries to make much economic headway, which spelled the death knell of socialism as a blueprint for development in the non-West. This period coincided in the West with the 'turn against the state' and the forceful affirmation of the superiority of market economics. And it is this combination of historical factors that propelled forward the new ideology of development advocating democracy as a prerequisite to economic development. So, it is well to remember that what passes today for development orthodoxy was in fact the result of a specific concatenation of factors. Until the 1980s, development ideologies had given a much more central place to the state and had assumed that the move towards more 'democratic' politics, if and when it occurred, would be halting and slow. If there was a general presumption that democracy was best, there was nevertheless recognition that Third World countries might evolve politically in diverse directions.

Therefore the theory that democracy was a requirement for economic development, which is now at the core of the donor agenda, should be seen for what it is: the latest in a long series of Western prescriptions for the progress of the non-West. Perhaps even more crucially, we should note that this theoretical position was evolved not from a newly found causality between democracy and development but from the conclusion that state-driven development efforts had failed in many parts of the Third World, most notably Africa. So it was the acknowledgement of the failure of the previous tenet about government-propelled development that gave pride of place to the political reformers. The state was now seen as the principal impediment to economic growth and the priority was to free the market from political interference. This required a democratic dispensation in which governments would both be accountable to the electorate and committed to market liberalism. And it was simply assumed that political liberalisation would ensure market liberalisation.

Thus, the key question is whether this assumption – democracy makes development possible – is based on good historical evidence. The short answer is no, and this for two reasons. The first is that the Western experience suggests the causality is the reverse: it was economic growth that created the social and political conditions favourable to the emergence of democracy. It is therefore surprising that the West should have forgotten the lessons of history and become so adamant about the new democratic development agenda. The second is that what is happening in those East Asian countries that have achieved the highest levels of economic growth also contradicts this theory. All had authoritarian states that took the lead in creating the conditions for economic development and enforced state-led solutions with the utmost vigour, if not ruthlessness. Where there is political liberalisation today – and this does not include all these countries – it has been brought about through the pressure applied by the (middle) classes created by economic development.

This may suggest, and it is an argument that has generated much controversy, that there might be historical and cultural – rather than political – factors that favour, or make more difficult, economic development. Of course, this argument was first mooted long ago by Weber in his discussion of the relevance of the Protestant ethic to the development of capitalism in the West.[51] More recently, in the case of Japan, and now South Korea, China or Vietnam, it has been argued that culture (and to some extent religion) was conducive to both aggressive economic activity

---

51. Weber, 1958. It is well to remember that there have been many objections to Weber's thesis. See, among others, Samuelsson, 1961; Lehmann and Roth, 1993.

The problem

and a long-term view of development.[52] In a discussion that is reminiscent of Weber's, the theory is that 'Asian' (Confucian?) beliefs and values offer a world-view that channels well-established social networks into productive investment. The family and kin links that bind people across borders provide a platform of trust that is akin to contract-based economic activities (such as trade) in the West.[53]

If that should be true, and there is no consensus, it would help to explain a number of otherwise puzzling situations: why Japan managed to develop thriving businesses based on a long-standing concept of 'filial' loyalty to the firm; why Chinese diasporas have been economically so successful; why these Asian countries are able to adapt market economics to their more 'traditional' socio-political arrangements; and why, for instance, China has been so rapidly able to incorporate Hong Kong (and, later, Macau) into its economic sphere ('one country, two systems'). What is interesting is that the argument about the possible relevance of cultural and religious factors only gained ground when it became evident that these Asian countries were able not only to match but also sometimes to exceed Western economic and technological achievements.

However, the converse is still not true. Where there has been little or no economic development, as in Africa, the Western mind has been reluctant to concede that cultural factors might be at work. Largely because of the guilt generated by the West's appalling colonial and racial record, it has become morally and politically unacceptable to suggest that Africa's failure to develop may have some local cultural/religious roots. Instead, the consensus has been that it is the long-lasting effects of slavery, colonialism, imperialism, racism and neocolonialism that are to blame for the

---

52. On Japan, the first of the East Asian countries to achieve high levels of economic growth, the cultural argument is well presented by Robert Bellah (1985).
53. See among others Tai Hung-Chao, 1989.

inability of the continent to make much economic progress. This is of course a very delicate issue, on which I have written elsewhere.[54] I will not here rehearse the arguments for and against. Rather, I should like to make two points: one historical, one conceptual.

The first point is that explaining Africa's predicament by its troubled history is not convincing since it cannot be denied that the history of, say, China was also affected by Western imperialism and internal violence. In Europe, too, the historical record is not particularly good. Nor can it be argued that the development of capitalism was made easier by the record of internecine and inter-nation violence committed against the Chinese by aggressive and imperialistic governments in the West. The second is that there is something odd in the denial of the causal relevance of cultural/religious factors when applied to the non-West since we know that they were important in the case of the Western experience. Indeed, the reason why Weber's thesis is so well known is precisely because it carries so much conviction. And the German sociologist's quest for the understanding of similar cultural or religious dynamics elsewhere in the world is evidence that he was convinced of their significance.

There is nothing mechanistic or deterministic in what Weber wrote. His was not the expression of an 'iron law' of development, even less a 'theory' that would make it possible to predict what would happen. Instead, it was a subtle and sensitive approach that laid emphasis on those non-economic characteristics of society which were likely to impinge on their socio-economic evolution.[55] So, the upshot of his approach to the history of economic development is not that China is bound to thrive and Nigeria to stagnate – although that may well be what happens in the near future. Rather, it is that their paths to 'modernity' are likely to

---

54. Chabal, 2009; Chabal and Daloz, 1999.
55. Weber, 1964.

differ greatly, in part at least because of the cultural differences between the two. And also that, whatever form their respective 'modernisation' takes, it is not necessarily going to be synonymous with Westernisation.

It would be surprising, therefore, if these differences did not also affect the political sphere. The politics of China or Nigeria will evolve as a result of the changes that take place in their respective economic conditions and in their relations with the world market. However, it is very likely that they will evolve in different directions. To imagine that the types of political accountability that will arise should necessarily, 'in due course', resemble those of Western liberal democracy is, it seems to me, historically unwarranted. To speculate further that only the onset of Western-style democracy in poor countries can provide the conditions for economic development appears even more unrealistic. Indeed, the current Chinese economic 'invasion' of Africa is likely to influence these countries politically in ways that are not palatable to the present Western aid agenda.

If this is the case, why is Western thinking presently so geared to the spread of (Western) democratisation in settings where there seem to be good historical and cultural reasons for doubting that it is workable, at least in the near future? I should like to address this question by examining more closely the theoretical underpinnings of the West's claim for the superiority of liberal democracy. There are, it seems to me, two pillars to the West's thinking. One is the assumption that there must be similar causes to similar effects: in other words, if we note a correlation between democracy and economic progress, then we must assume the one is the cause of the other. The other is that there is a linear logic to the progression from less to more advanced socio-political and economic dispensation: if the West is the pinnacle today, then Westernisation has to be the way. I will return to these two issues of theory later in the book. Here I merely want to show how they pan out in respect of 'democratisation'.

The first presumption is very limiting in this case because we have no solid ground on which to judge causality. It may well be that Western democracies are today the most 'advanced' economically – just as it may well be that they are at peace with each other – but there is no way of establishing 'scientifically' that democracy is the cause of economic progress or peace. History tells us that this is not necessarily the case, so we should be wary of accepting uncritically the application of allegedly scientific principles to politics. Of course, history may not be a reliable guide to the future but it is probably a better guide than the ill-digested extension of scientific theory to the conduct of human affairs. So, even if there is today a correlation between democracy and economic 'success', it may turn out to be evanescent *or* it may be that there are other correlations of which we are not aware.

The other assumption – of linear progression – is deeply rooted in our contemporary outlook on the world and, again, is the product of the influence of science on our understanding of human and social developments. Even if historically dubious, there is a strong sense in the West that the political evolution of our countries has been upward since the French and American revolutions. Whether it was the creation of the republic in France, the assertion of the power of the Commons in Britain, the extension of the electoral franchise to all classes and then to women, or the safeguards enshrined in modern constitutions, *all* point to the improvement of our political rights and the increase in our freedoms. However, we omit to take into account two important points. One is that there has been a far from linear movement in the emergence of present-day democracy. It is enough to compare Britain and France to realise the divergence in evolution and the differences in political practices. The other is that there is no guarantee that such 'progress' as has been made is permanent. Here it is enough to remind ourselves of the wholesale destruction of democracy brought about by Hitler's use of democratic procedures.

These caveats should serve as warning: we should not presume to want to 'export' our democracy when we do not know for certain how, or why, it has come about or whether it is causally as significant as we like to believe. Otherwise, it is possible that the translation of our 'best intentions' into a blueprint for the establishment of democracy in the non-West will come to a short, nasty and brutish end. Although NATO never claimed officially that it wanted to 'export' democracy to Afghanistan, the amount of resources that have been devoted to 'democratise' the Karzai regime is revealing of the assumptions the West continues to make about the most relevant and desirable political arrangements in the non-West. The assumption about holding elections is that it will assert the president's legitimacy. But, as with other such presumptions, the West has neglected to consider that a politician's legitimacy in Afghanistan is derived from a large number of factors, of which 'democratic' elections may turn out to far less relevant than has been assumed.

So maybe the time has really come to start rethinking the West.

TWO

Identities

WE SHALL SEE in due course that rethinking the West involves thinking *tout court*. But for now it is important to set the terms of the exercise more clearly. The aim of the book is not to give a simple definition of West and non-West but to examine how the terms of the debate between these (in some large measure imagined) parts of the world are recasting the theoretical, conceptual, ideological and political framework within which the West operates. This will mean both to expose the limits of Western rationality and to identify the factors that have troubled its long-established and still very self-assured sense of rational superiority. Of course, I do not mean to suggest here that the West is either losing its place in the current world order or that it is necessarily in despair about its future. Rather, I would like to explore why its moral and conceptual foundations are now under closer examination than before.

Although the distinction between West and non-West may appear artificial in the age of globalisation, and many find it misleading, it is in fact increasingly instrumentalised in our thinking – whether we like it or not. The age of instant communications and an enlarged European Union have, paradoxically to some, brought about greater uncertainty about our identities and greater resort to a dichotomous form of thinking: us and others, here and there, North and South, developed and underdeveloped, Christian and Muslim, locals and immigrants, and so on. The fact that the 'other', the South, is now well implanted in the West – in our midst, as the xenophobes point out – has brought this dichotomy closer to home and has made it more insistent in our ways of thinking. And our politics has reflected this – as we saw in the previous chapter.

This mindset has reinforced, rather than reduced, a way of thinking based on distinction and difference, which is deeply rooted in the 'scientific' theories we use to explain the world around us. In the next chapter, I shall examine in some detail what this binary form of reasoning implies for our understanding of causality and change. Here I want to look at how it affects our ability to rethink some of the key questions with which we now have to deal. We tend to view what I call the West and the non-West as relatively well defined and all too often as mutually exclusive categories. One is either Western or not. But a moment's notice makes clear that this approach is problematic. To point out only the most obvious quandary: is being Western a geographical or a behavioural characteristic? Is the British Asian who does not speak English more Western than the urbane, Oxford-educated and English-speaking Indian businessman from Punjab? Is being Western a state of mind? Or does it mean to be 'modern'? But, then, what does 'modern' mean? Is the above-mentioned businessman who slaughters a goat for good omens 'modern'?

The confusion is all the greater given that there is – and has been for some time – in Western countries a plethora of movements seeking 'wisdom' and different forms of rationality from non-Western sources. Many in the West are adepts of Zen Buddhism,

Indian Vedic medicine, voodoo, Kabbalah, yoga or African parapsychology – thus leading a life that is at odds with the Western precepts on which they were brought up. To them, none of these beliefs or practices is incompatible with being Western but the choices they make put into question the clear distinction between West and non-West. Not only does it evidence some disenchantment with the Western forms of religious or secular rationality, but it also points to a 'fuzzying' of the notionally clear-cut definitions of identity that are common currency in the West. But perhaps those who profess attachment to non-Western forms of thinking are still profoundly Western in that they have simply inverted the received wisdom: to them, non-West – rather than West – is best. Which is still a way of conceiving West and non-West in dichotomous terms. And if that is the case, then maybe these Westerners are not as subversive as they think they are. 'Their' non-West is very Western in nature.

A similar kind of distorted dichotomous reasoning is to be found among some ecological prophets, who sometimes argue that Africans who live in poverty are in fact 'happier' than competitive, materialistic and alienated Westerners. If only the West could learn from Africa in this way, they say, we would be improved spiritually.[1] The quest for happiness, to which the Americans are constitutionally bound, has often sought solace from the non-Western way of life. And, on reflection, this is not new. It follows on from the Renaissance view of the 'savage' as an exotic creature of comfort and pleasure – closer to nature than the now excessively mechanical Western man. This conception of the noble savage is still an important aspect of our vision of the world, and not just among anthropologists like Lévi-Strauss who bemoaned the inhuman consequences of modernity.[2] But here, as ever, that

---

1. See, for instance, Robert, 2004.
2. Lévi-Strauss, 1970.

conception of the world is built on binaries – in this case, 'savage' and 'civilised'.

Less obvious, but equally revealing, is the postcolonial trend in the human and social sciences. Here, dissatisfaction with the Western (read imperialist) historical account of the world and the theories upon which it is based has led scholars and activists to seek a 'non-Western' standpoint.[3] These alternative theories, ranging from literature to anthropology, reject (in part at least) the assumptions that underpin Western thinking. So, for example, they decry the notion of a literary canon – which they see as the crude assertion of the superiority of Western literature. Instead they advocate either a different basis for the appreciation of non-Western literatures or a post-modern approach to text, whether literary or not. More broadly, there is an argument that what passes for 'art' in the West confines creative expression to a limited type of artistic output whereas in fact a different understanding of what art is would bring to light other forms of beauty or achievement, which the Western approach does not take into account.[4]

Yet, this postcolonial argument can also be seen – and I would argue ought to be seen – as the flip side of a very Western approach. What seems to be at issue is the nature of the canon, *not* whether the notion of canon itself is a relevant means of assessing artistic output. It is about making place for different forms of *art*, not just those that are seen as quintessentially Western, *not* whether it is justifiable to segregate various forms of creative expression into 'art', 'craft' or 'artefact'. It is about berating Western arrogance from the safe confines of the Western academy on account of one's supposed non-Western standpoint; *not* about contributing a creative or intellectual form of expression that actually challenges the Western approach. And in this

---
3. See Chakrabarty, 2000.
4. See Thompson, 2005.

way the so-called postcolonial and post-modern challenge to Western theory should be seen as an offshoot, albeit critical, of that very theory. No one can read let alone understand Gayatri Spivak who is not already well versed in the arcane language and forms of reasoning of a particular Western (in this case French) philosophical approach to the world.[5] It is doubtful the actual, as opposed to imagined, 'subalterns' recognise themselves, or find an explanation for their lives, in the writings of those who profess to speak on their behalf. Indeed, Spivak speaks *from* the West *to* the West in very (esoteric) Western language.[6]

What this suggests, of course, is that what counts as West and non-West is complex, confusing and can easily be made simplistic. Here, what I am trying to convey, which is not properly recognised in the use I make of this dyad, is the fact that the conception of the world in dichotomous terms, including (I readily admit) West and non-West, is itself a very Western way of approaching reality. My claim, however, is not that I can think in a non-Western way, which would rightly be seen as suspect, but that I can try to make plainer the limits and contradictions of Western forms of thinking. I also aim to present, however sketchily, the nature of the challenge now faced in the West by what I call non-Western types of rationality. Therefore, in the remainder of the chapter I explore what it would mean to rethink some of the crucial questions we face today in ways that stretch the boundaries of current social science theories. I do so in the full knowledge that I, myself, speak from within the fort but that I do so based on a lifetime studying how people from other parts of the world (in my case, chiefly Africa) conceive of their existence.

---

5. See Spivak, 1999.
6. See, among others, Young, 2004.

Who are we?

This is obviously the first, and probably most difficult, question to ask if we are to think through the various forms of rationality we live by. From what standpoint, other than my own, can I ask what it means to be Western? And is it plausible to claim that there is but one way of conceptualising who we are? To break out of the vicious circle into which these two questions lock us, it is only possible to answer by way of a critical gaze on the assumptions that stand behind the standard approaches to the relationship between our understanding of identity and our conception of the world. What this means is that we should not take for granted either the definitions with which we work or the concepts we use to explain psychological, social and political behaviour. Nor should we accept at face value the claim that theories in the social sciences have acquired the same kind of scientific 'status' as those that have evolved in the physical (or hard) sciences.

So, starting at the beginning, we in the West think of ourselves as self-standing, autonomous and rational individuals, who have chosen the ways in which we live socially together. We see such a way of being as the logical outcome of the development of society since the Enlightenment and the rise of the scientific understanding of the world, which have led to the Industrial Revolution and the production of the technology on which our everyday lives depend. We consider the protection of individual human rights as the pinnacle of a civilised way of living, in which we value each other as persons and seek to protect both our individuality and our personality from undue interference from others or from the state. Therefore we view our conception of the human being and our arrangements for living in society both as the most progressive and as being possessed of the greatest potential for individual advancement and fulfilment. As we see it, it is because of the way we have managed to liberate and protect the individual that we make it possible for each person to seek the best for him/herself.

The political and social arrangements we have put in place and the economic market system that underpins our way of life are based on what we call the exercise of individual free will and on the ways we interact socially with each other. Although we recognise the importance of many social groupings – ranging from family to religious, ethnic or regional affiliation – we conceive of these as concatenations of individual persons bound together by history, tradition, language, kin, class or geography. Groupings are understood as aggregations of individuals rather than as bounded matrices within which the person is born, reared and socialised. In other words, we view human beings as separate persons who grow up and join society as equals, even if they are heavily conditioned by the particular characteristics of the groupings to which they belong at birth. As they are socialised, first by the family, then by the schooling system and finally by the social and professional worlds in which they function, these individuals detach themselves in important ways from the strictures of the groupings into which they were born. They become increasingly autonomous individuals, able and willing to make decisions on the basis of their needs and desires rather than on the traditions from which they come.

The core assumption of our Western ways is that we are what we become. And what we become is very largely in our hands. The liberty we have of making the choices of what to become is precisely the outcome of the progress our societies have made since the Enlightenment and the Industrial Revolution. It is through our efforts that we have created the conditions enabling us to have this free choice. Although the post-war existentialists argued that the exercise of free will could become a burden too heavy to bear, it is the general consensus within the West that it is in fact the greatest factor in the liberation of the individual from the horrors of material want, the constraints of metaphysical beliefs and the yoke of social conventions. The capacity of the modern-day Western individual to exercise free choice in his/her economic, social and political decisions is effectively enshrined in the constitutional dispensations that set the parameters of our lives in society. It is the result of the centuries of political struggles through which we have defined our individual rights and established the rules that would protect them.

The other key assumption about why we are who we are is that modern Western (wo)man is directly the product of a distinct path to 'progress', which we now profess to be universal. There is a dual supposition here. The first is that 'progress' is meant to be the extent to which human beings are able to exercise their free will as individuals. The other is that there is an identifiable, or recognisable, way in which this is achieved: individualisation by way of Westernisation, as it were. This interpretation of our history amounts to the widespread perception in the West that the present condition of our societies, for all their shortcomings, is to be adjudged as better than those that prevail in either less developed economically or less politically free countries. It may not be the intention of our social and political theorists, and it is certainly politically incorrect to say so explicitly, but the upshot of the view we have of ourselves inevitably generates a sense of Western superiority. We don't like to gloat or to make it too obvious but deep down we *do* believe that our social, political and economic arrangements are not just the best in the history of mankind but also, and this is crucial, the best in the present historical circumstances.

That we think in this way about who we are is clearly the result of the theories of change, evolution and progress that were developed in the nineteenth century and still inform our understanding of the world. It is indeed the combined impact of, among many, Darwin and Marx that consolidated our view of the evolution of individual and society. This is not to say that Darwin, who was deeply religious, would have acquiesced to the various, often simplistic, tenets of 'social Darwinism' that have sprung up since he lived. Nor is it to say that Marx would have had any truck with our belief that capitalism is infinitely able to reform itself and thereby to maximise individual and societal benefits. Nevertheless, there is little doubt that the nineteenth century cemented our conception of the evolution of society along a particular path, culminating in the liberal democratic and market order, which we now consider to be the best, or (more modestly) the least worst, and which we hold to be desirable for all.

I am less interested here in debating whether this Western economic and political dispensation is effectively the best than in looking at the consequences of such assumptions for the way in which we see ourselves and look upon others. For it is indeed the case that such a vision of our 'progress' implies a sense of distinction that puts distance between us and the others. And that distance is problematic in many ways. First, there is the conundrum of who belongs to this West: does one need to grow up in the West to be part of it or is it possible to acquire the characteristics deemed to be Western? Second, is our conception of the individual to be taken as the universal attribute of those who are most 'advanced' or is it merely the Western variant of the 'modern' person? Finally, how can we (in the West) assess the merit and indeed the future evolution of those who are *not* individuals in the sense in which we understand it? In the process of trying to address these questions I shall discuss more precisely what it would mean to rethink our identities.

My argument here is that the problem is not so much one of finding out how individuals in the West and non-West may be similar or differ as it is one of looking into the ways in which we *think* about the issue of what an individual person is. And why we do so. The idea that society is made up of autonomous free-standing individuals is one that is commonsensical and that no one – from the pensioner on the bus to the political philosopher in her ivory tower – disputes. It is the foundation stone of our social theories and yet *historically* it is not so straightforward. In point of fact, it is a very recent conception. Indeed, until the Enlightenment, the lands that today constitute Europe were governed by religious, metaphysical and 'traditional' beliefs that gave scant leeway to the person qua individual. The same was, and still largely is, true in the rest of the world. The notion of the individual was subsumed under the practical, ideological and religious realities of the grouping to which that individual belonged. In other words, what a person was did not primarily derive from his/her intrinsic personality but from his/her place within the community from which (s)he issued.

From that perspective, the individual in the sense in which we understand it today simply did not exist. What that means more concretely is that it was literally inconceivable to think of the person outside of the social tissue within which (s)he was born and lived. And even if that person migrated, (s)he remained defined by the characteristics of her/his original community. In the new environment, that person might in due course change her/his identity by acquiring some/many of the attributes of the host grouping. But (s)he would never be viewed, nor indeed think of her/himself as a freestanding individual, able to move across social spaces at will. Of course, each person was endowed with a number of individual skills and specific knowledge, which could be deployed in any community. But the point is that what the person was, and was seen to be, was not primarily the sum total of individual attributes but rather the ways in which these attributes combined within the environment to which the person belonged.

Rather like the chemical world, the social realm was seen as one in which the properties of the individual were only meaningful, could only be 'activated', when in relation with others. Just as it would not make sense to speak of electrons other than within the rest of the atomic structure, it was pointless to define individuals other than as part of the social world. From that standpoint, a detached individual was no more 'viable', indeed no more conceivable, than a detached electron. And if we were to follow this analogy a little further we would be led to say that the present view of the free-standing individual is a scientific *nonsense*. But we do not need to make spurious use of the parallel with chemistry in order to point out that the question of who we are, or rather who we think we are, is seriously dependent on the way in which we conceive of the individual in our Western societies. And that is historical and relative, rather than objective and scientific.

We do, of course, have an idea of what this other type of society might look like thanks to the work of anthropologists. Yet, we must remember that the very discipline was built on the assumption that its remit was to study what was at the time dubbed 'primitive' – that is, in my jargon, non-Western – societies. It is no coincidence that anthropology should have been born at the tail end of the nineteenth century, which I have already pinpointed as being the period when theories of evolution were consolidated and the social sciences emerged. It was indeed the accepted view that the West was now *developed*, which made it more imperative than before to understand what *un*developed societies looked like and how societies moved from 'primitive' to 'modern'. In this way, anthropology – the rise of which coincided with colonial expansion – sought both to understand the relation between the individual and grouping in 'primitive' societies and to conceptualise the trajectory from the socially bound 'traditional' person to the free 'modern' individual found in twentieth-century Western society.[7]

At best anthropology managed to explain both how individuals were conceived and how that definition derived from their place within the community in which they lived. Let me give some examples of how different conceptions might utterly transform the notion of the person. If, as in many African societies, the world is composed of the living and the dead and if it is understood that these two groups interact in some specific ways, then the notion of what an individual is must perforce include many invisible facets. If, as in India, there is a strong belief in reincarnation, then obviously one's own person is part of a long line of individuals (human and possibly non-human) of which one is only a particular representation. If caste is the defining characteristic of a group of individuals, then it is clearly the case that who they are, who they believe they are, and what others believe them to be, are 'naturally' prescribed. If, as Geertz noted in Indonesia, the personality of the newly born is determined by the name of the ancestor it is given, then here too the psychological and (especially social) make-up of that person is clearly 'overdetermined'.[8]

In all the cases above, for the individual to sever him/herself from the group is, quite literally, to become a non-person, to cease to be a human being. It is inconceivable. Now, faced with this state of affairs, our Western response is twofold. In the first instance, we associate such conceptions of the individual with 'primitive', 'backward' or 'not-yet-developed' societies, which will eventually change. Hence, we project our view that there is but one path of social modernisation, which will eventually result in a process of individualisation as occurred in the West. Second, we point to the countless individuals who have escaped the constrictions of such

---
7. See Barnard, 2000.
8. See 'Person, Time and Conduct in Bali', in Geertz, 1973.

'traditions' to no apparent harm and who have adapted easily to Western societies. Here we comfort ourselves with the idea that *individual* transformation is really akin to Westernisation. High-class Brahmins are now living in Silicon Valley, working at the cutting edge of technology and are married to non-Brahmins. Nigerian surgeons work in London and lead a life that has little in common with that of their community of origin. Clearly, these individuals are decidedly *not* non-persons – or at least they appear comfortable with the fact that they have broken with the yoke of 'tradition'. They are now like the rest of us.

All this is true but it is misleading. Our conclusion is based on the assumption that at heart we are individually all the same and that it is only the material circumstances of our lives that determine what sort of person we become.[9] This is correct in a general sense but it is simplistic in two important ways. One is that it presumes that those who behave like us *are* like us and, even more questionably, that they consider themselves to be like us. There is no good reason to believe this. The Nigerian surgeon may also believe in the power of his ancestors. The Brahmin engineer in California may also fear that the betrayal of his caste will rebound on his future life. Second, it gives far too little importance to the fact that we are made up of multiple identities, not all of which are consistent with each other. We project the fact that in the West our multiple identities are not excessively dissonant onto those of non-Western origin who live in the West and appear to be perfectly well integrated. But we have no way of knowing the extent to which the lack of fit between their Western and non-Western identities is a problem and how it may affect their sense of self and their behaviour. And we have precious little notion of how they think of themselves, of the

---

9. See Carrithers et al., 1985.

people among whom they live and of those to whom they are connected in their community of origin.

So, let us for a moment imagine what the study of society based on a different notion of the individual would imply. I start from two examples drawn from real life. The first is drawn from the case of the African businessman who returns home from the USA to set up a new business. In America he had gone to a prestigious business school, set up a very successful computer business, which he had sold at great profit, and now he wanted to start up a similar company back in West Africa. By all accounts his academic and business career in the USA had been spectacularly brilliant, very largely because he had mastered the latest financial and technological innovations that made his original investment so successful. He had already been approached by local investors, who wanted to buy him up and had received offers from competitors who hoped to harness his skills. In short, his future in the West seemed assured precisely because he had absorbed the West's ways so adroitly.

However, on his return to Africa he was soon beset with problems and the business, set up along the same lines as his first (American) one, began to decline. Within five years he was bankrupt and was forced to return to the USA to start all over again. The reasons he failed back home are complex but they boiled down to three factors. The first is that he was not able to run the business in the same way since both his employees and his customers refused to conform to the Western ways with which he was familiar. The second was that, once home, he had to operate with multiple identities, some of which impinged directly on his business, which he had forgotten or suppressed whilst living in a Western society in which these other identities were meaningless or redundant. Finally, he discovered quickly that back home the mark of success, the signs of prowess, the evidence of status, were not linked as straightforwardly to technical and financial wizardry, and ultimately to wealth, as they had been in the USA. In order to be recognised as a thriving entrepreneur he had to evince *communal* rather than *individual* 'substance', which meant spending his income on socially desirable grounds rather than investing it for economic gain.

Now, it might be thought that this case merely illustrates the fact that Africa has not yet developed enough to enable the proper flowering of the capitalist ethos but that this will eventually happen. And when it does, such African entrepreneurs will be able to return and thrive in their home countries. This may be true if we assume that Africa *will* develop in this way, but it leaves out the other side of the equation, which has to do with the sort of 'individual' this African businessman actually was. Although fully Western for practical purposes, and considered as such by his American peers, he found that in Africa the complex and multiple identities that combined to make him the person he was, indeed to make him a person, made it impossible to resist what the West would see as the 'traditional' social and financial pressures he faced. This was not so much because he was coerced but because he himself shared the beliefs from which these so-called 'traditional' obligations were drawn. He was not able to avoid giving employment on the basis of social/kin relations rather on merit because he was himself part of a network of reciprocity that marked his own identity. He could not resist the redistribution of his wealth to those who were socially dependent on him because he recognised the merit of the obligation placed on him as the most highly educated and financially successful member of his own community. In other words, his conception of what it meant to be a proper person was firmly shaped by the community in which he now lived again – despite the clear evidence that to allow such factors to affect his business would lead to ruin.

The second case, as mentioned in the Introduction, concerns a woman born in France of North African parents who decides to wear the *niqab* against her parents' wishes. This case is the opposite of the previous one: that woman was born in the West but appears to behave as would someone in the (Muslim) non-West. Here, as we have discussed before, the woman makes two claims, which seem to be contradictory to the Western way of thinking. The first is that she is choosing to dress in this way out of free will. The second is that she claims this sartorial choice increases her sense of freedom. We are willing to concede that she is entitled to exercise her freedom in the way she pleases, including wearing a garment that effectively restricts her everyday freedom and exposes her to discrimination. But we find it difficult to accept that her choice, which goes against the history of greater female emancipation, can possibly enhance her freedom in the Western society in which she was born and which is firmly hostile to a dress code widely seen as 'constraining' women. To many, this decision appears to be a step back in the perceived evolution of greater individual female freedom.[10]

And yet it is plain that such a move must be seen as 'modern' rather than 'traditional', in that it is clearly a response to the changing sense of identity among a number of second- or third-generation French Muslim women. By which I mean that the decision to wear the *niqab* is not a return to an ancient 'tradition' that had been abandoned in the West but the construction of a modern identity that relies on a reinterpretation of selected elements of a tradition that has continued to evolve, and evolve differently, in different Muslim societies. In that sense it is firmly an 'invented tradition', such as we commonly find in our Western societies. For

---

10. It may appear that the *niqab* is similar to the habit worn by nuns. However, there are two important differences. One is that the nun's habit is not claimed to be a religious 'requirement'. Some nuns dispense with it. The second is that there is no suggestion that nuns should also veil their faces. In effect, they are merely wearing a 'uniform'.

example, what shocks the majority of French people is not so much the 'myth' of the supposedly proper image of a Muslim woman as the fact that this image should so clearly go against what are seen as permanent advances in the status of women in France. Indeed, the legislation to ban the *niqab* in public places is partly based on the view that such covering of the body and face goes against the equality of men and women.[11]

But what would it mean to rethink this question in terms other than the present dichotomy — these women are either being forced or they seek political provocation — neither one of which is acceptable in our Western societies? It would mean in the first instance accepting that there is no inevitable 'progression' in the emancipation of women — at least as measured by the way they dress. In other words, the assumption that the historical march to greater freedom necessarily involves the gradual disrobing of the female body should be questioned. More significantly it would indicate that the relationship between identity and emancipation is neither linear nor irreversible. This implies, second, that the very texture of Western identity, the very nature of what we are, of who we think we are, can evolve in ways that do not fit the theory of a neat 'progressive' advance in the direction of what we take to be Westernisation. Third, it would imply the acceptance of a new 'modern' — as opposed to 'traditional' — Western way of thinking that is clearly at variance with the accepted consensus. Obviously, recognising that one can be at the same time Western and *niqab*-clad requires a revision of our conception of women. And in the end, this — rather than the claim that it is a sign of the ascent of fundamentalism — is why the decision by Western-born women to conform to this invented tradition is what most challenges the West.

---

11. For an argument against the banning of the veil, see Scott, 2007.

This is what the French mean when they say that the wearing of such a garment goes against their values.

From this viewpoint, the French decision to ban the *niqab* is a sign of a loss of nerve and of the inability to rethink the nature of some of the social changes taking place in society. The old nineteenth-century code by which politicians and intellectuals alike define what it is to be French and conceptualise present French identity is no longer up to the job of making sense of what is happening in today's France. The claim that the state must resist the challenges to the 'republican order' is vitiated by a framework of understanding that is not able to explain or to deal with a social and historical reality in which the notion of the individual is not what it had been assumed to be. If in the case of women's sartorial choices the dilemma is clearest in France, the same conundrum affects all Western societies. The belief in the clash of civilisations in the USA or the commitment to a form of multiculturalism in the UK, which does not seem to 'resolve' the key question of American or British 'identity', are similarly eloquent examples of the limits of our way of thinking in regard to the presence of 'others' in Western societies.

By implication, a rethink along these lines would suggest that we may not be who we think we are – or, in other words, that the way we define ourselves, our core values and central identity, may no longer be fit for purpose. If in the past, Western societies managed to integrate immigrants from (largely) Western countries, it seems that the presence of larger groupings of non-Western people, along with the spreading of other social logics that appear to defy our way of living, have taxed the methods by which we manage our societies. This is not merely due, as is sometimes suggested, to the conservative reaction of people who are jolted by what others do and believe. It is rather because the conceptual instruments we use to explain these new phenomena are no longer suited to the task at hand. And since these are based on the theories produced by the social sciences in the past century, it is to these that we shall have to return eventually.

What this means is that our difficulty in rethinking who we are is less the product of our blinkered, racist or xenophobic nature than of our inability to find the ideas, concepts and theories that would help make sense of what we are witnessing and living through. So what is read as a failure of nerve is in fact a failure in our thinking.

Who are the 'others'?

It is quite clear, however, that what we are, who we think we are, is intimately connected to who we think the 'others' are. Indeed, it is noticeable that surveys of public opinion in the West commonly point to the ways in which Westerners seek to differentiate themselves from those of the non-West. It is not enough to provide definitions of what makes us who we are – whether in terms of human rights, democracy or even race. We somehow need to anchor that response to a reference of how distinct that is from 'others'. As Sarkozy is famously reported to have once said, 'We in the West do not kill sheep in our bathtubs.'[12] And a much-hyped controversy in 2010 in France – a country not short of controversies in respect of its Muslim citizens – is the number of fast-food outlets that now sell (by definition only) *halal* hamburgers. One MP was quoted as saying that this constituted 'discrimination' against non-Muslims who want an ordinary, that is non-*halal*, meal.[13] The food chain aptly named Quick has now been forced to concede that it will provide non-*halal* hamburgers prepared and sealed away from the *halal* Quick outlet so as not to contaminate *halal* meat!

---

12. See http://galliawatch.blogspot.com/2007/04/marshall-plan-for-ghetto.html; accessed 7 February 2012.
13. See http://news.bbc.co.uk/1/hi/8524056.stm; accessed 7 February 2012.

What these banal, and ultimately petty, examples show is that the question of who 'we' and the 'others' are has now become more complex in Western societies. Instead of a difference, as originally set in the fifteenth century when Europe began to 'discover' the outside world, which consisted in identifying the 'other' in a geographically distinct part of the globe, we now have a situation where the two are fellow citizens. What we regard as the attributes of distant 'others', understood (if not necessarily endorsed) as part of different traditions, has now become part of our own societies. Polygamy, originally confined to certain parts of the world and vigorously combated by our missionaries, is now lodged in our midst. It is perceived to be such a problem that the Sarkozy government proposed in 2010 (a year of particular chauvinistic gyrations) that polygamy should be made into an offence justifying the stripping of French citizenship.[14] Even if these proposals were only meant to recapture part of the electorate that might otherwise have supported the National Front, they do reveal confusion at the heart of the French republican ideology. Furthermore, Sarkozy has received support not just from the right but also from a large section of the French political and intellectual elite.

The problem, in short, is not the distinction between 'us' and the 'others', a distinction that is found in any community, anywhere in the world. The problem for the West is different. It is, first, that the unquestioned sense of superiority between 'us' and the 'others' is now no longer so firmly unquestioned: 'we' have begun to wonder whether we are in fact so indisputably superior to the rest of the world – if only because it now looks as if East Asia might one day (soon?) overtake the West economically. Second, the very sense of our own identity – the superior 'we' – is now battered domestically. It may well be that 'we' do not kill sheep

---

14. See http://frenchtribune.com/teneur/10480-sarkozy-take-away-french-citizenship-criminal-offenders; accessed 7 February 2012.

in our bathtubs but that such could be done by our fellow citizens – even if, as is likely, the rumour has no basis in fact – has clearly shaken a particular kind of complacency. 'We' may still be clear that polygamy and genital mutilation are 'backward' practices that 'we' will not tolerate in the West. But the problem arises when 'our' fellow citizens choose to act in ways that go against both our social assumptions and our sense of identity – as is evident in the business of the *niqab*. The claim that one can be *both* Western and holders of values that 'we' find objectionable provokes utter confusion in the comfortable dichotomy between 'us' and the 'others' with which we have lived for so long.

The end result of this confusion is twofold. On the one hand, we may feel compelled to claim, and cling to, a notion of identity that harks back to an ancient, very largely invented, past – thus congealing a sense of self that is very reactionary. On the other hand, we may be tempted to move towards a form of cultural relativism: offering a picture of ourselves as tolerant of other practices on which we profess not to pass any critical judgement despite our *better* judgement. Examples of both are easily found. As concerns the former, in Britain, the British National Party (BNP) and the English Defence League (EDL) receive some popular support in their (very clumsy and confused) attempt to identify the very specific type of white English person that is 'indigenous' to the British Isles. Even if most people in the UK recognise the artificial nature of the exercise, they do not necessarily reject the quest for a definition. Regarding the latter, there is now a well-established current of opinion in the USA that supports the wearing of the Islamic scarf, and sometimes the *niqab*, on the grounds that it is an individual choice upon which one ought not to pass a judgement based on an assumed Western superiority.[15] Admittedly, that

---

15. See Scott, 2007.

argument rests on the view that the Western practice of individual choice *is* superior to other forms of social intercourse but it still confounds our sense of identity.

What this points to is a situation in the West where the very notion of a distinction between 'us' and 'others' is becoming blurred. This is partly due to this geographical shift, which has moved the divide from outside to within, or, to put it another way, which has made geography irrelevant as the sole marker of difference. But it is also because the fraying of this divide now occurs within our own *individual* sense of identity. That fact is often labelled by fearful reactionaries in the West as a 'loss of fibre' among the younger generations, now partial to rap and *beur* slang instead of remaining true to their 'European' heritage. Leaving aside the xenophobic subtext of such accusations, what is revealing here is the ways in which significant segments of European youth should now construct an identity that includes attributes more normally associated with the non-Western 'others'. This demonstrates not just that values are changing, and with them the notion of what it is to be 'fashionable', but also, and more importantly, that the 'other' could now be seen to be those who stand by the largely obsolete idea of what a Westerner is. Indeed, many young people (and not only in the alienated French *banlieues*) reject the Western values of the older generation.

As we have seen, this is partly a form of teenage rebellion – the contemporary version of *épater les bourgeois*. Ultimately, there is little reason for those who are concerned with such issues to worry: these young *bourgeois* will not easily turn their backs on the privileges they enjoy in present-day Western societies. However, what matters here is the form this defiance takes: it is no longer merely generational; it now touches on the idea of Western identity. What interests me here is the language of identity the youth employ and the attendant effects this may have on the debate about who the 'others' are. Will they have a different sense of the distinction between 'them' and the 'others' or will the integration of the present forms of 'otherness' they adopt reshape Western identity? Will the adoption of ostensibly non-Western clothes, culture, deportment and language have an impact on the emerging sense of difference the younger generation will live by in years to come? Is it more than merely a superficial fashion? Just as in Europe there are now more and more interracial couples, will there emerge a sense of Western identity encompassing many of the attributes that may appear today to be those of the non-Western 'others'?

The process by which a supposedly dominant society, in this case Western, adopts the ways of other traditions is nothing new. So what it is interesting to examine here is how the process now under way in the West affects Western rationality – or, to put it another way, how it may affect the assumptions underpinning our theories. Therefore, I now turn to a discussion of how we habitually conceptualise the 'other' both in commonsensical everyday fashion and in social science theory.

In everyday parlance, we hold people to be 'other' when we consider that their identities and their behaviour differ too radically from ours. But this is a very vague notion, which is tied to a large number of variables, not all of which are compatible. For instance, it could be a matter of origin, race, class, education, region or it could simply have to do with what is unknown to us. Moreover, we also need to pay attention to the question of whether the use of the term 'other' is meant neutrally, pejoratively or even with hostility, all of which can change over time or according to circumstances. So, the best that can be said is that the apparently commonsensical perception of the 'other' is a moveable feast, about which subjective opinion is all-important. And it is precisely the inability to identify who the 'other' is, other than in the concrete situation in which the question is asked, which points to the difficulty of extricating that question from that of the perception of who we are.

The upshot is that in everyday life the social and political consequences of identifying and living with the 'other' derive from the evolution of our own sense of self and our perception of who constitutes the 'others'. For instance, public opinion about the Jews who live in Europe has changed drastically over the course of the past century: anti-Semitism is no longer officially tolerated. However, levels of anti-Semitism continue to fluctuate according to domestic and international events: the recent rise in the UK and France is obviously connected to the increasingly hostile view taken of Israeli policies vis-à-vis the Palestinians. So, can it ever be said that Jews in Western Europe will cease to be viewed as 'others'? Well, we don't know; it will depend on circumstances. And the same applies to all recognised minority groups in any Western country. The recent controversy about the French treatment of the Roma from Romania and Bulgaria illustrates the fact that, although notionally European, the members of that community are widely perceived as being alien in France. They are obviously treated with greater disdain than other migrants from the European Union, which no doubt is due to their perceived marginality and their alleged refusal to live in 'normal' society.

Indeed, the plight of the Roma confirms the view that the perception of the 'other' is predicated on the ingrained assumption that in all societies there are always, there always have to be, some who are different, who 'go against the grain'. Perhaps only in this way can we be reassured about who we are: we are not like 'them'. And if that seems the only reliable way of identifying who we are, it stands to reason that there is no possibility that the 'other' will ever disappear from our radar. The only question is who that 'other' happens to be in the current circumstances. This very simple, and somewhat pedestrian, observation has considerable implications for the public policy of what is variously called assimilation or integration. Just as we know that poverty can never be eradicated in our societies since it is defined in relative (rather than absolute) terms, it would appear that not all members of society can be like 'us'. We *need* 'others'. And if that is the case, the best that can be hoped for is the devising of policies that make it possible to live together more, rather than less, harmoniously. So, perhaps it is time we should do away with the myth of 'assimilation' or 'melting pot'. Living together is a never-ending business that will always cast some out, to serve the role of the 'other'. Assimilation is relative: some groups are considered to be assimilated more rapidly than others and some groups appear not to assimilate.

These myths, by which we live, are not simply common sense. They also arise from the social and political theories which inform our way of life and our policymaking. The conceptualisation of the person, as discussed in the section above, entails a particular understanding of the relationship between the individual and the group. The assumption of the supremacy of the individual, the single person, over the grouping from which (s)he hails is the bedrock of our social theories. Indeed, we conceptualise the group as being a congregation of individuals bound together by social, cultural, linguistic, religious and other codes, which mark them out as a community. There is no place in social science – except in the anthropological study of distant 'other', usually less advanced, societies – for the reverse hypothesis: that is, the possibility that the individual is defined *by* the community. This has two serious consequences. The first is that we cannot make sense of Western individuals who subscribe to such a notion of group, or ascriptive, identity. That may be why we are tempted to cast them out, unless they change their ways. The second is that it creates a well-nigh unsolvable tension in theory between the conceptual primacy of the individual and the obvious relevance of the group, to which some might claim the strongest possible allegiance.

As a result, Western countries adopt contradictory policies, none of which is likely to 'resolve' the problem of integration, since the difficulty arises from the incompatibility between prevalent social theories about the individual and the realities of what might be called group psychology. At one extreme, the French insist that merely to acknowledge the existence of ethnicity or recognise the importance of communities is actually to create *communautarisme*. The upshot is that they can only contemplate policies that tackle individual social and economic inequalities, even when the problems are clearly related to racial, ethnic or religious – that is, group – discrimination. At the other extreme, the Americans believe in devising social policies along the lines of ethnic or community logic so as best to safeguard the interests of what they call minority groups. As a consequence, virtually all American citizens have come to define themselves in terms of their communal origins: African Americans, Cuban Americans, Irish Americans, and so on. Individual advancement, or the protection of individual rights, is believed to be best promoted by reference to such communities. Paradoxically, therefore, the American melting pot is made of apparently non-soluble blocs, living side by side and united only in their belief in the American ethos, whereas the French policy of individual assimilation is blind to the most obvious causes of inequity arising from group discrimination.

These differences between France and the United States clearly have their roots in their different historical trajectories. But since both have produced constitutions they believe to be models of how best to combine individual freedom with living together in society, it is interesting to look in more detail at the limits of their policies in terms of managing the presence of the domestic 'other'. Although they have opted for radically different options, what these two countries share is a belief in the primacy of the individual. Indeed, their constitutional framework is geared to protect individual rights and to guarantee equality. Where they differ is in their understanding of what an individual is and in their outlook on the relationship between the individual and the state. The Americans want to be protected *from* the state; the French to be protected *by* the state.

This has led them to different safeguards: the Americans stress individual legal protection; the French emphasise the rights of citizens. It is an important distinction. In the United States, individuals are conceived as having all the rights that are not denied them by the constitution. In France, citizens are thought of as having obligations, particularly with regard to the state, which are bound to restrict in some ways their individual rights. So, in practice, the French accept the supremacy of the (freely chosen and legitimately constituted) state over the individual, so long as their rights as citizens are preserved. The Americans do not: they believe in the need constantly to limit the reach of the state, the legitimacy of which is always to be renegotiated within the existing constitutional parameters – and these are liable regularly to be tested in court.

The differences, which have a bearing on how each country deals with the question of 'them' and 'us', are well illustrated in the contrasted stance taken on the question of secularism. On paper, the two agree on the separation of Church and State. Indeed, both ban religious education in state schools and religious symbols from public buildings. But here the similarities end. Secularism for the French means the private right of worship as protected by the state. In turn, the state is duty-bound to prevent religious interference with the lives of the *citizens*, who are supposed to be equal before the law. In the United States, secularism means that the state will not interfere in the religious beliefs, or practices, of the individual members of society. So, here we have confirmation that the key to the difference lies in the distinct vision of the role of the state. The founders of the American Constitution wanted to guarantee religious freedom from political interference. The fathers of French republicanism intended to protect the state, and thereby the citizens, from the interference of the Church, which combated the revolution and then the republic to the bitter end. So whereas the Americans place religious freedom above the purview of the state, the French uphold the absolute pre-eminence of the state in guaranteeing the citizen's right to practise any religion and to be free from religious interference.

This distinction, although quite clear and historically understandable, seems largely to escape those in each country who berate the practices of the other. The French do not understand how the United States can tolerate the unending demands of the various religious groups to have protected status for their practices, feasts, holidays, dietary or sartorial requirements, and so on. For their part, Americans are baffled by what they see as the French overreaction to such demands, which they see as belonging to the private sphere and, therefore, of no particular threat to the fabric of society. They cannot understand why the French should approve heavy-handed legislation to protect the republic's secularism. The French see mortal danger in the publicly sanctioned expression of religious (or ethnic) differences. The Americans believe that religious (or ethnic) tensions are best assuaged by allowing them their full, albeit private, expression. Hence, the complete failure of the Americans to appreciate why the French government decided, after lengthy consultation and with all-party support, to ban the Islamic scarf in secondary schools and, more recently, to ban the *niqab* (or face-covering *burqa*) in public places. Whether these decisions were foolish or not will become clearer in the future, but their rationale had everything to do with the prevailing consensus about the meaning of individual rights.

The comparison between the two is clear enough and it makes for an interesting contrast in Western secularism, but it does not explain either why both countries continue to have problems or why the attempt to 'resolve' them is vitiated by the limitations of social theories. The failings of the French approach are plain enough. The refusal to acknowledge that religion is now used by some minorities to combat what they perceive as ethnic racism makes it impossible for politicians to confront the issue directly. But state 'repression' is a blind alley. On the other hand, the American tendency to allow full expression of ethnic and religious demands has resulted in a spiral of particularistic claims, which weigh heavily on the social fabric. If the strength of the 'creationist' movement – with its impact on school curricula – is the most obvious face of this problem, the impact of religion on politics is probably even more fateful. The electoral weight of religious and ethnic lobbies can, and does, lead to policy choices that are clearly counterproductive: witness the effects of anti-abortion campaigns on health provisions or the influence of the Jewish lobby on US foreign policy in the Middle East. More generally, the fragmentation of the 'political voice' into myriad particular interests is clearly a threat to the cohesion of American society.

In both instances it is difficult to see how policymakers can escape the ideological and conceptual yoke that traps them. The French way to think through the problems is to set the discussion within the terms of the republican myth – that is, to redefine for the present time what those 'timeless' post-Revolution principles and values mean. So, for instance, it is thought possible in France to come to a firm conclusion about what constitutes a 'French identity', regardless of the fact that circumstances today, not least of which is the importance of the European Union, make it difficult to see what a concept of ur-Frenchness would be. In the United States, change takes place by means of the evolution of the legal landscape. Particular interest groups and individuals test the limits of the constitution, which is reinterpreted according to the changing social, political and cultural environment. Here too, therefore, the reference is to some ur-principles, setting the parameters of permissible change. But in both instances, the problem is less with the constitution than it is with its contemporary interpretation, which rests in the final analysis with those who are in charge of making policy. And here the difficulty is that politicians are unable (incapable or unwilling?) to contemplate policies that are unpalatable to public opinion. Policy advisers are told to guide their recommendations according to what is 'politically feasible'. This policy conservatism is obviously a bulwark against potentially radical change but it is also a brake on the process of rethinking that is so clearly needed in the West today.

So what would it mean to rethink who the 'others' are? And how would that make a difference? As I have already intimated, one way out of the blind alley would be to reconceptualise the notion of the individual. This would mean in the first instance to take into account that a person is *at once* and *simultaneously* a separate human being and a member of a number of social groupings. So what makes up the individual is constituted both of the person's singular characteristics and the social make-up, which grows out of a constantly changing interaction between the person and the various circles of sociability (from family to region, by way of religion, sport, leisure, ethnic, etc.). The mistake would consist in believing either that the individual attributes – whether physical, mental, psychological, cultural or economic – are cast in stone or that these circles of sociability are immutable. Both are liable to change, evolve, according to circumstances and therefore affect the specific notion of the individual that prevails, or is relevant, at any particular time. The upshot of this first point is that today's identities in the West should be seen as eminently changeable, unstable and fluid.

The second point would be to move away from the excessively sharp distinction between self and other that is at the heart of our social theory. Or, to put it another way, to consider that in today's Western societies the distance between 'us' and 'them' is both less clear and more fuzzy than our theories allow. As I have shown, one of the features of contemporary life is the extent to which what the 'other' is, or represents, is increasingly being adopted by ordinary people, particularly the youth. This is due to the fact that individual identities are less marked than before and the attributes of those who are otherwise labelled as 'others' are slowly becoming part of the mainstream. This process becomes unassailable when it is not recognised for what it is. An amusing example of this is when 'ordinary' parents, who might otherwise be racist, come to believe that dreadlocks are merely a youthful fashion accessory to which their sons are entitled. Not infrequently, they may defend this as part of 'their' identity, just as they did when male earrings came back into fashion. The inability to detect the 'other' in oneself is clearly an indication that the 'other's' influence is strong, and probably growing.

Following from this, a third factor in this process of rethinking would be to visualise the relationship between 'us' and the 'others' in a different way. Instead of starting from the premiss of separation, difference or dichotomy, it should be possible to conceptualise this relationship in terms of continuum. That is, to work on a theory of social relations built on a different premiss: individual human beings are changeable characters oscillating constantly in the extent to which they view themselves, or are viewed by others, as separate or composite. In other words, and returning to a scientific analogy, the 'properties' evinced by individuals should be conceived as infinitely variable rather than, as now, as the *given* attributes of each person. Here one would work with a principle of instability, rather than stability, the parameters of which would be determined according to circumstances. So, to take one example, the assessment of the relationship of a member of the BNP or EDL with members of the African community could not be made simply on the basis of that political allegiance. It would have to be seen in the complexities of the many situations in which this white EDL activist interacted with black people: hostile when seen as 'immigrants' but good mates at work, in the union or as sport partners. This is why the study of racism can never be conclusive. The results cannot be consistent since its existence is situational.

What this would mean, finally, and I will return to this in the next chapters, is that our social theories operate with excessively rigid units of analysis, which often hamper our research and constrain our understanding. If, as I have suggested, the focus on the individual as the single most important unit of analysis makes it more, rather than less, difficult to conceptualise what racism may mean in our contemporary societies, then we need to revise our analytical ways. This is what would happen in the physical sciences, where concepts and theories are discarded if they fail to account for observable realities. But the problem in the social 'sciences' is that it is less easy to accept that theories are at fault because the material with which we work, human beings, is infinitely more complex and malleable than theory can account for. As a result, it is all too easy to continue to assume our long-established concepts and theories are still relevant. So, to return to our example, a different approach would make it possible to understand racism as relational and situational rather than as a particular attribute of individual human beings.[16] This implies that we should cease to try to ascertain whether people *are* more or less racist but study why they *behave* in more or

---

16. On racism in the USA, see Sollors, 1987.

less racist ways depending on circumstances. If that is the case, then it is the circumstances, rather than the individuals, that require analysis. The same would be true of other issues, such as Islamophobia.[17]

Clearly, such rethinking would have major relevance to policy-making since a change in the unit of analysis would entail a change in the focus of policy. Instead of an attempt to refashion the individual, through education or psychology, it would entail much more work on the situation within which the problem emerged in the first place. It would imply the need to work with groups rather than individuals, and to place emphasis on group dynamics rather than on personal psychology. It would also force the acceptance of the fact that problems arising from the relationships between 'us' and 'others' are indeterminate, unstable and relative. This would change the very definition of what constitutes a 'problem', which would have a major impact on how it is conceptualised and what remedies might be applied to alleviate it. Banal as this observation may seem, its application would entail a wholesale revolution in how policymakers analyse, explain and attend to the major social issues with which they are confronted. If, say, politicians were able to acknowledge that, as hinted above, racism is inevitable they would perforce have to concentrate not so much on how to 'root it out' from obdurate individuals, but on how current living and working conditions bring about a particular form of racism (Islamophobia, xenophobia, etc.), with particular consequences for social cohesion. Incidentally, this would also make it easier to explain why each country thinks it has a better handle on such problems than its neighbours – since it would entail looking at one's own stance from the perspective of the 'other'!

---

17. For a wide-ranging discussion of this issue, see Sayyid and Vakil, 2010.

Why is the West more 'advanced'?

The very notion of who we in the West are today is premissed on a sense that we stand at the pinnacle of a series of converging scientific, technical, moral and social developments that make us more 'advanced' than the rest of the world. This very common, and commonsensical, idea rests on a vision of development that binds together these various scientific and socio-political advantages. Therefore the assumption is that the West is 'advanced' not just because it is the product of cutting-edge science, but because its form of development combines technological, social and political features in ways that are demonstrably superior. Or, to put it another way, our 'development' has been successful because it is grounded in a juxtaposition of scientific and societal advances, which have secured for us the framework within which we have been able to make such assured progress. So, in less politically correct language, we have managed to mesh scientific, social and political improvements in a uniquely *productive* way. That, rather than merely GDP, is what puts us 'ahead' of the rest of the world.

Yet, there are today a number of issues that test this simple, though powerful, idea of what the 'advanced' West is. Because in the minds of so many – and not just among ordinary people – progress is equated with material wealth, the obvious economic success of a number of Asian countries, particularly China, is a challenge to the West's sense of superiority. Equally, the fact that Asia's mastery of sophisticated technology is making rapid strides strikes at the long-held view that the West is, and will likely remain, the centre of technical innovation. At the same time, there is clearly in the West a sense that the search for material satiation is beginning to undermine society. This is perhaps best illustrated by the undeniable epidemic of obesity now afflicting Western societies and, increasingly, those countries where fast food has established a foothold (often on the paradoxical ground that being Western it is more 'modern'). But it is also visible in the widespread increase in mental ailments such as depression. Not surprisingly, this has led to the argument that it is the inexorable rise of secularism, and the attendant decline in spirituality, which has conspired to deprive Western societies of the spiritual qualities that underpin a healthy morality. Is secularism the price all societies pay for technology-driven progress? Or is this a peculiarly Western problem?

However, the biggest question of all is that of the environment. Is the increasingly sophisticated knowledge we now have about the effects of global warming an indication that economic growth and survival are incompatible? Are the assumptions the West has long made (and in many ways continues to make) about the ability of science and technology to find solutions to ecological problems still valid? Can we uncover the science that will produce the technology to preserve the future of the planet whilst *at the same time* allowing the non-West, or South, to develop economically? Or are we going to have to come to terms with a notion of progress that does not rest on continuous economic growth? And, if so, do we have the theoretical tools we need to make sense of this new form of rationality? Are we hampered by a way of thinking that combines theories of development and assumptions about progress that are increasingly at odds with present realities?

Therefore the questions we need to ask are twofold: what are the assumptions underlying our notion of development and what are the connections between development and 'advancement'? The first requires that we look at the very theoretical pillars of our physical and social sciences – which in effect means that we revisit our notion of progress. The second implies that we examine the material and moral basis of our societies, with a view to asking how we have come to define well-being in the way we have and what this means for our understanding of development. As ever, I am less interested here in trying to assess the nature of the West's malaise, or its supposed turn away from materialism, than in the thought processes that affect how we come to view ourselves as more or less 'advanced'. And I want to try to tease out the extent to which these are shaped, or influenced, by the non-West. In so doing, I try to go beyond the commonsensical but superficial observation that, for instance, Westerners need to turn to Asian spirituality because they live in aggressively secular societies. This may be relevant but I am more concerned here with the ways in which Western rationality (that is, its theoretical baggage) may be reaching its limits and how it may be challenged by other forms of rationality.

The reason why the West thinks it is more 'advanced' is not simply due to its undoubted scientific, technological and military superiority, since the historical experience of the main Western countries shows that their domination may fluctuate. Many in the West are prepared to countenance the possibility that the USA may in future no longer have the preponderance it once enjoyed. They might even be willing to concede that other, non-Western, countries will soon also be 'advanced' in this way. However, and this is the key, the assumption is that they would become 'advanced' *because of* their ability to follow the development path already blazed by the West. In other words, at bottom the West's sense of its own superiority is rooted in the belief that there is but one way of developing that can secure at one and the same time economic progress, material benefits and a socio-political arrangement that makes possible the most efficient use of the (material and moral) resources we need in order to progress in this fashion. That belief rests on the assumption of a *unilinear* form of development, which effectively translates into Westernisation: modernity is *ipso facto* Western.

In turn this assumption of a unilinear development path rests on three main pillars: scientific, socio-political and moral. The first is the least contentious since there is little debate about how scientific progress is made. Theories about the physical, biological and chemical realms are tested, their results are replicated and their predictions are confirmed in the real world. Development in this area is made when new theories afford more precise understanding of the phenomena under observation or are invalidated by new theories. In any case, advance is finally secured when the technology is developed to confirm or disprove what are at first merely theoretical speculations. And even when the theory is still incomplete, the success in translating theoretical hunches into workable techniques counts as progress. Indeed, we may know empirically why something works without being able at first to specify the theoretical reasons why. However, the presumption is that explanation will derive logically from the theoretical knowledge extant. In this sense, it is easy to show that there is in fact a *linear* form of progress in the sciences that demonstrably results in 'advancement'. When such 'advancement' ceases, science moves into another linear type of reasoning. Thus it has the capacity to remain critical vis-à-vis the theories it uses to secure 'advancement'.

The difficulty arises when this assumption is applied to the socio-political, economic and moral realms. In the socio-political field, the presumption is that the West has devised forms of governance and of living together that are both superior to earlier templates and more 'progressive' than those found elsewhere – that is, the non-West. As concerns morality, the theory here is that the move to a secular type of society, one in which religion (or the Church) no longer controls behaviour and politics, is at the root of a system of civil and human rights, which has vastly increased our freedoms and our ability to push the boundaries of enlightened thought. This enabled the move from the metaphysical to the scientific, thus making possible the technological and industrial revolutions. So here too there is a presumption that morality has progressed from a metaphysical posture of fear to a more liberating science-based secularism. And although the latter has been fiercely contested – not least in the recent 'science versus religion' debates – in practice our social legislation is based on notions of civil rights that rest on individual and secular foundations.

But here there are three problems with our rationality. The first has to do with the presumption that development is unilinear. The second is the belief that such development is cumulative and progressive. And the third is the notion that, as seems to be the case in the physical sciences, progress in the human and social fields is also irreversible. I take these in turn.

(1) The assumption that development is unilinear is based on two key arguments. One is that the huge improvements that have been made in the West have brought improved living conditions and economic well-being, which confirm an evolutionary vision of progress. The other is that this form of progress is validated by the theories of economic, political and social sciences that underpin our analysis of the modern world. In other words, both the realities of our achievements and the theories used to explain them point to a singular path to development. The collapse of Communism is said to have removed any competitor to the market economy. The inexorable adoption by non-Western countries of apparently democratic forms of governance is in the process of invalidating other political dispensations. And the ostensible growth of rights-based social systems demonstrates the advantage of secular and individual arrangements for the expression of free choice.

However, there are at least three obstacles to the apparent triumph of the theory of the single path to development. One is that in all three areas – social, economic and political – there are vast differences between national models within the West. For example, it is debatable whether the Swedish and Italian models have much in common and whether they will converge in the future. The other is that there are now clear limits to the prospect for further development in the West. There is today the beginning of a debate on the need for 'degrowth', which obviously would go against the present economic rationale and affect how countries evolve in the future. And, finally, there is evidence that economic success is neither predicated on, nor necessarily a prelude to, Westernisation in a country's political and social arrangements. Indeed, it is questionable whether China, for example, will become politically and socially more 'Western' despite rates of economic growth that match the best the West has ever experienced. And in any event, what would it mean for China to be 'Western'?

If there are, or can be, forms of economic, political or social development that are both successful and at variance with the assumed Western template, then this throws down the gauntlet at our social sciences. To take only one example, our theories posit that development involves a gradual but continuous process of individualisation. As societies become more affluent and more secular, it is argued, 'traditional' social ties loosen and metaphysical constraints dissolve. People conceive of themselves, and increasingly behave, as separate autonomous individuals who make decisions primarily on the basis of personal choice. Over time, the weight of social, family and community pressure diminishes and individuals detach themselves from the webs of social bonds that enmeshed their parents, grandparents and ancestors. It is customary, therefore, to describe modern developed societies as being more atomised than the so-called traditional ones. And as a crude rule of thumb this is true.

However, it is by no means clear that, even in the West, this general process of individualisation has had similar outcomes. It is obvious, to pursue our previous example, that family ties in, say, Italy are both much more deeply rooted and more socially relevant than they are in Sweden. Furthermore, this is not (as some might argue) because Italy is less 'advanced' than Sweden. It is, rather, because family ties in Italy have not evolved, 'modernised', in the same way as they have in Sweden. This may be because there are clear societal differences between Catholic (southern) and Protestant (northern) societies or it may be because economic development in Italy has taken a course that is distinct from that of Sweden. There may well be a whole number of other reasons to explain this difference in the role of the family. But it means there is no obvious uniform type of social development that must necessarily result in a form of modernity in which the family matters less, or not at all.[18] The assumptions made in this respect are clearly based on a narrow, and biased, theory drawn from the experience of some (mostly northern and Protestant) societies – which presumes, among other things, that what we see in the USA today is what we will have in Europe tomorrow.

And the process of individualisation in Asia, for example, makes this point even more obvious. Although there are now many countries in that part of the world where levels of economic development are close to those of the West, social relations, and in particular the role of the family, have not evolved in the same ways. Outstandingly successful Chinese entrepreneurs continue to rely on family- or community-based forms of economic partnership, with no apparent ill effects on their businesses. Equally, ethnic ties bind very successful, and in every respect very modern, Nigerian businessmen. Thus, although it is broadly true that economic development eventually leads to greater individual autonomy, the forms that such individual autonomy takes remain congruent with

---

18. Now that birth rates are declining in Italy, it will be interesting to see whether the role of the family evolves in the direction of the Nordic pattern.

the social and cultural foundations of the society concerned. In other words, economic 'advancement' may take different social, and even political, paths – not all of which are similar to or even compatible with the Western template. Nor is it at all clear that the citizens of these non-Western societies automatically aspire to the Western condition of individualism that is assumed in our social science theories to be the 'natural' outcome of development – and hence of modernity. There are indeed many ways of being 'modern'. And there are many ways of being an 'individual'.

(2) The belief that social and political developments are, as in the sciences, both cumulative and progressive is a very powerful tenet of our theoretical armoury. Indeed, it is at the core of our Western rationality. To follow on from the previous example, it is generally assumed that the process of individualisation is sharpened over time: it becomes an increasingly prominent feature of being modern. It is also presumed that it is *progressive*, meaning here that it is an 'advance' on personal freedom, choice and therefore an improvement on the social conditions of those who came before us. Leaving aside the debate about whether it is morally better to be more individualised, I want to look at the theory behind this widely accepted aspect of our Western rationality. I have already explained why it is simply not tenable to posit that there is but one path to individualisation. Let me now examine the assumptions underlying the claims that such change is cumulative and progressive.

The first difficulty here has to do with the distinction between social and psychological change. Even if it were true that individualisation in the West has accrued cumulatively, which is debatable since it is likely to have accrued in leaps and bounds, it is clear that the process is not the same for the individual person. In fact, since mobility across continents is now a feature of the modern world – on a scale unmatched before – there are an increasingly large number of people who transplant themselves from non-West to West. And among them there is a wide range of adaptation to the Western norms of individuality – from those who become immediately comfortable with the individual-based lifestyle to those who become even more entrenched in the supposed communal traditions of the societies whence they came. So, the theory that people are socialised cumulatively into a given type of Western 'individual' is too simplistic to account for what actually happens. There is a gap, sometimes very large, between the psychological and social processes of individualisation that goes against the plain assumption of smooth evolution in this respect.

Similarly, it is questionable whether it can be demonstrated that such Western individualisation is 'progressive' or even that progress in this area can be objectively measured. No one denies that the protection of individual human rights is a positive development. But, above and beyond this civil advance, there are a number of aspects of individualisation that might be viewed as 'regressive'. Some social scientists point to forms of atomisation and alienation in society, which are pernicious for the individual and destructive of the social fabric. Others point out that the twin process of market consumerism and individualism leads to a restricted, and in extreme cases addictive, type of existence that undermines people and society. So it would seem somewhat presumptuous, and premature, to declare that Western individualisation is simply to be marked as progress. However, although we are quite willing to recognise the negative features of this process, we are still in thrall to social theories presuming to demonstrate that individualisation is necessarily liberating for the individual, and hence 'progressive'.

The picture is even more muddled if we consider the relation of individual to community in various Western countries. Although the USA is generally considered to be the society in which this process of individualisation has gone furthest, it is paradoxically a country where most people identify themselves by way of a communal or group allegiance. A century ago, it appeared that migrants to the USA sought above all to integrate and become 'real' Americans, to join the melting pot. However, today, as we have seen, everyone – including those who have been settled for several generations – feel compelled to present themselves in composite terms: African Americans, Italian Americans, Mexican Americans, and so on, or in terms of gender, sexual orientation and race. Indeed, so strong is this social pressure that it is those who do *not* identify in this way who are now beginning to argue they feel discriminated against. So in this brave new world of supposed free individuals, it has become necessary to situate oneself within a (real or invented) ethnic or 'lifestyle' community in order to be complete as a person and, perhaps more importantly, in order to compete successfully for resources, support, employment or education.

Now, this may or may not be considered a desirable, or progressive, development – analysts tend radically to disagree here – but it certainly does not fit the standard theories of individualisation. Far from being cumulative, the process of individualisation in the USA might be seen as circular – by which I mean that an excess of individualisation within a context of a multi-origin society is now calling forth a movement towards 're-communalisation'. The same might be argued about the role of religion in the USA. Although the country is secular, and that is not about to change, there are grounds for thinking that religion today plays a more significant role in American politics than it did, say, in the 1930s. Americans have commonly been more ostensibly religious than their European counterparts but what is noticeable today is how public, political and aggressive the expression of religious sentiment has become. That stance is forcing the issue of religious affiliation, belief and practice to the forefront of what constitutes individual identity in the country. So here again it seems difficult to subscribe to theories of social development that posit a cumulative and 'progressive' increase in degrees of secularism.

(3) This takes us to the final assumption: that is, the belief that social 'progress' is irreversible. What I mean here is not so much the conviction that such progress cannot be undone – as clearly it has been during wars, crises, invasions, and so on – but that the features of such advances once acquired are here to stay. Barring accident, therefore, the West would not expect, to take one example, that universal suffrage would ever be reversed. A reversal could be forced on some people under some circumstances, but the knowledge that universal suffrage is a basic human right would never be willingly jettisoned. By the same token, anti-Semitism re-emerged acutely during the Second World War but the recognition that such discrimination is unacceptable has now permeated society to such an extent that it can never again be made lawful. In other words, social progress once achieved becomes internalised by individuals and societies alike so that the legislation promulgated to protect it is seen as perennially legitimate and thus to be applied whatever the current political dispensation.

The issue here is not whether there may be temporary setbacks on this progressive evolution – times when circumstances allow the reappearance of illegitimate practices such as 'legalised' anti-Semitism – but whether the very notion of what is progressive is as irreversible as it appears to be. In other words, the question is whether it is possible that there may be political or social policies that do not accord with the theories of progress or advancement we employ.

Consider the case of co-educational schooling. It came to be seen as socially undesirable that the sexes should be taught separately and as socially progressive that they should be mixed in state schools. This was based on research pointing out that mixed schooling would enhance social integration and help achieve sexual equality for women – both of which were considered progressive and the mark of modernity. Today there is research to suggest that in fact co-ed schooling can be detrimental to the academic success of both girls and boys.[19] Both, but for different reasons, achieve less than they would in single-sex education. If this new theory were to gain further ground, it would overturn decades of education policy. It would show that single-sex schooling, which was the norm until the 1950s, was preferable, albeit for reasons completely distinct from those that prevailed in the mid-twentieth century.

Similarly, theories about social integration might also have to be revisited. If, for instance, it turned out that the very worthy policy of multiculturalism was counterproductive, then that would cast asunder a large body of social science theory which has long appeared unimpeachable. Consider the possibility that the careful attention paid to ethnic and communal origins, allied with a policy of channelling funding along these lines, is actually *aggravating*, rather than alleviating, social divisions. The widespread assumption that individual satisfaction in society is enhanced by official recognition of ethnic, racial or group differences would be turned on its head. Instead, one would have to consider policies, which appear regressive today, of 'forcing' citizens to confine their individual roots and group traditions to the private sphere – even if this appeared to make them victims of discrimination. Or it might suggest that it is the very open, and at times excessively public, display of one's specificity (say, by wearing the *burqa*) that generates the discrimination, of which those asserting such identity claim to

---

19. For a summary of a Cambridge University study on the advantages of single-sex schooling, see www.singlesexschools.org/evidence.html; accessed 7 February 2012.

suffer. So much, then, for the argument that social 'progress' is either easily identifiable or irreversible.

The real-life ambiguities about social progress, despite the confident assertions of many of our social theories, are made more manifest today precisely because of the growing proportion of citizens of non-Western origins in Western societies. So, if it is the case that there are multiple paths to modernity and that non-Western social modernisation is significantly different from the Western ways, then it is not surprising that misunderstandings and clashes should occur. It is one thing for Swedes to live with Estonian or Lithuanian immigrants; it is quite another for them to accommodate Sudanese and Somalis. Although the tendency has been to attribute Africans' difficulties of integration to socio-economic deprivation and ghettoisation, there are undoubtedly other, more socio-cultural, factors that conspire to maintain a socially divisive gap between them and the local Swedes.

This is not to say that there are obvious and clear-cut cultural attributes that make integration difficult, although that is sometimes the case, but rather that notions of what is socially appropriate to being 'modern' in Sweden may differ radically from the local norms. For instance, it may be the case that gender relations for second-generation Sudanese Swedes remain sharply at odds with the prevailing social consensus in Sweden. To insist that such a gap will in due course dissipate through 'integration' may well be to blind oneself to differences in conceptions of *modernity* that will continue to challenge the Swedish model. Already the realisation that second- or third-generation Muslim women choose to wear the *niqab* and even more that women converts opt to do the same, raises serious questions about the assumptions underlying female emancipation.

But, although the most frequently mentioned, this is by no means the only area in which such apparently regressive social behaviour occurs. For example, the current craze for the widespread tattooing of parts of the body that are easily visible (arms, neck and even face), as opposed to the more discreet traditions of old, which appears to have engulfed numerous and diverse social groups is arresting. Unlike sartorial decisions, which can always be undone, this massive display of tattooing will continue to give the person a distinct identity. Tattooing on that scale can easily be considered odd, even if today it is made fashionable by overpaid footballers, and could well blight the tattooed person's social and professional life. So, by all accounts, the decision to reinvent oneself as a 'savage' in this way might be considered to be socially regressive. It goes against theories of modernity and individualisation, which posit that social development leads to greater individual freedom from ascriptive, racial, sexual or ethnic constraints. And yet, supposedly free, modern, individuals choose to chain themselves in ways that will make their later life more, rather than less, socially difficult.

More generally, therefore, it might be argued that these and other examples bring to light two processes that fail to accord with simple theories of social 'progress'. One is the assumption that the characteristics of social 'modernity' – for instance between European citizens of Western and non-Western origins – will *necessarily* converge. They may or may not, and that in itself is not an indication that the ones are less modern than the others. They are simply modern in different ways – and sometimes ways that may not be easily compatible. The second is that it is not credible to assume that individual social behaviour will *necessarily* conform to the accepted norms of social progress, which Westerners commonly presume are the defining marks of modernity. There are many modern types of behaviour – and not just tattooing! – which go against the grain of theories of modernisation. The most obvious is secularisation.

If it is broadly true that fewer and fewer in the West now attend church services, there is on the other hand a distinct interest in forms of 'mystical' beliefs, some of which, like paganism, pre-date the emergence of the main monotheistic world religions. Now, it might be argued that this is confined to the private moral sphere and therefore does not interfere with what would otherwise conform to 'modern' social behaviour. And yet, if people make life-changing decisions on the basis of sundry mystical or cabbalistic beliefs, then it is to be wondered whether there can be a simple definition of modernity in this respect.

My intention here is not to engage in a debate about cultural relativism or sterile discussions about the merits of Western modernity. Rather, it is to look at some of the assumptions that underlie the West's view of itself as being more 'advanced'. What is in question here is not the fact that the West should consider itself superior. That, after all, is a widely shared characteristic among powerful nations or empires – as is evident from the history of China. What is of interest is the basis upon which the West defines its 'advances', particularly in relation to the non-West. Here, my argument has been that the encounter with the non-West, as well as the present influence of citizens from non-Western origins in our societies, has conspired to challenge both the nature of the West's view of its superiority and, ultimately, the foundations of its social sciences. But whilst there is growing recognition of the need to be sensitive to what are usually labelled 'cultural' differences, we have yet to come to terms with what that means for our notions of progress and modernity. And the theories on which we rely to define progress and modernity *as well as* explain the historical processes of modernisation are now increasingly found wanting.

Therefore, in order to rethink why we believe we are more 'advanced', it will not be sufficient to confine ourselves to the postcolonial agenda because that agenda merely contests the claims of Western superiority on political and ideological (rather than conceptual) grounds. Its key argument is that, because the West is guilty of imperialism, its norms and values have been imposed on the rest, particularly non-West (formerly colonised) societies. But that argument is very much the other side of the Western coin in that it accepts the (very Western) notion of the persistence of a clear-cut dichotomy between Western and non-Western values.

My point is that the present West is made up of both West and non-West and that this complex reality challenges our notions of modernity and our theories of development. So, the business at hand is not merely to decry Western presumptions of superiority but to work out what aspects of Western assumptions are now demonstrably unable to account for what is happening within Western societies themselves. And the difficulty lies in being able to think outside the Western box, which I would argue the post-colonialism critique does not. As noted before, postcolonial theories speak to the West in the West's language of rationality. They do not question the West's rationality since they are very much part of it. Their critique starts from, and ends with, the standard critique of the Western approach to the non-West – that is, the West's inability to take seriously the non-Western standpoint.

Why is the non-West a 'threat'?

To go further in our investigation of the ways in which the postcolonial situation is challenging Western rationality, we need to look at the dark side of the West's self-perception. That the West feels threatened by the non-West is clear enough, so what is of interest is not so much the discussion of the nature of the perceived menace but the reasons adduced for being threatened. After a brief review of how the threat is presented, I will focus my attention on how it is thought through, how it is conceptualised. This will lead me to study how this affects the social and political theories we use to explain the nature of the 'threat' and to devise the policies we employ to tackle the problems we believe it creates. Therefore, the aim will not primarily be to discuss whether the perception of 'a' threat is justified but to explain why it is identified as it is.

Long before 9/11, the West had begun to feel under pressure, if not beleaguered, by the non-West. If the very first premisses of that perception originated in the decolonisation period, when colonial superiority was wiped out, the more serious anxiety arose when European economies began to suffer in the 1970s. As growth stuttered and unemployment grew, Western European countries began to take note of the presence of the many non-Western immigrants in their midst: the 'problem' of immigration was born. This had happened before, of course, but the difference now was that these immigrants were not European: they came from the former colonies and they had a 'culture' that differed more markedly from the European. So the combination of culturally different immigrants and unemployment led to the theory that 'outsiders' were now threatening to take the jobs of the 'locals', who were suffering as a result. The key point about what happened is that this perception of 'otherness' arose in a context where most of these early immigrants were in fact rather well integrated – or in any event genuinely sought integration.

The most compelling statement of this threat is without doubt Enoch Powell's 1968 'Rivers of Blood' speech – for which he was sacked as shadow defence secretary. The speech was not primarily on immigration; it was largely a response to the Race Relations Act 1968 introduced by the Labour government, which Powell opposed. Whatever the merit of the speech, which brought the metaphor of blood by way of a reference to Virgil (Powell had been a professor of Classics), the real issue is why it struck such a chord. Both the fact that Powell received large popular support and that the established political parties reacted so strongly against his speech proved he had touched a raw nerve. His crime was to have brought to the fore what were by then clearly two contentious and intertwined issues: racism and the dangers of immigration. Looking 'in horror' at what had happened in the USA, he argued that a further increase in non-Western (here, primarily from the Commonwealth) racially different immigration represented a mortal threat to the West. Leaving aside the clear racist tenor of his argument, what is most noticeable is the notion that the presence of culturally (and racially) different 'others' was in itself a threat – and this despite the fact that Europe had always been a land of immigration and that in the late 1960s it was still booming economically.[20]

Powell's discourse made explicit what has now become a standard perception of the non-Western threat. Although the speech is habitually marked down as an act of gross racism, it is probably more significant for having brought to the surface the postcolonial malaise that gripped the societies of the former imperial powers. If race was the obvious vehicle, the more subtle message was that Britain would not survive the 'melting pot' experience. In Powell's view, and he had many supporters, the strength of the nation issued from its cultural and historical homogeneity. And a dilution of that homogeneity would be fatal. So, Western societies were now threatened by a process of internal deliquescence that would strike at their very essence. In the postcolonial period, Powell suggested, the West ought to retrench to its core constituencies and fundamental values, which he felt Commonwealth immigrants would dilute. Paradoxically, or perhaps not, his notion of what constituted a threat to the West has now become more, rather than less, prominent in popular and political circles. Mainstream parties

---

20. On Enoch Powell, see Heffer, 1989.

all over Europe – including in hitherto unaffected countries like Sweden – are facing electoral challenges from right-wing outfits that place such arguments at the very centre of their political message.

The events of 11 September 2001 as well as the continued threat from al-Qaeda and other Islamist groups have focused attention on two specific aspects of the perception of a general threat from the non-West.[21] One is the fact that Islam would somehow represent a greater threat to the West than other religious or cultural challengers. The other is that Muslims within are now also a direct threat by way of terrorism in their European country of birth. The first feeds on centuries of conflict and competition between the West and the Muslim world, which are now an integral part of the Western imaginary about the Muslim 'other'. However, in that imaginary, the threat was always external and, provided sufficient attention was paid, it could be kept at bay. However, the second factor, which is new, is the belief that supposedly integrated Muslims in the West can 'revert' to a foreign allegiance to those Islamists who now profess to fight the West. The result here is that integration is powerless to stop such an allegiance and the argument is that a Muslim presence in the West is, and will always remain, a clear and constant danger.

Despite vigorous campaigns against Islamophobia and the constant attempts by Western governments to make a distinction between the vast majority of 'law-abiding Muslim citizens' and a tiny minority of Islamist activists, there is in Western countries a growing belief in an internal Muslim danger. Official denials of a *Muslim*, as opposed to a *terrorist*, threat seem to have had little success in convincing the wider public that there is no connection between the two. And, indeed, it is no longer politically taboo for

---

21. For an argument that al-Qaeda is a receding threat, see Gerges, 2011.

parties to campaign on the specific issue of Muslim immigration, even in such traditionally liberal countries as the Netherlands, Denmark, Norway and Sweden. What this points to, therefore, is a perception that religion has become a more salient issue than race in present discussions about the dangers of immigration to Western countries. Moreover, this view is increasingly shared by North Americans, who (given their historical trajectory) have traditionally been much more tolerant of multi-ethnic societies. The so-called Islamic threat appears to affect the West generally. It harks back to an old European demon, which has most recently reared its ugly head in the conflicts that bloodied the former Yugoslavia. The message now is: Muslims can never be trusted.

The most elaborate explanation for this state of affairs has undoubtedly been Huntington's clash-of-civilisations thesis – which may appear all the more convincing for having been articulated *before* 11 September 2001. Although the argument, at least in its 1996 book form, is not nearly as simplistic as it is often made out to be, the gist of the thesis is clear: it is the religion/culture nexus (which Huntington calls 'civilisation') that will determine the conflicts of the twenty-first century. Leaving aside debates about Huntington's definition of 'civilisation' and the divide he makes between what he believes to be the more important such groupings, the argument boils down to two key notions. The first is that civilisations are indeed discrete and that, despite the fact that some countries do not fit neatly into his scheme, their core characteristics can be identified – which implies that such features are not just visible but that they remain distinct *over time*. The second is that, however much these different civilisations modernise and advance technologically, they will not become more similar to the West. In other words, there will *not* be a convergence of civilisations, as development theorists have long asserted. According to Huntington, these two historical 'facts' put together presage conflicts that will only be avoided if the distinct interests of these separate civilisations are taken into account. For him, attempts to Westernise societies by force or to ignore their separate 'civilisational' attributes are bound to fail and could lull the West into a false sense of security.[22]

The further consequence from this view of the world is that civilisations can live side by side without blending. Like oil and water, they remain separate. The melting-pot hypothesis, on which the American experience is predicated, is but an illusion: the ur-civilisations do not mix. Huntington's later book, *Who Are We? The Challenges to America's National Identity*, confirmed that the author did indeed extend his analysis to the future fate of those Western countries where migrants from these other civilisations came to settle.[23] Although the focus of the book is on the threat posed by the increase in Latin American migrants, the argument underlying the analysis is very much about the corrosive effects of large-scale immigration from different cultural/religious groupings. And in this respect it is no different from the view in many European circles that *Muslim* immigration is indeed a threat to the Western identity of European countries.

Whatever the racist implications of such reasoning, it is worth paying attention to Huntington's theory – if only because his body of work is academically of high quality and the issues he tackled in these two books have turned out to be relevant to the ways in which we in the West both perceive and conceptualise the threat of the 'other'. Furthermore, the fact that Huntington reached such a pessimistic conclusion about the USA, a country built on immigration, should make us reflect on the potential limits of integration. In brief, since Huntington was a scholar and not a crank, his theories are of some importance. In any event, they

---

22. Huntington, 1996.
23. Huntington, 2004.

represent the most elaborate conceptualisation of the non-Western threat to the West.

Against this, standard social theories posit a process of individualisation and integration that results in the creation of various forms of hybridity – by which societies absorb immigrants and evolve at the same time. That, in a nutshell, is the theory underlying the melting-pot model. The United States might be made up of people from myriad origins but they all change and adapt, so that in the end they all become American both in belief and behaviour. In the process, they redefine what it means to be American, even if all believe in the American 'dream'. However, the fact that Americans increasingly feel the need to identify themselves as composites, and members of distinct communities with roots outside the country, would tend to show that the melting-pot metaphor has its limits. People do not dissolve into a notional mixture; they partake of the myth whilst insisting on differentiating themselves from the 'others'. This should act as a warning against the assumptions of unilinear social development: the process of coming together does not evolve into a process of social dilution. And the continuing reference to ethnic/national/religious differences does have an impact on social and political relations within the country.

Huntington's thesis subverts existing theories of social development in two fundamental ways. One is that he claims individuals are defined as members of 'civilisations', which are historically, religiously and culturally distinct. Therefore, even when they migrate, they continue to identify with those original groupings and to accord their behaviour to their norms. So, whereas the integration of different nationalities within one 'civilisation' is easily achieved, the integration of different 'civilisations' is problematic, when not impossible. This is a powerful, and worrying, argument. The other is that these different 'civilisations' develop differently: they may modernise successfully and even rapidly but that does not mean that they are thereby Westernising. Therefore Huntington goes against theories positing that economic development implies social and political convergence. According to him, the world is, and will continue to be, divided into identifiable and self-sustaining 'civilisations', which will evolve according to their own historical, religious and cultural logics, even when they partake of a seemingly ubiquitous globalised material modernity.

Although Huntington's arguments have been roundly rejected, partly on political and partly on historical grounds, the fact that they provide a theory to explain relevant contemporary sociopolitical phenomena and that they elicit widespread popular support should make us pause. My point here is not to support the author's views, many of which are indeed contentious, but to highlight the significance for theory of the ways he conceptualises what he terms civilisation. Admittedly, notions of immutable divides based on religious and/or cultural differences are shocking to the way in which the West imagines itself to be. To be a culturalist, or even worse an essentialist, has virtually become taboo in our societies. We pride ourselves on being sufficiently enlightened to accept the individual, whatever his/her race, colour, creed or *origin*. And yet this satisfying self-perception is battered by two uncomfortable realities. One is the fact that so many of our fellow citizens actually believe there are some (religious, cultural, social) differences that cannot be erased, no matter how successful integration has been. The other is that this belief is actually shared by many who come to settle, and integrate successfully, in the West. The latter is of course grist to the mill of the former, since it makes obvious the point that some differences are just unbridgeable.

Whether we like it or not, the question of Islam has come to symbolise the 'threat' as it is currently perceived. However, the issues raised by Huntington go well beyond that conundrum. The recent controversy about the Roma in Western Europe, as we have seen, has brought back into view the situation of those, like the Travellers, who are both citizens of a country and prefer a way of life that is at odds with their contemporaries. Is the 'problem' with the Roma that they originally come from a 'civilisation' (India) that continues to affect their beliefs and behaviour or are they primarily to be seen as nomads, with kindred spirits in many parts of the world? On the other hand, the beliefs and behaviour of well-integrated Muslims in the West do raise questions that go beyond superficial common sense. And the reasons those questions are both important and not easily brushed aside is that they link this particular religious grouping in the West to what Huntington calls a civilisation outside the West. But this is not enough. After all, there are millions of Chinese settled in the West, who also hail from and are linked to their 'civilisation' of origin. So why should they constitute less of a 'threat' than the Muslims? Is this primarily due to Islamophobia or are there more serious reasons for the West's unease – reasons that have more general implications, above and beyond the so-called Muslim 'problem'?

I do not intend here to tackle this question in the depth it merits. I will only use it as an illustration of my more general point about the limits of Western rationality. Leaving aside the many historical reasons why the Muslim world and the West have been, or feel they are, at loggerheads, I should like to focus on the contemporary arguments. The nub of the problem boils down to two specific issues. One is the fact that there is now a Muslim political movement (al- Qaeda) that is violently hostile to the West and claims to work for the establishment of a World Caliphate. However minuscule and poorly supported that movement is, its claims comfort the view in the West that Muslims seek world domination, not accommodation with, and even less integration into, the West. That view is instrumentalised politically in the West to instil fear and justify the war against 'terrorism'. In that way, it fits neatly into the world-view that pits an embattled West against a multiform enemy which is exploiting political Islam – much as the Soviet Union used communism as the rallying anti-Western cry. It supports a dichotomous view of the world and provides the external enemy the West so patently seems to need.

The other, which is potentially more threatening to the West's rationality, is the argument that in order to accommodate the Muslims who now live in their midst, Western societies must reconfigure their norms, values and practices to make it possible for Islam to express itself freely in its *own* ways. That argument points to an insuperable contradiction that drives a stake at the heart of the West's self-perception: in the name of their core values of democracy and equality, Western societies must accept that a group of their citizens may choose to live in contradiction with the West's professed norms. Although each Western country has reacted differently to this question, they are all ultimately confronted with an unpalatable choice: to accommodate demands that violate their socio-political norms or to violate their political principles and impose restrictions that amount to discrimination. This is why the debate in France on whether to ban the *niqab* has been so significant. Far from being, as it is often seen in Britain and the USA, an overzealous quirk of the French particularistic conception of republicanism, the issue is in fact a deadly serious argument about the perceived threat to the French republic.

The grounds on which the French wanted to ban the *niqab* turned around the primacy of secularism; but they also included the rights of women. What that means is that the prevailing (social and legal) norms of *laïcité*, including sexual equality and women's emancipation, collided with those who claimed that to wear the *niqab* was an expression of their freedom of choice. Set in those terms, there was no possible compromise. The argument of the *niqab*-clad women is a radical challenge to the historical, moral and cultural foundations of the existing sexual equality legislation in its French version. Yet, to deny women the right to dress as they choose is also in utter contradiction with the legislation on freedom of choice. Whatever their reservations about the enforceability of such legislation, French MPs have concluded they cannot allow such a challenge to the prevailing social and cultural norms to stand. To do so would be to open the gates to a succession of related demands, which would ultimately degrade human rights and social customs in France. But in banning the *niqab* in public places, they have imposed a more restrictive application of the prevailing norms of democracy than they perhaps would have liked to do. And that decision does have serious political implications, which may come to haunt the legislators. What was at first merely a discussion about the covering of women has now become a political argument about the limits of democracy.

But the question of the *niqab* is not the only one that appears to support Huntington's thesis. For example, the long-standing debate about whether Turkey should be admitted into the EU raises very similar issues. Whatever the *official* reasons adduced by politicians in a number of European countries (such as France and Germany), the underlying popular basis on which the refusal to admit Turkey rests is that of the incompatibility between a Christian West and a Muslim would-be European state. But since such an argument is not really compatible with the criteria for admission into the EU, the arguments given for delaying Turkey's application turn on other more political conditionalities. Only in those countries, like France, where it has been made clear that Turkey's admission would be submitted to a referendum, is it plain that politicians are shielding behind popular opinion to justify the long-foretold reluctance to consider Turkey a European country.

And what is at stake here, regardless of official pronouncements on the matter, is the fear that the admission of a Muslim country into the European comity of nations would engender the same sort of difficulties already experienced at national level by the demands Islam makes on ostensibly secular and democratic societies. In other words, there is a belief that Islam implies an interlinking of religion and politics that is not acceptable in the West. How widespread is this belief is difficult to gauge, but Geert Wilders's campaign in the Netherlands, for which he was brought to trial at the very moment when his electorally successful party became the conservative coalition's kingmaker, is surely a sign here. So, as we have seen, are the statements of Thilo Sarrazin, the Bundesbank member whose anti-Islam book *Deutschland schafft sich ab*, arguing that Muslims cannot integrate into Western countries, earned him the sack.[24]

These political tremors, which are becoming more regular and of greater magnitude in Western Europe, are the symptoms of the limits of our rationality. The conundrum of 'Islam' in the West is but one point of friction which exposes the contradictions in the West's conception of itself. Regardless of the future of violent political Islam, which has probably already reached its peak, the questions raised by the demands for reform made by some European Muslims will probably not go away. The arguments of someone like Tariq Ramadan, couched as they are in the language of Western rationality, will continue to act as an irritant to the West's self-perception.[25] Is this merely a passing phenomenon, made more salient by the al-Qaeda question, or are we to take this challenge to Western rationality seriously? Huntington's later work, which centres on the question of distinct 'civilisations', is probably a good pointer here, since it raises issues that are not comfortable for either politicians or social scientists. Many instinctively dislike what he writes, but the questions he raises will not go away. So,

---

24. Sarrazin, 2010.
25. Ramadan, 2010.

the threat to the West is not primarily that of immigration. It is to its ideologies and theories.

Much as it may enrage those who decry Islamophobia, I suspect that the very painful debates initiated in France about the meanings of secularism are a portent of things to come elsewhere in the West. The point is not really to ascertain whether French legislation is right or wrong – from what standpoint anyway? – but to pay attention to the ways the issues concerned have exposed contradictions in French rationality. Whatever the long-term political future of the new legislation, the debate has at least had the merit of forcing the country to make explicit its assumptions, norms, values and prejudices (all of which make up what I would call culture) and to make clear the rationale underlying its ideology of secularism and human rights. It has forced a re-examination of the constitution – since the legislation was scrutinised by the Constitutional Council – and provided a reconceptualisation of modern women in France. And, in the end, the argument that Muslims ought to have separate civil and political rights did not wash.

However, that very public and systematic debate has also exposed the rationality of Western social theory. First, it has ripped to pieces the French assumption that ethnicity does not exist, since it is clear that the public display of religious clothing is not just a religious statement; it is also an assertion of *beur* identity. By dressing in an ostensible Muslim way, second- or third-generation men and women are publicly embracing an *ethnic* identity (Muslim of North African origin or even convert to Islam), which offends the French assumption that they are all assimilated citizens. Second, the fact that the vehicle for this ethnic statement is religion has struck deep at the French concept of secularism. That concept is underpinned by a theory of development that assumes an inexorable evolution towards the increasing separation of religion and politics. Third, it has exposed an unexpected contradiction in the theory of sexual equality since, as we have seen, the rejection of the *niqab* on the grounds of women's rights clashed with the rights of women to express freely their sartorial choices. More generally, this has raised the issue of women claiming that confinement at home is an expression of personal freedom. Fourth, and perhaps most significantly, it has raised the possibility that the land of human rights is discriminating against those who refuse to conform to the Western norms prevalent in their country of residence. In other words, legislation curtails the cultural rights of some on the grounds that social theory does not recognise the possibility that modern Western individuals should deliberately choose norms which appear to contradict constitutional human rights.

At the same time, the common appreciation of Geert Wilders is that he is a right-wing (fascist?) agent provocateur. As such he is dismissed as an extremist maverick. His statements on the Quran are seen not just to be well beyond the pale but also to be ignorant of the religion itself. Were he not able to garner as many votes as he does, he would be ignored. Yet, he clearly expresses opinions that are widely shared in Dutch society. And here again we come face to face with the limits of Western rationality. There seems to be no possible, or logical, defence of Wilders's argument that the Quran is equivalent to Hitler's *Mein Kampf* other than madness or criminal provocation.[26] Our liberal and secular societies are supposed to have evolved beyond the stage of book burning! All this is true but the question Wilders (and others like him) pose is the following: are Western societies entitled to discriminate against those they believe challenge the secular foundations of the country? Is there a place for discrimination in our rationality? Posed in this way, the answer is a self-evident no, and yet in the privacy of the polling booth other views are now being expressed.

---

26. And clearly makes an odd reading of the Pura.

But looked at another way, it remains a challenge. Can our social science theories account for individual and collective behaviour that appears to go counter to the assumptions of social and political development we hold to be true? Yes and no. Yes, if we relegate the reasoning of either the *niqab*-wearing women or Geert Wilders to the fringes of rational thought – akin perhaps to those who still believe in witchcraft or the flat-earth theory. No, if we view their respective positions as legitimate variants of the freedom of choice we so cherish. What both assert – the one being the flip side of the other – is that secular societies are no more 'advanced' than faith-based ones. The choice of the former to place ostensible religious obligations over women's rights amounts to a rejection of the logic of Western secularism. The decision of the latter to ban the Quran amounts to an expression of the fear that a religious book can induce behaviour inimical to our Western ways. But that debate was supposed to have been settled long ago. So how can we explain that it is becoming increasingly strident as we appear to be moving into the post-modern era?

Well, we can only explain it if we accept that modernisation is neither straightforward nor unilinear. That is, if we consider that the movement towards social and political emancipation[27] is liable to take different routes, some of which may not be compatible. This would imply that we have to take seriously the notion that societies, though apparently becoming more homogeneous, are in fact prey to the separate evolution of groupings that move in different directions. And that some of them may develop according to logics that do not conform to the dominant social theories. This would require reconceptualising society as composed of individuals and groups that may not cohere or integrate, thus taking into account a vision of a social body that is neither as well defined nor as well

---

27. By emancipation I mean the acquisition of greater personal freedoms.

ordered as social theories would have it. It would also, and this is important, imply a conceptualisation that would allow for the non-linear, or non-evolutionary, movement of society. Finally, it would demand a rethinking of the notion of the individual that encompassed the realities of what are multiple, fragmented, changing and contradictory identities. In other words, individuals are not 'logical persons' but the concatenation of many types of *identities*, each one of which evolves according to its own logic.

THREE

Ideas

THE ISSUES that arise when we consider how to rethink the questions raised in the previous chapter point to the need to revisit some fundamental concepts in our (Western) social and political theories. As I have suggested, the conundrum Western societies face today is not so much the inability to identify the key problems they face but the instruments they deploy in order to tackle them. These instruments are limited because they derive from theories that can no longer satisfactorily conceptualise and explain what is happening. In other words, the confrontation with the non-West and, even more importantly, the consequences of the implantation of the non-West into the West have exposed the limits of the forms of thinking that had served us well until the 1970s. But in the postcolonial age, when the empires gained a foothold in the metropolis, and immigration brought a complicated mix of peoples to inhabit the West, old certainties began to vacillate. As we have seen, the West gradually came to feel threatened and its rationality was called into question, even as it remained unaware of it.

Paradoxically, therefore, what is stake is the identity of the West, not primarily that of the non-Western immigrants. As is well demonstrated by intense discussions about 'Englishness' and 'Britishness'. To some, English identity is now an issue.[1] Until recently, it was the other nations – Ireland, Wales and Scotland – that engaged in national(ist) soul-searching. The immigrants from the (largely colonial) non-West had to face the question of who they were, now that they and their children lived away from 'home'. Were they Asian English or British Asian, African English or British Africans; and did it matter? The postcolonial questions on identity triggered by the presence of so many second-generation 'non-Western' Englishmen and women has now forced a debate. This in itself is proof not just that the British in some sense feel 'threatened' but that the loss of their status as colonial masters has finally compelled them to reconsider who they actually are. And the process of doing so has been complex as well as painful.

The same is true of the United States, for so long the uncontested world leader, but now confronted with the possibility that China will overtake it – economically at first, but perhaps in other ways later. The very realisation that China has the potential to become a leading superpower compels the Americans to rethink who they are and in which ways their dominance could be challenged. Hence there is a flurry of studies on the Chinese resurgence (for they were once a superpower), their ability to mobilise their resources and their determination to regain top status in a world so long controlled by the imperial West. It is now common to read books in the West that forecast the coming Chinese supremacy, explaining why the combination of economic, sociological and cultural factors make it likely that the Eastern 'giant' will eventually surpass the 'declining' West. China's status as the USA's largest creditor is seen as the gathering dependence of the West on China.[2]

---

1. See, among others, Paxman, 1999.
2. See, for example, Friedberg, 2011.

What these two examples show is that the theories we have used to explain Western dominance have now been overtaken by events. They did not, indeed could not, forecast that a superpower could emerge that did not follow the Western path of development. On reflection this is not surprising. Our explanation of Western supremacy is tied to the historical context within which it has been developed. A change in the circumstances that appeared for centuries to comfort the notion that the West had unlocked the mystery of modernisation has induced a reexamination of the theories that explain this evolution. Ultimately, the reason why the British are having a crisis of identity and the Americans a rethink on the potential for continued world dominance is the same: they are no longer exactly sure they are who they assumed they were. Or, to put it another way, until they were challenged, they did not question their status and accepted as 'scientific' the theories purporting to explain Western superiority.

But if social scientists appear now to be at a loss, historians have long been aware that empires rise and fall, countries are reconfigured, ruling classes are displaced, economies falter and trade ascendancy is fragile. Indeed, historians are generally sceptical about generalisations but they operate within an intellectual and cultural environment that conditions their research, and in particular the questions they ask. They too are influenced by the changing trends in the social and political sciences, as they are by the events they study. They may write about the past but the way in which they reconsider that past is affected by the present in which they are trained and work. So, they may have more sophisticated explanations about the origins of English identity but the reason they may be called upon to speak on that question is, for them too, a result of the present uncertainties about national identity. In this way, the discussion about flying the flag of St George is not just the preserve of sport aficionados; it becomes a relevant historical question.³

Furthermore, historians, who are otherwise well aware of the *longue durée*, also work with the conceptual and theoretical instruments extant – even when they claim resolutely to be only interested in the empirical. For example, they all today use the notion of class, or capitalism, without referring to Marx. Similarly, they all employ the sociological concepts developed by Durkheim, Weber, Michels or even Foucault without necessarily feeling the need to explain why it is that these concepts are useful to historical research. Over time, then, we all carry a theoretical baggage, the origins of which we may not even know, and which we take for granted. It is part of the intellectual and analytical armoury we deploy to think historically.⁴

But how to think about history has changed a great deal in the last thirty years. In some ways it could be argued that historians have been more attuned to the impact of the non-West upon our way of thinking than their counterparts in the social sciences. Whilst they have tried to grapple with the contradictions and complexities introduced by the postcolonial age, many social scientists have taken refuge in an increasingly quantitative, rational-choice, type of theory, which is often radically divorced from realities on the ground. The aspiration of social scientists, it seems, is to become more 'scientific' whilst historians remain wedded to the need to account plausibly for what has happened or even what is happening. So, in this way, historians may well be more sensitive to recent societal changes than social scientists, who claim ceaselessly to focus on those changes.

---

3. The flying of the flag of St George (particularly on cars) has now become common whenever England is taking part in a sporting tournament, such as the football or the rugby world cups.
4. See Burke, 2005.

Of particular relevance to recent developments in historiography are what are commonly referred to as the cultural and linguistic turns. The first was a reaction to the long-standing dominance of social history, whereby the focus was on the socio-economic drivers of historical change. For its part, the cultural turn sought to recentre history around 'ordinary' people and 'everyday' life. Historians no longer focused on the dominant modes of production, the forces of history or the social classes that were supposed to matter most. They now wanted to understand how the more cultural aspects of people's lives affected their place in society and their socio-political outlook. New avenues of research opened, which privileged micro-approaches and the study of the activities, artefacts and opinions of those who had hitherto not been seen as the main historical actors. Social history moved the discipline away from the narratives of the great and the good.[5] Cultural history moved it into what was labelled 'quotidian' life, making legitimate research into such areas as clothing, sports, deportment, leisure and furnishings. Underlying this shift was the strong belief, which came in part from cultural anthropology, that understanding the stuff of everyday history required a much more refined appreciation of the cultural context within which people lived and worked.

The linguistic turn was more radical still. Largely under the influence of postcolonial and post-modern approaches, a number of historians began to challenge the very notion of historical *account*. Of key importance here were the question of the standpoint and that of language. The bedrock of this new approach was the argument that reality, historical or otherwise, is only given meaning in so far as it is expressed by means of language. What matters about reality is not so much the physicality of what is out there – the

---

5. For a critique of social history, see Cabrera, 2005.

preserve of the scientists – but how it is perceived, understood, articulated and above all enunciated. So, in history, there could be no account of past events that was not determined by the language used to give them discursive body. Conversely, historical events (such as the French Revolution, which was discussed extensively by some of these historians) could not have materialised until there arose a 'language' in which the actors involved could conceptualise what was happening to them and, more importantly, what might happen as a result of their actions.[6] In this reading, then, events do not happen because the 'right' socio-economic conditions prevail but because there arises the ability to conceptualise and articulate them in terms that can impel human action.

Whatever the import of these two major turns (and of those that have followed, like post-social and post-cultural history), their merit is to have made explicit the fact that 'doing' history in the post-colonial age required rethinking the discipline's premisses.[7] However, there is much less evidence that social science has been as self-critical as history in this respect.[8] There are several reasons for this but the principal factor is the perennial will to emulate the physical sciences. The attempt to produce and refine theories that are more credible 'scientifically' has led to a move towards increasingly reality-poor quantitative approaches. The need to simplify social and political life so that causality can be identified by means of a limited number of variables susceptible to quantification has meant operating on axioms and premisses that are increasingly detached from the complexities of the real world. Predictably, the assumptions of rational choice and perfect information, which are

---

6. See for instance, Baker, 1990.
7. As evidenced, for example, by the work of the French historian François Furet. See Furet, 1995.
8. Except anthropology, a sizable proportion of which is now concerning itself with 'every day' life in the West. One should also mention sociologists like Bauman and Alexander. See, for instance, Bauman, 1978; Alexander, 2003.

at the heart of economic theory, have served as the foundation of these social theories.

The obvious discrediting of the scientific pretensions of economics made manifest in the post-2008 financial crisis has at least raised the awareness that theories of the market are very crude. If the proximate trigger for the crisis was the mathematical modelisation of risk-hedging activities alarmingly devoid of reality checks, the larger problem lay in the assumptions about market behaviour in standard economic conceptualisation. What that financial catastrophe revealed was the danger of quantification, which requires a simple model of economic activity that is amenable to mathematical manipulation. But what the patent failure of prevalent market theories to account for the *real* economic world shows is the danger of quantification in social and political theories, where the grounds on which to modelise reality are even shakier than they are in economics. Of course, many economists will dispute the conclusion that the recent crisis was due to a failure of theory, pointing instead to the unethical and unsustainable consequences of risk-hedging run riot. They see it as a policy rather than a conceptual issue. But, as we will see below, other than in the simplest of cases, markets are not capable of self-regulation.[9]

This detour by way of the travails of economics was only meant as an illustration of the limits of our economic, social and political theories. The problem is not primarily, as is usually argued, that we need to refine our theories more effectively – by which is meant test newer hypotheses against real events. The problem is that our theories are not capable of taking into account the fact that many of their fundamental axioms and assumptions are no longer sustainable – if they ever were. We have developed very sophisticated statistical models and applications, which are useful

---

9. On the ongoing economic crisis, see among others Reinhart and Rogoff, 2009.

and which do provide a wealth of information about our societies. That is not what is at issue here. What is at issue is how we decide what information we collect and how to make use of this statistical material in ways that provide greater analytical acuity. In other words, it is both the conceptualisation and the theorisation of social and political realities that are at stake. If, as already suggested, people can hold multiple, including contradictory, forms of identity, then theories that rest on the assumption of a single, or at least dominant, identity will be unable to account for some of the phenomena we are witnessing today. Similarly, if people can be concurrently religious and secular, then our theories desert us since they do not provide us with any means of conceptualising such a state of being. Finally if, as now seems to be the case, most of us make economic decisions on a combination of 'rational' and 'irrational' grounds, then economic theory is left bereft of its primary assumption.

In the rest of this chapter I try to illustrate the difficulties faced by current social and political theories in reconsidering six key concepts, the assumptions of which are rarely subjected to critical scrutiny: *individual*, *society*, *freedom*, *faith*, *market* and *change*. Whilst it may seem difficult to understand how discussing such vague and general notions can be relevant to our current predicament, I will try to show that without an attempt to reconsider what appear to be 'givens', we stand little chance of thinking beyond theories that are increasingly failing us. It is precisely because these notions belong to our axiomatic baggage that it is imperative to tackle their meanings and significance. I do not claim that the choice of these six concepts is anything other than subjective and, indeed, there are other important notions that might well be equally relevant. My claim is only that they belong to the primary, or basic, concepts, which form the building blocks of our theories.

Individual

As I have already indicated in previous chapters, the idea of the individual is both the starting point for many discussions of contemporary problems and the core of our social theories. In the West, our everyday lives as well as our reflections on the human condition are tied to a very specific notion of what an individual is. That concept has a long genealogy and it is seldom tackled explicitly. It is also at the heart of the assumptions we make about who we are, what we do and how we relate to other people. It is in fact so engrained in our consciousness that it would seem odd, not to say perverse, to ask people what an individual is. We know: each one of us is an individual and the person who stands in front of us is also an individual. So, what could the question possibly mean?

An appropriate 'scientific' stance in respect of what appears obvious, or given, should be inquisitive scepticism, a stance social scientists seem not to have borrowed from their counterparts in the physical sciences – whom they otherwise seek to emulate. For instance, the evolution of atomic physics since its inception shows that our notion of what is 'out there', objectively, or what matter actually is, has changed over generations, as our science of the physical world has developed. Or, to take another, more contemporary, example, recent strides in neurobiology and the study of artificial intelligence have led to claims that the brain is nothing other than a chemically activated computer – hence the claim that artificial intelligence may soon emulate human brain power. Of course, brain power is not the same as consciousness but, nevertheless, some scientists do now believe our very conception of what an individual is will be reshaped by the uncovering of the brain functions.

However, regardless of these claims, it does seem odd that social sciences (as opposed to the philosophy of science) rarely reflect on the meaning of the individual and operate on the basis of a simple idea, which forms the basic axiom of its theoretical elaboration. The working definition is that the individual is a discrete person making choices on the basis of free will according to his or her own distinct preferences within a socio-economic and political environment upon which he or she can act through, among other things, the vote and the market. Now, like most definitions in the social sciences, it is a reasonable approximation of observable reality for the general purpose of studying society, but it ought to come with a number of caveats, some of which are of no little importance in our contemporary world.

Although we give due recognition in our theories to the sex, age, origins, social class, education, work experience of the person, the assumption remains that what is of analytical interest are the individual characteristics of the people concerned. In other words, it is presumed that we can conceive of individuals as equal, or comparable, building blocks in society. Indeed, as I shall discuss below, society is commonly conceptualised as the aggregate of all individuals. This assumption, which makes sense in strict sociological terms, is recognised to be limiting in other respects.[10] For instance, psychology works on the presumption that it is the differences between individuals, as produced by their own separate emotional development, which matters most. It is admitted that, because of psychological problems, some people might in fact not be 'proper' individuals, in that their behaviour is based on the belief that they are *not* the standard single discrete person but, for instance, the reincarnation of something else or the embodiment of several spirits that have taken possession of their psyche. For example, acute paranoia is a condition that turns a person into a

---

10. Even the sociology of 'community' is built upon the same notion of the individual.

combination of various personalities, thereby erasing its presumed singularity.

The point of such psychological insights is to confirm that those who suffer from these conditions are not 'individuals' as we conceive them. Only a handful of psychologists have argued that the so-called mentally ill are normal people like everyone else.[11] Otherwise, they are seen as abnormal, deviants, the exceptions that confirm the notion of what a regular person ought to be. So the 'science' of psychology, like the medical science it emulates, holds that individuals develop and mature in broadly similar ways, going through similar stages, and become adult persons who see themselves as discrete and possessed of free will, even as they have to cope with their own familial, social and emotional baggage. In a very concrete sense, psychology sets the boundaries of our conception of the individual and gives a 'scientific' explanation of why those who are too far off the norm cannot be considered normal *persons* – or in a juridical sense responsible for what they do.

Similarly, sociology and political science start from the premiss that society is composed of separate persons behaving at home, at work or at the ballot box, in the expected ways of the individual. Like psychology, they recognise that some people might conduct themselves abnormally: refusing to work because they do not consider themselves adult; rejecting the vote because they believe that the individual vote makes no difference; refusing payment for their work because they hold that people ought to work for free. But, again, the fact that such people are clearly 'deviants' comforts the view that the accepted assumption of what an individual is remains the best approximation we have of the way in which people live and relate to each other in modern society. At most, our theories will allow that people are not yet adapted to modern society or

---

11. Of whom the most famous was R.D. Laing. See Laing, 1960, 1961.

have not 'modernised' fully, but they will stick to the view that once they are 'modern' they are individuals like everyone else.

Therefore, what is obvious in that conception is that the individual is seen as the progressive outcome of a linear process of modernisation, which results in the acquisition of the characteristics we take as given in social theory. The assumption is that social science today has conceptualised the individual in as close an approximation as possible to the real 'existing' people who live in society. But the further assumption is that this approximation holds for all people, wherever they are, in so far as they have become 'modern'. And so the final assumption is that all people will 'modernise' in ways that will make them susceptible to this conceptual simplification. Now, this may be broadly true but, as we have seen already, 'broadly' may no longer be good enough. Just as Newton's theory of gravity was true on its own terms, it was eventually shown by Einstein not to be true enough for the new questions that arose in scientific research. So, the issue now is whether this ubiquitous idea of the individual, with which social, economic and political sciences work, has now reached its limits.

In economic theory, much of the most recent innovative work is on the significance of the findings in (economic) psychology to the effect that individuals do not behave rationally when making decisions – which, if correct, would overturn one of the key axioms of the discipline as it is presently being taught.[12] The same would be true of rational-choice theory, which has wide applications in political science. The long overdue realisation that decision-making is, to a significant extent 'irrational', in the sense that it is not the outcome of a detached and well-informed analysis of the quantifiable cost–benefit consequence of the decision, is of course fundamental. Not only would it confirm that the 'development' of

---

12. Ariely, 2008.

man does not result in a self-evident acquisition of the 'rational' mind it was presumed to bring about, but it would also open up the possibility that that there are different kinds of '(ir)rationality' with different impacts on decision-making.[13] At the very least it makes plain that we ought continually to revisit the idea of rationality, in this instance Western rationality, which is another concept we seldom discuss, but which is at the heart of this book.

Returning to some of the points raised in the previous chapters, there are sensitive issues related to immigration in our contemporary societies that challenge the accepted notion of the individual. The first issue is that identity might be made up of various forms of identification that are not easily compatible: for example, French *and* Algerian or German *and* Turkish. Here, many in the West argue that some aspects of the respective non-European culture – say, polygamy – are simply not acceptable. At the same time, second- or third-generation immigrants claim that rejecting these 'essential' aspects of their culture is an attack on their human rights as citizens of a Western European country. I will return to the question of faith below but I want here to suggest that this argument is likely to force Western governments to consider whether they need to incorporate specific cultural attributes to the definition of the individual citizen. If this were to happen – and recent French legislation suggests it might – it would recast the notion of the Western individual in ways that could be highly subversive of the existing conceptual consensus – and would be seen by some as progressive but by many others as regressive.

The second issue is the perception that some immigrants identify themselves not as discrete persons, as per Western assumptions, but as 'communal individuals', whose behaviour is primarily

---

13. For a discussion of the meanings of rationality in the social sciences, see Elster, 1983.

determined by the group. This is not new: for instance, Gypsies and Travellers have long refused to conform to the norms of individuality, preferring to see themselves as a community guided by other social criteria. What is new is the decision by some locally born citizens of foreign origin to begin now to subscribe to a vision of the individual that is secondary to that of the grouping to which they pledge allegiance – the Muslim *ummah*, as we have already seen. Here, it appears that the assumptions of social science theory simply cannot hold true since behaviour dictated by a notional supranational community is not readily compatible with the presumption that individuals are discrete persons making choices based on purely personal preferences. Of course, it can be argued that to dissolve one's person into the *ummah* is a personal choice but this is a circular argument with little practical purchase.[14] One who does not conceive of him/herself as an individual cannot be presumed to be an individual in the sense in which we normally define it, especially if the notion of individual used is that specified by external normative or religious criteria. In any event, what sort of individual one is, is ultimately determined by the society in which one lives. So, what is problematic for the West is the presence of people who choose to identify themselves as 'communal individuals' in an individual-based society – the definition of which we now need to re-examine.

Society

The concept of society used in our social sciences is thus predicated on the notion of the individual discussed above. What marks out our Western theories is the idea that society is best conceptualised as the aggregation of such discrete individuals making choices on

---

14. See, for example, Hansen et al., 2009.

the basis of free will according to personal preferences within a socio-economic and political environment upon which they can act. It is this vision of an ensemble that is, in definitional terms, nothing other than a conglomeration of separate persons, which underlies our analysis of social processes, and which is the fundamental working assumption of the social sciences. Society exists only in so far as individuals come together to offer a given group a legitimate existence and provide it with the political means to govern itself. In democratic theory, only consent can justify the political architecture of society. And the arrangements that govern the workings of society can only be changed by political means legitimated by the citizens – that is, by individuals.

This notion of society is congruent with the belief that primacy always rests with the individual. Because it is individuals who act to construct society, it is they who constitute the underpinning of what is only an artificial grouping which they, as discrete persons, have elected to bring to life and sustain. There may be a distinction here between the more libertarian and more socialist political doctrines but there is no fundamental disagreement on the logic between individual and society. The former see society as the most minimal binding together that is required for the national grouping to function: all that is not specifically attributed to the state, the political guardian of society, belongs with the individual. The latter argue that the well-being and improvement of the individuals rest with the social and political arrangements that bring them together and regulate their lives. This is, of course, a very important difference but not one that offers a different conceptualisation of what society actually is. These are merely two opposite views of how individuals can use society to their best advantage.

Nevertheless, the question of whether personal betterment is best achieved by individual or collective efforts marks the current opposition in present conceptions of society. These are ideological differences. In reality, however, Western societies are all of a fairly common type, the two extremes of which would be the United States and the Scandinavian countries. The one believes that the individual must always trump the state – that political arm of society – whereas the latter assert that individual well-being is best guaranteed by a strong state, so long as it remains politically legitimate. In all Western countries, however, the state is huge and it imposes very substantial taxation on all citizens, whose liberties it carefully delineates and constrains. Although it would appear that the Scandinavian model brings a higher quality of life to *all* its citizens, what matters here is what the individuals concerned believe. In that sense, well-being is also very largely a matter of self-perception. A poor individual in the USA who believes in the American dream of infinite self-advancement may feel herself more empowered than a materially satisfied Swede who has become blasé on account of an excessively comfortable welfare state.

Thus present political debates about society turn around the extent to which individuals should entrust their welfare to the state – not around the relationship between society and individuals. There is a libertarian extremist fringe that refuses to acknowledge the legitimacy of the concept of society, arguing that any social and political arrangement of that type is an attack on individual freedom. To them, there is no such thing as society, only abuse of power on the part of the state upon the citizen. However, their views are in keeping with the Western assumption that, in what is effectively a parallel with the place of the atom in physics, the foundational block of society is the individual person. Nowhere is it envisaged that this may not be the case. And yet there are now a number of issues confronting us with dilemmas that are not easily resolved within this standard vision of what a Western modern society is.

The first has already been mentioned: it is the claim by some (perfectly 'modern') members of our society that their identity as individuals is determined by their communal affiliation to a greater 'community', such as the transnational Muslim *ummah*. What this means is that they do not consider themselves to exist other than in a symbiotic relationship with a notional group, which extends far beyond the society in which they live. In this they share a vision of all those who profess that their religious belief implies the dissolution of the individual into the religious grouping. However, unlike those religious orders that create a new, and confined, mini-society in which these religious devotees can live outside 'normal' society, those who claim an *ummah*-based identity as individuals want to recast the world in their image. They see their duty in terms of the creation of a society in which the collective trumps the individual. To them, membership of that community and the obligation to abide by its rules are not open to choice: they are a requirement of being born a Muslim.

I shall not debate here whether this conception of the *ummah* is valid or not. I leave this discussion to scholars of Islam. My point has to do with the claim made by locally born Western citizens who profess to make the individual subordinate to a supranational concept of society. That very claim, however confined it is to a minuscule or marginal group, raises the issue of whether our conception of the relationship between the individual and society is the only possible one for the modern world. Is this a relevant concern or an irrelevant phenomenon? I will take up the question of faith below, so I want here to concentrate on the issue of whether the social science conceptualisation of the relationship between individual and society is not just axiomatic but also immutable. It is the necessary corollary to the process of socio-economic and political evolution the West has undergone since the Enlightenment. And that process of individualisation is irreversible since it is the keystone of our modern Western societies.

Historically, this process of individualisation was underpinned by the assumption that economic development was not just self-sustained but also potentially infinite. The emergence of capitalism was made possible by the Industrial Revolution, and its march onwards would rest on the constant technological improvements and the endless modernisation of industry. With some caveats, this is still the current presumption. However, the question is now open as to whether the very serious resource and ecological constraints the world faces undermine this economic logic. If that were the case, we would obviously have to rethink the notion of development. We could no longer assume that the evolution of our societies is sustained by the economic and industrial progress that makes possible the financial and technical improvements on which we have come to depend. The very idea of the society we could expect to inhabit would have to be recast.

If that were to pass, it would very likely contribute to a necessary reconceptualisation of the relationship between individual and society. Indeed, if we start from the premiss of a limited, rather than unlimited, process of economic development, then this changes the notion of individual as it is understood in current social theory – and this for several reasons. The first is that the individual would no longer have free choice, since the result of the aggregation of all such 'free' choices could lead to a society that is no longer sustainable. If electricity production reaches a limit, for instance, the whole of our use of electronic equipment will be threatened. The second is that the 'collective' dimension of the individual would again come to the fore. What individuals are would depend not just on the nature of the society in which they lived but also on the links between that society and other communities. The present situation where water is becoming a scarce resource and neighbouring countries redefine their priorities accordingly would then become universal. Equally, the rise of sea levels due to climate change would force millions to see themselves differently: not in regional but in global terms.

In other words, society could no longer be seen *merely* as the agglomeration of the individuals who are its recognised members. It would have to be conceptualised in terms of the matrix within which there would be a need to renegotiate the relationship between citizens and state. The long-term future of the individuals would now be subsumed under the need for society to ensure survival, not just domestically but internationally. So, the end of the (largely unstated) assumption of unlimited growth removes a key pillar from the foundations of theories of society based on individualist presumptions. Perhaps Malthus was not entirely wrong after all! The pursuit of individual preferences, including that of procreating, would no longer be viable. And society could be seen no longer as the arena of free choice but as the expression of the socially acceptable limitations to the individual 'pursuit of happiness'. The present debate about the long-term viability of pension arrangements in the West can perhaps be seen as a harbinger of much more drastic constraints to come – constraints that would radically alter the Western notion of the free individual, living in a society that is chiefly designed to serve *his/her* needs and demands.

Of course, it can be argued that it is individual consciousness of the likely limits of future economic growth that is contributing to this redefinition of society. And it is true that a large number of people are now becoming aware of the need to change their lifestyle. But what I am suggesting is more radical, for it points to a recasting of social *theory* – a paradigm shift in our conceptualisation of what society is. The prevalent causality would have to be reversed. Society would no longer be what individual citizens make it. Individuals would become what society makes possible for them to be. Such a complete reversal would obviously impact on political theory, which also starts from the individual. Just as when, in the special circumstances of war, the state is granted special dispensation to limit the rights and privileges of individuals in order to safeguard the whole of society, there would now have to be a rethinking about what democracy can mean in a state of permanent penury. The tendency for authoritarianism would be strong and the possibility of abuse would be great. So, this raises the question of the importance of beginning to think about how radically revised assumptions about society would bring about the need to safeguard individual rights and enable proper political accountability in a situation of 'permanent crisis'.

Freedom

Existing notions of individual and society imply a certain conception of freedom. Not only is liberty thought to be one of the highest achievements of our modern Western society, but it is also a defining feature of the claims for the superiority of our democratic political arrangements.[15] Our understanding of present-day individual freedom is seen to be the culmination of a long process of social and political emancipation that started with the Enlightenment and accelerated after the Industrial Revolution. It was consolidated by the gradual emergence and strengthening of the democratic political order. In such a socio-economic and political arrangement, freedom is conceived in two ways: one substantive and one individual. Or, to put it another way: freedom *from* want, tyranny and poverty, freedom *to do* as one pleases within the constraints imposed by society – perhaps best embodied in the individual right to the 'pursuit of happiness' enshrined in

---

15. See here Berlin's two concepts of liberty, in Berlin, 2002.

the American Constitution. Liberty in this sense is the outcome of the historically felicitous establishment in the West of the most productive link between individual and society.[16]

Therefore the question arises as to whether the possible renegotiation of this relationship, as discussed above, is likely to affect the concept of freedom by which we currently live. The argument that Western freedom is nothing but the selfish expression of capitalist individualism is not new. There has always been awareness that our liberty was only viable because we had exploited the rest of the world to ensure our material comfort. Western freedom, in this view, was the other side of the coin of imperialist domination. The centre was made rich by the plundering of the periphery. However, that critique of our way of life was concerned with the economic inequalities generated by the expansion of the world capitalist system from the imperial core to the rest of the world. It did not address the question of freedom *per se*. The political implication of the critique was that all peoples of the world should be afforded the same freedoms, *not* that the Western concept of freedom was in question. From this perspective, it was very much a Western critique of the exploitation of the non-West.

A non-Western critique of the Western concept of freedom could be more radical yet, for it might arise from a different notion of individual and society. For instance, it can be seen that in Africa today the fact that the person is conceptualised partly in terms of the ties of reciprocity that bind him/her to the community means that the understanding of liberty is very different. For those who find comfort in this societal condition, freedom means the exercise of fully fledged community rights: land, marriage, production. For those who reject what they see as this excessive communal burden, freedom would mean the ability to operate as an individual in

---

16. See Macfarlane. 2000.

the Western sense. But as that is difficult in Africa, they have to emigrate to achieve it. However, even then, as we have seen, they would continue to view their identity abroad as being linked to the economic 'duties' that still bind them to their community. To refuse to send remittances back home, for instance, would mean to break their link with their community – that is, to cease being a person in the context of origin.[17] And such a break might not be experienced as freedom, no matter how it may appear to our Western presumption.

In this way, Africans who live in our midst may appear to us to be 'irrational' in that they fail to seek the freedoms we believe our societies afford them. Although Africans living in the West are as keen as we are to partake of the material benefits of modernity on display, they are simultaneously prone to consider that freedom entails obligations to their family, kin and community back home. In standard social science, that attitude is normally considered a 'leftover' from the sense of belonging that continues to link them with their community – an attitude that ought to wither in due course as they become more Western. However, this is a short-sighted and inaccurate perception that rests on the (unstated) assumption that there can only be one form of modernity – the Western – and one form of freedom – that of casting away communal obligations. It is, of course, one of the tenets of our societies that we are free to choose our freedoms, as it were – implying thereby that we are also free to choose 'un-freedom'. But that remains at heart an individualist conception, which cannot account for the necessary expression of a 'communal' freedom. We view all constraints on individual freedom as obligations, hence as restrictions on our liberty.

---

17. For a discussion of the politics of being and belonging in Africa, see Chabal, 2009.

It is for this reason that we fail to make sense of the fact that Western women should want to cover themselves for ostensibly religious reasons, thereby in our eyes restricting their freedom. Our societies allow for people to make 'unreasonable' choices, which are ostensibly inimical to the flowering of the individual freedom of those making such choices. However, there is very little acceptance of the fact that these choices might be the result of a different concept of freedom. The choice to curtail one's individual liberty for the sake of one's religious commitment is accepted as the option of a tiny minority of people, who can only live their faith in this way. But the decision by a woman deliberately to curtail her 'emancipation' in aid of a debatable interpretation of Islam, or even worse accept a practice like genital mutilation, simply does not sound right to us. So the argument by some feminists that women ought to have the right to cover themselves if that is their choice exposes the contradiction of our notion of freedom. Or, rather, it shows the degree to which we have come to make a fetish of *individual* free choice.

The debate about euthanasia restores some perspective to this question, since (with few exceptions, such as Switzerland) present legislation does not condone the exercise of choice when it comes to dying or to assist in the death of another person. The issue of where freedom lies in the debate of these two very different questions – the *hijab* and assisted suicide – pushes at the boundaries of free choice. It reveals both the assumptions behind our idea of freedom and the limits of our tolerance of unbridled liberty. In this reading, it is permissible to tolerate the *hijab* but it is not acceptable to help those who want to die. And yet both sets of actors are claiming the right to exercise the freedom to choose. Clearly, the reason why we take a contradictory view on these two different claims is because we view the one as 'exotic' and the other as too close to the bone. Indeed, the discussion of euthanasia is plainly one in which we see the need to pay heed to the limits of individual freedom. And, incidentally, one in which we make religious and moral assumptions we fail to find as objectionable as those of Western Islam.

Be that as it may, the most searing challenge to this individualist notion of freedom comes at the moment from modernist Muslims (such as Tariq Ramadan) settled in the West.[18] The core of their argument is twofold. First, Muslims settled in these countries must abide by their laws. But, second, these countries need to revise their conception of the public good by allowing Muslims to behave according to their own religious norms and injunctions. So, for instance, there is no justification for the French decision to ban the *niqab* in public places since it curtails the wearer's fundamental human rights – that is, her freedom to dress as she pleases. This argument strikes at the heart of the Western notion of freedom because it exposes the contradiction between two equally valid claims: freedom of choice and women's emancipation. This is so because the West, especially France, makes a sharp distinction between the social and the religious, whereas Islam provides a view of the world in which the personal, the social, the political and the religious are interrelated.

By putting forward this argument, these Western Muslim theorists demand a revision of the notion of freedom, which would place the requirements of the community (*ummah*) above those of the individual. In other words, and according to them, individual Muslims can only be 'free' when they choose to abide by the notional rules of social life that are an integral part of the believers' faith. If some of these choices collide with the precepts of Western societies, it is for these societies to make adjustments to their social codes. The approach, therefore, consists in using

---

18. For a discussion of Muslim intellectuals, see Kersten, 2011.

the Western constitutionally enshrined rights of the individual in order to challenge the social or political restrictions their governments would want to place on the actions of Muslims settled in the West. The conundrum for our societies is that an acceptance of the primacy of the communal over the individual would undermine the foundations of the individual freedoms which we hold to be both an irreversible social advance and the linchpin of our current legislation.

From a Western point of view, then, an acceptance of the Muslim theorists' argument would be tantamount to allowing two competing notions of freedom within the same public space. The demand that there should be recognition of Muslims' need for a different approach to social legislation would obviously go against the equality of all citizens, which is another core principle of Western political theory. But the real challenge to our Western concept of liberty is not simply that Muslim activists should seek to advance their quest for a different notion of society, and hence freedom, but that some citizens in these Western countries should demand *communal* rights on the basis of their *individual* human rights. This deliberate claim by (Western-born) individuals to curtail their individual freedoms in favour of a communal notion of liberty is not susceptible to a 'rational' resolution within our own social theories.

It is of course simple, if not easy, for Western legislatures to reject these claims, as the French have done, but it may not be as simple to live with the political consequences of such decisions where, as in France, the Muslims represent such a sizable minority. The further French decision to ignore the realities of ethnicity, and thus the potential mobilising force of the community of Muslims, will do nothing to ensure that Muslims speak as individual citizens rather than as members of a religious grouping. It might even be thought that such a denial of group identity would merely encourage it to grow, especially in a context where Muslims (rightly) feel discriminated against because of their names. But this is the political battle, which might in due course affect legislation in Western countries. Here I am more concerned with the implications for theory of this challenge to the idea of liberty – a challenge that can only grow if, as in a situation of growing scarcity, we need increasingly to worry about the survival of society, even at the expense of individual freedoms.

The claim made by Muslims that the practice of their religion requires special social dispensation, which appears ostensibly to constrict individual freedom, represents the most serious attempt to redefine the boundaries of Western social theory. Until then, the only comparable situation was that of the rights of the indigenous peoples in the New World dominions. Their claims to different *communal*, rather than individual, rights were placated by granting them actual geographical territories upon which they were entitled to exercise jurisdiction according to their own 'traditional' customs. In those cases, Western states conceded not just that these peoples were entitled to land but that they were also permitted to organise their social life according to norms that might not conform with the dominant Western ones. Indeed, that concession did admit that some inhabitants in the West were at liberty to abide by different rules. It was a belated recognition both that they were the original inhabitants of that part of the world and that Europeans had conquered their lands by force, thus abolishing their freedoms by fiat. However, the present Muslim claim is different in that those who are making it are of immigrant origin. And they are making the claim by using the very constitutional norms that sustain the notion of individual freedom in the West. Whether that challenge will result in the changes Muslim activists want is a moot point. What is more relevant here is that the argument about the limits of individual freedoms will not go away.

Nor can it necessarily be assumed, as social theory does, that the present gains in personal liberty are irreversible. For example, the attempt by pro-life activists to overturn the legislation on abortion in the West is showing no signs of abating. Here the argument turns on the individual rights of pregnant women against the putative rights of the unborn foetuses – or, in other words, the rights of notional beings (foetuses) that are not part of society as currently defined. Therefore the claim that those unborn babies have in principle the same rights as actually living individuals redefines what society means and what freedoms it bestows on women. A reversal of present legislation would undoubtedly be a curtailment of women's liberty in so far as it would give their status as 'begetter' precedence over their existence as human being, equal in law to men, who do not suffer the dilemmas of pregnancy. In that sense, it would thus undoubtedly be a step back from the present belief in the equality of men and women.

The discussion of the Muslim claim to the supremacy of the community, the *ummah*, and of the Catholic implacable objection to abortion, raises the issue of the role of faith in our Western societies.

Faith

One of the key features of modern Western societies is that they are secular – by which is meant in the first place that there is a clear constitutional separation between religion and power. Indeed, the hallmark of the political development of Western countries since the Enlightenment was the gradual but inexorable emergence of a state over which the Church no longer had any direct control. The ideology of the state and the instruments it evolved to regulate politics became firmly secular. Even in countries like the UK, with an established Church, there no longer is any challenge to the absolute sovereignty of the elected parliament. In political terms, the UK is as secular as France or Germany. Of course, religion continues to exercise strong influence on society, not least in Catholic countries, where the Vatican's view on marriage, divorce, contraception and abortion weighs heavily on any policy of social change. But officially, at least, in the West matters of faith are considered to belong to the private sphere.

So, what is at stake in the West is not so much the political influence of religion as the nature of secularism. Here, yet again, it is the Muslim argument that has unsettled the working assumptions, which had enabled peoples of different faiths to live together in relative harmony. Of course, religious discord in Western and, especially, Eastern Europe has brought about frequent political and violent confrontation. Catholics and Protestants in Northern Ireland, Orthodox and Muslim communities in the Balkans, among others, have resorted to armed violence over many years. Yet these were essentially political disputes, rooted in long-standing nationalist claims. They were not the result of the ambition by one side to do away with secular politics, even in Kosovo, where the conflict was savage. It is only recently that in the former Soviet Caucasus groups of Muslims, heavily influenced by Wahabi ideology issuing from the Middle East (chiefly Saudi Arabia), have been calling for the re-establishment of religious political dispensations, or, even, the Caliphate. Yet, even there, they face implacable opposition from other 'nationalist' Muslims, who reject that ideology. It has now become a multi-stranded civil war, in which the Russian state supports the secularists.

The debate in Western Europe is very different and it hinges on two separate, though related, issues. The first is the nature of secularism and particularly its implications for political and social legislation.[19] In other words, how relevant is secularism to

---

19. For a strongly felt review of present debates, see Eagleton, 2009.

the decisions we make about 'living together in society'? The other is whether the demands made by Western Muslims should lead to changes in our legislation. Here the question is how best to accommodate the demands of Islam in societies that are predominantly Christian in belief but secular in practice. Both aspects of that debate have exposed the limits of our rationality. They have shown up the contradictions between, on the one hand, our ideology of equality and rights-based policies and, on the other, the claims made by Muslim theorists that Western legislation is fundamentally discriminatory against those who want to live their Islamic faith unhindered as *individual* citizens of Western societies, in which they were born and where they choose to live. I discuss these in turn.

With some important variations, there are basically two 'models' of secularism in the West: the French and the American. They both enshrine the separation of State and Church in law and they both protect religious freedom. But the meaning of that separation is entirely different, largely because the historical experience of each country is so distinct. The French achieved secularism after centuries of church involvement in politics. They wanted to be able to live in the new post-revolutionary society free from clerical and papal interference. The Americans designed secularism to protect themselves from the long tradition of state intervention in religious matters they had inherited from Britain. They wanted to be free to worship without fear of persecution.

In France, secularism means the protection *of* the state from church intrusion and the protection of individual human and social rights by the state. Here, therefore, the key is quite clearly the role of the state, which must be shielded from the Church so as to safeguard the rights of all citizens to live in liberty. In exchange, the state protects all religions from segregation and warrants the freedom of religion to all citizens, so long as it is confined to the private realm. This translates into a rigidly secular type of education but, perhaps paradoxically, allows for state funding of religious buildings. In any event, the state is constitutionally bound to avoid discrimination between religions and to ban all individual discrimination on grounds of faith. In France, therefore, the challenges to secularism, whatever their origin or form, are by definition challenges to the state. Or, to put it another way, they are automatically political, since the state stands at the apex of the constitutional edifice that secures the country's secular identity and protects its citizens.

In the USA, secularism means the protection of religious freedom *from* the state. The constitution is designed to enshrine and secure individual rights against political abuse. It is that constitution, and the independent judicial system that buttresses it, which protect the citizens from the state, assumed to be incapable of restraining itself from abusing individual rights. In such circumstances, what is asked of the state is that it stays out of religion, limiting its reach to the legal protection of all faiths and all forms of worshipping. The nature of secularism in the USA, and the complexion of the relationship between secularism and religion, are neatly encapsulated in the motto 'In God We Trust'. That statement of religious belief would not be tolerated in France, the land of Revolution, where the dominant icon is Marianne, the secular image of individual liberty. American secularism, then, rests on deeply religious historical foundations, upon which the erection of a legal framework to secure the exercise of individual freedoms is deemed to be sacrosanct. As a result, American society is probably far more religiously grounded than most Western European ones. Secularism does not stand in opposition to religion, as it does in France, but in aid of it. It is thus no surprise that today it is in the USA that are found the most fundamentalist expressions of Christian faith in the Western world.

On the face of it, therefore, the USA is better equipped than France to deal with present Muslim demands for the social and political expression of their religion. The supremacy of individual rights allows Muslims to act as they wish and to wear what they please, so long as their behaviour does not infringe on the rights of others. A very strictly enforced freedom of speech also enables Muslims to express themselves in ostensibly political terms, whereas such statements might be considered inflammatory in Western Europe. Furthermore, the right to private property puts very few obstacles to the building of mosques or madrassas in the USA, whereas it has already led to legal and political wrangles in Western Europe.[20] It is no surprise, then, that the wearing of the *hijab* has not provoked the same reaction as in France, Germany and Belgium. So far, there has been no test case on the 'legality' of the *niqab* in public spaces and it is probable that, other than in special cases (such as official photographs), there will not be in the USA the same compulsion to ban the garment in question.

However, it is also true that the proportion of Muslims in the USA is small compared to that in Western Europe. Islamophobia, though growing, is limited, and segregation according to religion is of little import in that country. Because politics in the USA turns around individual rights rather than the state, American Muslims have not so far felt the need to question the country's political architecture, the role of the state or the legitimacy of the constitution. They, like everyone else, are protected *from* the state and, so long as they do not suffer overt discrimination on grounds of religion, they needn't protest. Nevertheless, the American authorities are worried about the possible influence of modernist Muslim intellectuals, whose claims for a distinct political theory they are reluctant to entertain. Indeed, it is they who prevented the Swiss

---

20. The controversy about opening a mosque near Ground Zero did not hang on the *right* to do so but on whether it was desirable to ignore the symbolic significance of the 9/11 site.

philosopher Tariq Ramadan from taking up an academic position in the USA, whereupon he was offered a visiting professorship at Oxford and an invitation to join Tony Blair's advisory council on Muslims.

In point of fact, the reasons for being, or not being, suspicious of Tariq Ramadan's views are at the core of the dilemmas Western societies face today as they try to respond to the Muslim challenge. The difficulties are twofold. On the one hand, our social theory tells us that, as they modernise, societies become increasingly more secular. But what does that mean in practice? Does religion become less important to the individual or is it the religious argument that is deemed to have lost its impact on our social and political theories? On the other hand, our constitutional arrangements dictate that religion should be the preserve of the personal, and not the public political, sphere. Or, to put it differently, faith should impinge on our political judgement no more and no less than any other belief. Faith holds no higher ground in the ethics of how we live than other moral imperatives. And, clearly, not all morality issues from religion. This is where we are now but some Muslim theorists, like Ramadan, are crying foul. Your ways, he avers, are inimical to my religion, which does not accept the assumptions you make. The freedoms you claim for all citizens must allow Muslims to 'live' their faith in their own way, even if it means you have to revise your views on religion. What you call secularism is oppressive of our faith.

The claim about the increasing secularisation of society is open to question, and at the very least needs to be approached from different angles. It is true we have secular constitutional arrangements but this is where clarity ends. Quite plainly, religion continues to impinge greatly on our ethics, as is evident in the discussions about abortion, IVF, euthanasia, stem cell research and cloning. If philosophers and social theorists are often asked to join ethics committees, the boundaries of their discussion are usually framed by religious beliefs, whether they are avowed or not. Similarly, many of the assumptions currently made in Western societies about charitable work have their roots in religious injunctions about the need to care for those who are less fortunate. Much foreign aid is also justified in this way. We may not attend church services in large numbers but we continue to propitiate our grief through religious rituals, whatever our faith. Secular we might be in our commitment to government by men rather than God but we continue to believe in some God-like rationality to make sense of our lives.

In the first place, then, it is well to remind ourselves what secularism actually means in modern Western societies. Whilst social theories do accurately reflect a historical move away from metaphysical explanations, they do not readily account for the changing nature of faith from religion to spirituality. If the scientific revolution that has made our modernity possible is grounded in the increasing 'rationality' of our social and political theories, it has done nothing to change the apparently insatiable need for some sort of faith in the world beyond this one. So, if the role of formal religion has lessened, the space vacated by the rituals of established religion has been occupied by various forms of spirituality. Furthermore, there has been an upsurge in new religions, like Pentecostalism, particularly among 'southern' immigrants. Finally, we have witnessed a wave of scripturalist or fundamentalist interpretations of spiritual and social life, especially among Protestants, the proponents of which have gathered large numbers of followers.

Thus the reaction to modernity in our Western societies has led to the rise of new religions, sects, fundamentalist offshoots of established faiths and a limited, but significant, turn to non-European faiths like Buddhism, Hinduism and, today, somewhat paradoxically, Islam. These developments do not affect directly the secular nature of our political systems, but they provide avenues by which groups of citizens apply pressure on the social fabric of our communities.[21] Of all the recent changes, the two most significant are probably the growth of Christian fundamentalism and the conversion of Westerners to Islam.

The former is interesting because it is a move away from secularism, back to the past, in that guidance is sought in texts that were written centuries ago but that are claimed to provide a 'true' way of life. It is a turn against modernity, which is seen to have confused the basic verities of human existence with an excessively loose interpretation of the parameters of the 'good' life. It is thus no surprise that Christian fundamentalism should be most popular in the USA, since (as we have seen) the foundations of individualism are rooted in religion and the search for meaning in a chaotic and fragmented world harks back to the early certainties of the country's myths of origin. The expression of faith, and religious beliefs, are as central to the politics of that country as they were two centuries ago. And the move to replace evolution with creationism is a reflection of the distinct ways in which some Americans wish to challenge secularism. The key point here is not so much whether they will prevail but that their self-evidently 'anti-science' theory speaks to so many.[22]

However, it is undoubtedly the conversion of Westerners to Islam that raises more pointed questions about the nature of secularism. Whatever the motivation for the individuals who convert, they choose to enter a religion that conceives secularism in a radically different fashion. There is nothing in Islam that prevents Muslims from adopting ostensibly secular political systems (as in Turkey), in which political and civil rights are granted to all, including

---
21. See Dawkins, 2006.
22. See Armstrong, 2001.

non-Muslims. Although there are large numbers of secular Muslims in the world, including many who would profess no belief at all, I am concerned here to examine the Muslim notion of faith. In that context, being a Muslim precludes the option of restricting religion to the private realm. Just as it is not open to a Muslim to renounce his/her religion, there is no leeway in the interpretation of what is required of the 'good' Muslim. Islam is a prescriptive religion, which offers not just spiritual meaning but also a whole way of life. From this perspective, therefore, it cannot be denied that Westerners who convert to Islam are committing themselves to a resolutely non-secular existence.

Islam is also distinct from Christianity in that it is not open to a conceptualisation of society in which the public and the private or the social and political can be dissociated. To live one's faith is fully to accept the precepts of the religion. Whilst in principle Islam allows non-Muslims both to practise and to live their faith, the same freedom is not afforded those who were born Muslims or converted to Islam. This is not to offer a simplistic view of Islam and even less to deny the long tradition of reformists who have argued that Islam should modernise and allow more secular expressions. Nor is it to enter the debates between modernists and reformers, which I am not qualified to do. It is merely to explain how Islam as a religion is a conceptually different expression of religious faith from other less prescriptive religions.[23] And it is the theoretical impossibility of transforming Islam into a religion of individual choice – including renouncing one's faith or working to limit religion to the private sphere – that challenges the West's notion of secularism.

Therefore, the main point is to explore why those who dispute the West's ideology – whether as individuals or as exponents of the faith – do so in terms that preclude the possibility of a

---

23. Except for orthodox Judaism and scripturalist Christianity.

secular Islam. And the real question has to do with the Western response to this challenge. The argument here turns on the claims by Muslim intellectuals like Ramadan that the West's notion of secularism (which some call 'militant' or 'fundamentalist') is oppressive of Muslims, whose religion cannot partake of such a concept. Similarly, women converts to Islam who opt to wear the *hijab* declare that they suffer from discrimination because Western society considers modernity to be incompatible with clothing taken to condone the oppression of women. In both cases, the argument is the same: it is the West that cannot countenance a non-secular interpretation of religion and seeks to protect itself by means of legislation. And in so doing, it discriminates against Muslims.

The claim that Western societies are Islamophobic, or that Islamophobia is on the increase, is also interesting from the conceptual viewpoint. Indeed, what is defined as Islamophobia is usually the ostensibly commonsensical popular view that Muslim behaviour marks them out as people who do not wish to integrate into Western societies. So, the argument is circular. Popular opinion is fashioned by what people see and hear – that is, more and more women wearing the *niqab* and the pronouncements of Muslim extremists who wish to fight the West in the name of Islam – and such perceptions lead them to view Muslims differently. At the same time, the argument by some (and some only, it must be pointed out) Muslim intellectuals that they should indeed be viewed differently reinforces the view that 'being a Muslim' is not compatible with Western modernity. This cannot but lead to the view that Muslim 'exceptionalism' is not due to the slogans of the extremists but to the very nature of the religion itself. And it is this argument, which harks back to the old European demonisation of Muslims, that feeds Islamophobia.

But the reason the debate about Islam in the West has so much resonance is not just because of the threat of Muslim terrorists.

It is also because the questions raised by Muslim intellectuals like Ramadan find an echo in the current questioning of the West's secularism, or its relation to faith. Ramadan is perceived as 'threatening' because he argues from within the West, both in terms of the social theories he addresses and in advocating that Western Muslims must abide by existing legislation. His argument is that it is the West that will need to revise its conception of secularism in order to accommodate Muslims who want to 'live' their faith in the Western countries in which they were born. And it is precisely this argument that is deeply disturbing, since it cannot be reconciled with our social theories. It must either be rejected wholesale or else it must lead to a fundamental recasting of our vision of the evolution of Western societies into 'modernity'. In either case, it challenges Western rationality and the social theories upon which it is constructed.[24]

Of course, the most likely outcome is that the issue will be finessed in the hope that the dilemma will go away, on the assumption that the Muslim 'question' in the West will dissipate as political Islam weakens and terrorism is checked. However, the issue of the role and significance of faith in the West is unlikely to vanish. The heated debate between the so-called 'militant' atheists, such as Richard Dawkins, and the religiously inclined may in retrospect not be seen as proof that the former are winning the argument, but the reverse. If the renewed enthusiasm among the youth for religion is anything to go by, then the end of the twentieth century may well turn out to have been the heyday of secularism. Matters of faith might increasingly make their presence felt again. If that happens, then the so-called Muslim question will no doubt continue to resurface. It could well be the portent of the limits of

---

24. See Ramadan, 1999, 2003, 2004.

our secularism, which in due course will have to be revised, thus forcing a reconsideration of our theories of modernisation.

Market

In the West our understanding of the economy hangs on what is a virtually anthropomorphised notion of the market. In fact, we have lived with this concept for so long that it has become utterly familiar: we speak of the market as though it was a benign old friend, an uncle perhaps, who looks after us in good times but scolds us when we go astray.[25] The market, that 'grand old man', is tough but fair. He gives us the means to manage our affairs wisely but is ever vigilant lest we allow ourselves to overstep the boundaries of propriety and good sense. He provides us with the narrative of the good life but warns us that we have to listen to the wisdom it distils. He has issued us with the secular text of the modern religion: capitalism. Of course, the market is not a god but it is the closest approximation we have of a *deus ex machina*. Indeed, the belief in the market is also an article of faith, even if economists have told us that its workings can be explained rationally.

So, when reconsidering the concept of the market we need to address two radically different questions. One is the 'scientific' reality of the relationships and causalities economic theory provides: explanations of why and how production, prices, trade and growth take place. The other, no less important, aspect is the symbolic value it has acquired in our explanations of how individuals, societies and countries behave. Here the issue has to do with the subjective idea of the market, along with the influence such an idea has on our individual and collective behaviour. Although our Western rationality has made it possible to develop the science we

---

25. Although some undoubtedly see the market as an 'enemy'.

need to live well, the reality is that much of what we do does not find its origins in strictly rational action. Therefore the study of the market provides a good opportunity for the re-examination of the meanings of Western rationality in the contemporary context.

Conceptually, what is most interesting about economic theory is the claim that the market is self-regulating. Starting from simple premises, that theory develops a model of how economic relations between individuals pursuing their self-interest and maximising their preferences will result in what is often called an 'optimal equilibrium'. In plain language, this means that producers and clients, buyers and sellers can settle on a fair price, which reflects the value of the products they purchase or exchange. The theory of market equilibrium explains how supply and demand will set such a fair price independently of the subjective wishes of either party. What is just about that price is that it reflects the amount buyers are willing to pay sellers in the circumstances. At its most basic, therefore, the theory of the market shows that, under 'normal' conditions, the price of the item that is exchanged is a correct valuation of its scarcity and desirability – although, as Marxists point out, not necessarily of the labour invested in its manufacture or of its 'use value' for those who acquire it.

The other key mechanism that makes possible the market's self-regulation is competition, that other sub-*deus ex machina*. Neoclassical economic theory shows that where competition is unhindered, both the costs of production and the prices of commodities will settle at the lowest possible level – to the benefit of the consumers. Again, that conceptualisation of the market makes it plain that interference with competition, whether for political or ideological reasons, will result in disruption to the process of production and exchange, which will lead to higher prices and/or less efficient output. Economic theory does not concern itself with the reasons why 'perfect' competition might not be possible; it merely demonstrates that the more 'perfect' competition is, the more advantageous to consumers the equation between production and price will be.

There is, of course, much research in economics dealing with the effects of imperfect competition, which offers great refinement in our understanding of how markets can work in practice.[26] Equally, there is excellent work on the limits of the market's self-regulation, considering the complexities of domestic and international constraints on production and exchange.[27] Much effort too has been devoted to an analysis of how governments' fiscal and monetary policies impinge on the operation of the market and how socio-economic legislation places firm limits on the labour market. Similarly, economists are well aware that the financial markets are substantively different from industrial ones – with clear implications in terms of how they ought to be regulated. Of course, we now have learnt the hard way that trading in virtual or invisible commodities is not the same as exchanging actual goods. Nevertheless, there is in theory nothing to distinguish the former from the latter and many economists argue that regulation of the financial markets will merely distort competition and skew prices, to the detriment of profit and investment.

From my perspective, however, what is of greatest interest is the economists' claims of 'scientificity'. Although they are perfectly willing to concede that real-life economies are subjected to myriad forces that cannot all be incorporated into the models with which they work, they insist that their axioms and assumptions are justifiable conceptual simplifications. The implication is that economics is dealing with the same type of 'objective' reality as are the physical, chemical or biological sciences. Even if economics is the study of *man's* activities, it is nevertheless susceptible to

---

26. The first systematic discussion of imperfect competition was probably Robinson, 1969.
27. In 2008 Paul Krugman received the Nobel Prize for his work on imperfect competition.

the same type of theory-making as physics or biology. What this means is that it is legitimate to develop predictive models based on certain fundamental assumptions about economic activity. Of these, the notion that markets, like gravity, are a fact of life and the presumption that markets, like heat exchange, are self-regulating are fundamental.

The debate about the merits of various economic theories – for instance, classical versus Keynesian – is not my concern here. I want instead to address the reasons why this ostensibly 'scientific' approach to the market may well have reached its limits – or, to put it another way, how its limitations may be due to its 'scientific' presumptions. Indeed, the assumption that markets are self-regulating rests on a number of debatable premises, of which I examine a couple. One is that, confronted with the same set of circumstances, consumers and producers will behave in similarly rational fashion. This presupposes not just that they have the same aims but that they interpret the objective and subjective 'information' they have in similar ways. At a very crude level this may broadly be true. But is it true enough to comfort the theory of self-regulation? Clearly not, as we know from what happens in the real world. Individuals make decisions on the basis of a number of factors, including what is now called 'irrational' or impulsive grounds, that go against assumptions of rationality.[28] Businesses too must pay attention to 'non-economically rational' factors like loyalty, fairness, local pressure, politics, favouritism and corruption – forcing them to prioritise actions that may be detrimental to the pure pursuit of profit.

The other core assumption is that competition is sufficient to regulate the market. Again, the reasoning here is in theory impeccable, since it rests on the plain fact that potentially profitable

---

28. Ariely, 2008.

economic activity will inevitably attract operators, whose success will undoubtedly depend on their competitiveness. But in real life, the conditions under which this competition takes place are far from perfect and the distortions induced by domestic and international circumstances may well make a mockery of self-regulation. We know, for instance, that without anti-monopoly legislation there would be a tendency for capitalism to turn into monopoly capitalism. In other words, competition has to be controlled by tough laws otherwise it will be abused by the bigger players. Equally, we have been made well aware that hedge financial trading may result in an artificial competition that puts the entire financial system in danger of meltdown. The pursuit of short-term gains at all costs runs the risk of a pyramid-scheme type implosion, as was illustrated by the subprime market collapse in 2008, which ended in disaster. It is also highly questionable whether the speculative trading of derivatives can self-regulate.[29]

The issue here is not so much that markets are not really self-regulating. After all, governments have done much to ensure that competition and markets operate as they should precisely because they know that the presumption of self-equilibrium is far too crude. The problem is that our economic theory starts from the premiss that these assumptions are true. This means that the study of how markets actually work is hampered by a type of conceptualisation that is too simplistic to provide the required analytical tools. Progress in understanding markets is dragged back by a theory that is hardly fit for purpose.[30] In the physical sciences such a theory would be discarded. But since in economics there is little to suggest a more heuristically useful approach, the discipline's very scientific ambition forces its practitioners to hold on to a largely obsolete

---

29. See here Taleb, 2008.
30. And the study of social or cultural factors affecting markets would threaten the autonomy of the discipline.

instrument. However, the cutting edge of research into economic theory today is in part to be found in the work of scholars who invalidate some of the discipline's core assumptions: for instance, showing that consumers are not 'rational' actors.

But the market is not merely to be considered in its 'objective' reality; it must also be seen as an incantation. It is not just a cynical wizard; it is also a benevolent uncle. Adam Smith's representation of economic activity as the 'invisible hand' managed to capture two essential aspects of our relationship to the concept of the market – with which, paradoxically, he might not have agreed. The first was obviously the theory that it was self-regulating – the import of which continues to this day. But the second, and no less important, is the notion that left to their own devices the economic relations between people would find their appropriate equilibrium. It provided an 'objective' representation of the hunch social philosophers had about human activities: the sum total of the behaviour of individual agents would result in a 'rational' economic outcome. Production and exchange would find their right levels. It was the beginning of what is now known as classical economic theory, which still dominates the discipline today. But it was also the foundation of what might be termed a 'secular religion': if we believe in the self-regulating properties of the market, then the market will take care of itself. The theory of the market is thus also the credo of capitalism, the rationality of which depends on our belief that it will do us right. It is in that sense that its effectiveness also hangs on the continued invocation of its powers.

So long as capitalism was challenged by communism, the commitment to a market economy was both a statement of ideological intent and the claim to a more efficient economic system. Now that communist economics is dead and that China is showing itself so proficient at letting a hundred capitalist flowers bloom, our notion of the market is changing. The ideological battle is fought on the role of the state. Free-marketers, predominantly in the USA, want to limit political interference in the market to the minimum. Social democrats argue that only state regulation will ensure the market does not engender gross socio-economic inequalities and repeated financial crises. There is now a see-saw movement between the two: the apparent victory of the former between the 1980s and 2008 was followed by a brief revival of Keynesianism after that financial crisis. As was to be expected, books have now appeared explaining why the crisis was inevitable and why the financial markets are not capable of self-regulation.[31] There are attempts to agree international regulatory frameworks (chiefly within the G20[32]) that will restore sanity to global financial activities. However, it is already clear that the market ideology is recovering and it won't be long before the theory of market self-regulation is restored to health, once again set as the default position.

The point here is to highlight the fact that the arguments adduced by both sides regarding the market rely in part on belief and in part on incantation. As all governments know, statements about the economy have immediate impact: in the common jargon, they 'affect the market'. So, the flip side of economic 'theory' is clearly the belief that professing faith in the properties of the market will make it more likely that this anthropomorphised actor behaves in the 'right' way. Yet there is nothing in theory to curtail the behaviour of, say, speculators. Their actions can have a devastating impact on the performance of the market and cripple a country's economy, as happened when Britain was forced to leave the European Exchange Rate Mechanism in 1992 because of speculation against its currency. So, markets are also prone to fluctuate according to self-fulfilling prophecies, making them all the more difficult to control or manage. And economic theories

---

31. See for instance Reinhart and Rogoff, 2009.
32. The G20 is the grouping of the largest twenty economies in the world.

cannot help here, since they can only tell us that 'in due course' all currencies will find their equilibrium.[33]

The problem lies in the fact that the behaviour of the market is partly to be explained by the degree to which the theories are *believed*. Where faith in its properties dissolves, its performance becomes increasingly erratic and the effects of such unpredictability can be devastating. It is in this respect that one can point to the limits of market theories and, thereby, of economic rationality. Economic 'sciences', then, have not progressed towards greater refinement in the ways that their physical or biological counterparts have. However confident the claims of economists that advances in mathematical modelisation now make it possible to refine predictability, it remains as true today as it was a couple of centuries ago that market theories are inherently limited – and will remain so. The difficulties Western societies face lie in the limitations of an economic theory that rests on the *faith* in the inherently self-regulating properties of the market – a belief that is no more 'scientific' than wishful thinking. Faith is of course very comforting but the problem with the market is that the consequences of its misdemeanours are felt in this world, and not the next.

Change

Attention to the market points to the obvious observation that our notion of economic success rests on the underlying assumption of change. Although economic theory purports to explain how the market brings about productive equilibria between production and consumption, savings and investment, the need for growth demands continuous change. Whether driven by supply or demand, economies must move forward or contract. This requires, and

---

[33]. To which argument Keynes rightly said that 'in due course' we are all dead.

brings about, technological and manufacturing transformation, which drives the search for resources, new methods of production and engineering innovation. New products are introduced both because they satisfy a need and because they nourish the apparently insatiable desire for what is novel. In this race against time, publicity becomes a key driver of change, creating demand or feeding the wish to be up to date. The badge of modernity is the possession of the latest technology, the use of which is almost entirely supply-generated.

The modernisation of all societies as being driven by the desire for the latest technological innovation is now a well-accepted feature of globalised modernity. In point of fact, several Asian countries (such as Japan, South Korea) are ahead of the West in that technological game.[34] However, what is of interest here is the place of the *idea* of change within Western rationality – rather than the pace of change itself. At the heart of our present social science theories is the belief that societies are in a constant state of flux, the direction of which can be manipulated by our understanding of the processes of individual and collective development brought about by scientific and technological advances. Social theory thus rests on a set of assumptions which link economic, political and social *change* with the ceaseless progress of our mastery of the material world in which we live.

It was one of the fundamental shifts brought about by the Enlightenment that the condition of man could be improved by the drive to exercise agency upon the physical world – rather than accept one's fate within it. The displacement of the hegemony of the metaphysical by the belief in the pliability of the physical freed Western thinking and made possible the theoretical work that would eventually result in the development of modern science.

---

34. See Pomeranz, 2000.

What is singular about the West, therefore, is not so much the mastery of technology, which is widely shared throughout the world, but the impact of that experience. At the heart of the West's conception of itself is the legacy of the profoundly liberating moment when modern science was born, enabling the development of the theoretical knowledge that paved the way for the Industrial Revolution. Although that scientific moment was made possible by the accumulated knowledge of many other societies – most notably Chinese, Indian and Arab – the West considers that *it* was responsible for the final, and most significant, breakthrough.

The self-image of the West is that *its* modernity is a reflection of its unique ability to embrace and manage change. That view is reinforced by the idea that other societies, most particularly in the non-West, are hampered by an inordinate adherence to traditions – traditions that make it difficult for society to adapt or mutate. Indeed, there is even a sense that some societies, as for instance in Africa, are positively unable to change. Of course, this belief is not usually formulated in such stark language. It comes out most readily in the assertion that Western societies are particularly adept at innovation, as is evidenced by their scientific and technological dominance. East Asians are acknowledged as the masters of transformation and production but the West holds on to the notion that it rules over the creative impulse behind change.

In fact, this belief in the importance of change is so central that it permeates most aspects of our lives. Theories of social organisation, business and management all stress that success is the outcome of the ways individuals and groups are able to confront, understand and master change. Flexibility is key. Employers seek and reward those who are adept at embracing and generating *productive* changes. The widespread idea that the private sector is more dynamic than the public is precisely because the former is held to embrace change whereas the latter is believed to resist it. And since the private sector is seen as the engine of economic growth, the link between well-being and the advantages of change are clear enough. So, the West posits that progress is made possible by economic growth, which is the direct result of the ability to achieve and master scientific and technological innovation. Whatever facilitates this process is 'good'; whatever hinders it is 'bad'.

This dichotomous view of the world pits change against tradition – the latter assumed to be an obstacle to the former. Indeed, this idea of a 'hierarchy' among societies is also to be found at work *within* the West itself. The USA not infrequently sees itself as the land of creativity and innovation precisely because it is less burdened with 'traditions' than old Europe. And within Europe itself, there are suggestions that some types of tradition are more inimical than others to change: broadly, the South appears slower to adapt whilst the North seems more receptive to innovation. However based on prejudice these ideas might be, what they make clear is the extent to which change is seen as positive and tradition as negative. Equally, there is a strong belief in the West that Western societies attract those individuals from the rest of the world who believe in the modernity of change and seek the freedom it bestows by migrating to the West.[35] So, not only is the West the space of change par excellence; it is also the land of opportunity for those who understand the importance of innovation to a type of modernity that is liberating.[36]

This view of Western modernity is blind to the fact that what it calls change is nothing other than the transformation of the traditions that go back to the Enlightenment. The willingness to embrace change, or at least the belief that such is the mark of

---

35. And in Britain that belief includes the assumption that state interference in private life is wrong.
36. For a critique of the West, see Appadurai, 1996.

the West, is but the outcome of the influence of science on our conceptualisation of individuals and societies. It is the primacy of scientific rationality in our social and political theories that leads us to view change as the key to the improvement of our lives. From this observation comes the idea that change is good *per se*. However, this is a misreading of scientific evolution. Clearly, the assumption among scientists is that theoretical, or paradigmatic, change should occur when (and only when) new evidence shows that existing theories are failing in their presumed predictive properties.[37] Change, therefore, is conceived as an enabling instrument, and not as a primary good in and of itself. Furthermore, the paradigmatic revolution does not occur in a gradually managed fashion but in a stochastic and often unpredictable way. Traditions are not good or bad; they are the foundations upon which scientific research proceeds in its messy ways.

The justification in the social sciences for a model of continuous individual and societal developments, then, is a caricature of the way in which change takes place in the physical sciences. But there is more: it has also become an article of faith, which may now have become an obstacle to the resolution of some of the challenges with which I am concerned in this book. The reasons why this is so have less to do with the question of whether change is inherently desirable or not – which is a debate I shall not take up here – but with the issue of how the presumption of the superiority of 'change' over 'tradition' affects our thinking. Here again, the impact of the non-West on politics and economics, and especially the presence of so many immigrants of non-Western origins, have brought to the surface tensions that are not easily understood, let alone resolved, within the boundaries of our present thinking.

---

37. See Kuhn, 1962.

I illustrate the limits of our conceptualisation with reference to both domestic and international issues. The first example has to do with the notion of multiculturalism; the second with the relationship between culture and development in the non-West.

The idea behind multiculturalism is that peoples from different backgrounds will live better together if they are allowed to maintain, cultivate and express their different cultural norms, values and practices.[38] Britain is perhaps the country that has been most fully committed to this idea in Europe. The assumption behind the vision of a harmonious life is rooted in the belief of a particular type of evolutionary social change. It rests on three assumptions: one is that immigrant 'cultures' are not incompatible with the dominant norms of society; the second is that these cultures will evolve, modernise and eventually converge with that of the locals; the last is that the suppression of such cultures would likely result in resistance and thus a greater reluctance to accommodate to the new society. The advocates of this policy, therefore, do not see the need actively to engineer, even less force, integration. The focus instead is on allowing that transition to be made by natural osmosis, as it were, on the grounds that the benefits of integration are self-evident to those who settle in the West. Immigrants, it is believed, will come to see that change is the best way forward.

The problems of integration in contemporary Europe, not least the issue about Islam I have already discussed extensively, have now cast doubt on this argument. All three assumptions are being questioned. It is clear that all European countries have come to believe that some of the immigrants' 'cultural' practices are indeed incompatible with those of the West. Polygamy, 'arranged' marriages, 'honour' killing, genital mutilation, and a wide range of abuses against women, are all practices that are testing Western

---

38. See Taylor, 1994.

societies. Of course, it might well be argued that these actions are the preserve of a tiny minority and that, in any event, they are already penalised by law. But the difficulty arises when such practices continue over generations, including among those who are born in the West.[39] Should they be attributed to the leftovers from foreign 'traditions' that are upheld by a minority of ill-educated immigrants? Is it not just possible that some immigrants find in those 'cultural' attributes a way of acquiring an identity within a society in which they feel marginalised? This would suggest that they have now come to reject integration and find in tradition a meaningful way of asserting themselves. The upholding of norms clearly incompatible with those of the West would then become an instrument of community politics that undermines multiculturalism.

The assumption that the immigrants' culture would ultimately 'modernise' and thus converge with that of the West is equally problematic, for it rests on the presumption that modernisation amounts to Westernisation. Leaving aside the more disturbing practices mentioned above, there is a vast array of non-Western cultural norms that might well evolve within the West without converging with the prevalent Western values. The reassuring image of the go-getter immigrant who becomes more Western than Westerners in pursuit of the good life in the host country obscures many other forms of adaptation to life in the West. The majority of non-Western immigrants are not the highly educated and ambitious Indian computer scientists moving to Silicon Valley. They are those, unskilled or poorly skilled workers, who were encouraged to come to the West or who have made their way there to do the jobs that Westerners no longer want to do. Today, they are often illegal or economic migrants. They leave their countries of origin to escape poverty and despair, not primarily because they want to become Western.

---

39. Some second-generation Asian immigrants argue that they prefer 'traditional' arranged marriages. See Gell, 1995.

Their interest is not in adopting Western cultural norms but in making a life for themselves and their families. They usually send most of their hard-earned cash back as remittances. They work in the West but they 'live' in the expectation of returning home. Far from wanting to become more Western, they cling to their identity in the (largely forlorn) hope that, having made it rich, they will resume their home way of life.

The fact that many will never go back, if only because few make it big, means that they live in limbo, often in a twilight zone, with few rewards except their (increasingly romantic or distorted) belief in the value of their culture of origin. Living precariously in an environment that is increasingly hostile to immigrants, they find refuge in what they believe to be the more elevated values in which they were brought up. Theirs is a home-bound gaze, which is unlikely to make them more Western in outlook. Their way of life may modernise, in the sense that they live an increasingly Western material and professional existence. But that process of 'modernisation' is at variance with Westernisation: they see themselves as both 'modern' and faithful to their community of origin, not by the Western standards they often come to resent because of their marginalised position within the host societies. And it is their children, born of disenchantment, who feel they have entered this world as second-class citizens and against whom the odds are stacked, who may well become the more militant defenders of their parents' traditions – now seen as the only true expression of dignity in such a hostile environment. Continued discrimination against second- and third-generation children of immigrants incites a rejection of *Western* modernisation and thus of multiculturalism.

Finally, the assumption that suppressing non-Western culture can only generate resistance is consistent with the more liberal vision of how best to encourage immigrants to adopt Western ways. However, in recognition of the fact that such laissez-faire approach may not work, all European countries (including Britain) now advocate much more dirigiste policies. Having realised that the inability to speak the language leads to the creation of 'cultural ghettoes', in which immigrants continue to live totally disconnected from the West they inhabit, there is now greater emphasis on language competence. Similarly, most European countries now impose lessons in history and citizenship as part of the process of legal immigration. Some even require a formal commitment to abide by Western social norms as sanctioned by legislation. These tentative and as yet still limited steps to 'force' integration are nevertheless an indication that it is illusory to expect that living in the West is in and of itself sufficient to induce the cultural changes that will eventually result in the Westernisation of the individuals concerned.

The theory of multiculturalism ultimately rests on an assumption about the cause and direction of change, presumed to result in Westernisation. There was once good ground for thinking that it was the best way to ensure the integration of immigrants at minimum cost and disruption, since so many generations of newcomers (Huguenots, Jews, Poles, Italians, etc.) had melded in this way into the local culture. However, the arrival of immigrants from the non-West has brought about a new situation in which the assumptions of gradual and automatic integration cannot be taken for granted. This is not because these later immigrants are any less industrious or any less willing to integrate but because the host nations have looked upon these post-colonial 'strangers' as being more different and less liable to assimilation. In that situation, the old assumptions about multiculturalism are tested to their limits. The process of change, based on theories of socio-economic and cultural integration, has turned out to be different from that adumbrated by social theory. And despite our commitment to a liberal tradition that claims to welcome all manner of 'differences', we are now confronted with a situation in which a number (admittedly small) of our fellow citizens effectively refuse to change in the ways they are expected to do. They claim the right to modernise in their own ways.

This obviously calls into question the rationality of our theory of integration, since it could well mean that multiculturalism has become an impediment to the cultural change we assume will take place. It also puts into perspective the British critique of the French method of 'forced' integration. Indeed, some recent surveys suggest that the French way may well result in a stronger sense of belonging since a greater proportion of French Muslims have indicated they feel nationals first and Muslim second than in the UK.[40] Their problem is that they feel they are second-class French citizens. The limitations of French policies, which are largely due to the denial of the fact that *beur* alienation is also a problem of (ethnic and religious) identity, are plain to see. They also rest on assumptions of social change that are not warranted. But these problems may not in the long run be more severe than those of countries where multiculturalism has been the preferred integration policy. Indeed, the statement in 2010 by German chancellor Angela Merkel that *multikulti* had failed was a shock, and not just in her country.[41]

The question of the relationship between culture and development in the non-West also exposes the limits of our assumptions about socio-economic and cultural change. It has been a mainstay of our development theories that the development of capitalism was made possible by a transformation of 'cultural' outlook in the West – which Weber dubbed the Protestant ethic – that paved the way for individual entrepreneurship. If the scientific and industrial

---

40. For an EU overview of this issue, see http://fra.europa.eu/fraWebsite/attachments/Manifestations_EN.pdf. For an American summary of the 'Muslim question' in Europe, see www.fas.org/sgp/crs/row/RL33166.pdf.
41. See www.bbc.co.uk/news/world-europe-11559451; accessed 7 February 2012.

revolution provided the technological means for economic change, it was in the end the emergence of a capitalist 'culture' that made possible the rise of the market economy on which it thrives. The assumption here was that processes of socio-economic and cultural change were causally related and acted to bring about a certain type of society, the Western, with the most coherent and productive type of modernisation. Therefore the presumption was twofold: capitalist 'take-off' depended to some degree on a prior cultural change that would make possible private enterprise; and the emergence of successful capitalism would in turn lead to the (implicitly Western) cultural changes that would best sustain the further development of capitalism.

Those assumptions, as we have seen, have influenced our view of development aid to non-Western countries, resulting in the latest Washington consensus to the effect that the capitalist ethos and democracy were causally related. At the same time, however, we have had to concede that the sudden and manifest success of capitalist development in East Asia has taken place in a cultural context radically different from the Western. That success has been so stark that it has generated theories about the role of Asian 'culture' . The assumption of a causal relationship between culture and capitalism has led Western observers to seek in Japan, China, South Korea and Singapore the 'values' that have made possible such rapid economic progress. Far from being seen as 'traditional' drags on modernisation, as they once were, Buddhism and Confucianism were now taken as having provided the moral and individualist equivalent of the Protestant ethic.[42] Was there common ground between the cultural norms of Japanese, Chinese and Singaporeans that could explain their economic success? Whatever those may be, and many still deny that culture is relevant to development,

---

42. See an enlightening discussion in Tu, 1996.

the emergence of Asian capitalism has put paid to the assumption that Western values were indispensable.

Moreover, it is not clear that rapid economic modernisation in those countries will lead to cultural Westernisation. The Chinese and South Koreans may be avid consumers of Western products but they are from unanimous in aspiring to a Western way of life. Or, rather, the all too obvious aping of Western ways – perhaps best epitomised by the construction of replica Western cities in China – does not translate into a change in values that is as radical as might at first appear. The same is true of India, where for instance the influence of caste is as strong among the apparently highly Westernised as it is among their less outward-oriented fellow countrymen who are still mired in extreme poverty. In other words, the assumption that the acquisition of a Western material veneer is proof of profound cultural changes is much exaggerated. In point of fact, it is often among the most economically successful and Westernised Asians that there emerges a strong adherence to a 'traditional' (if often largely invented) set of beliefs with which to secure their identity. And members of the wealthy diasporas not infrequently assume a distinctly non-Western identity that comforts a longing for their culture of origin.

Furthermore, the emergence of market capitalism in communist countries like China and Vietnam also tends to undermine the assumption of a causal relationship between political and economic liberalisation. Economic and political changes are distinct processes, which although intertwined can result in a number of different paths to modernisation. It is plain that the experience of economic development in Asia does not confirm the assumptions made by the West about the political causalities undergirding market growth. The presumption that Western-style democracy is the political framework most consistently conducive to capitalist development is disproved by the economic success of these non-democratic Asian countries. Of course, it does not mean that democracy would not be a more desirable political dispensation than communist authoritarianism, which is another debate, but merely that it is no prerequisite to capitalist 'take-off'. And it remains very uncertain whether Asian capitalism will lead in due course to a Western form of democratisation or whether it will eventually be undermined by the absence of Western-style democracy.[43]

This brief discussion of the complex relations between change and culture ought to make plain the limits of theories assuming that both the pace and the direction of change follow predictable pathways – or that change is inherently beneficial. All movement is change but not all change is positive. Traditions and stability may also provide the basis for social, economic and political betterment – which is an argument that the Chinese are fond of putting forward. But above and beyond these considerations about the links between economics and politics, it is the very approach to the idea of change that is at issue. Western societies are prone to view change *per se* as desirable; non-Western societies are often more prudent and appear to value tradition more profoundly. And in point of fact, the notion that tradition and change are but the two sides of the process of evolution is one that may provide more secure foundations for development in Asia than the frantic worship of a resolutely anti-tradition concept of change as the ultimate public good. Be that as it may, it seems obvious that our approach to the problems we face today will require rethinking what change means. And that process will probably make us more aware of the merit of some of the non-Western conceptualisations of the relationship between tradition and change, which we have hitherto assumed would wither away under the relentless march of (Western) modernisation.

---

43. On the American democratic 'mission' in the world, see Smith, 1994.

FOUR

Interpretations

My argument so far has been that our social, economic and political theories are no longer adequate. Yes, the research methods and statistical instruments we have developed serve us well enough for the run-of-the-mill business of compiling facts and evidence about our societies. Yes, we have become masters at seeking correlations and offering basic answers to some of the common questions we need to answer in order to manage our work, life and environment. Yes, we are adept at explaining what we do by means of theory-clad reasoning: all governments produce elegant plans for reform that are 'fully costed' and for which the putative results are outlined in great detail. Therefore we are accustomed to profess understanding of the causes of social, political and economic change on the basis of the advice we receive from the experts. We pretend to live in a post-ideological age in which policies are merely a matter of working out the most effective way of reaching particular outcomes.

Ours has become the age of expertise and management; the justification for our policies is always presented on the grounds of good research. Indeed, the current catchphrase is 'evidence-based' decision-making – as though that were both a way of silencing any possible critique and giving proof that what we do is backed up by solid 'scientific' work. The fact that different policies can be put forward based on the same set of data, using similar analytical models, does not seem to present problems for our politicians – in part it has to be said because there is so little public or institutional memory. When the new plan appears, there is little or no reference to the previous ones. So, what we have in effect is the manipulation of quantitative evidence by means of models that correlate different variables in different ways. But this is bad science because the choice of which correlations to study is based on political, or ideological, proclivities rather than on new, or more compelling, evidence. In other words, science is invoked to give an 'objective' gloss to decision-making.

That politicians should be inclined to use social theories in this way is not surprising; nor is it shocking. What is more questionable is the fact that social scientists are loath to explain how the caveats to the theories invoked in this way are such as to make difficult any firm conclusion, let alone prediction. On the contrary, it seems that the profession is convinced its theories are not just valid but are being refined all the time. The implication, even if it is not stated that boldly, is that over time these theories will become increasingly better at accounting for the real world and at suggesting ways of improving how we live in society. The gradual quantification of the social sciences is part of a trend, which implies on the part of social scientists a belief in the growing 'scientific' stature of their disciplines.[1] In this way, policymakers and social scientists conspire to put out the message that policies are now backed up by better and better 'science'.

---

1. See, for instance, in respect of political science Morton and Williams, 2010.

The only significant exception to this trend is in medicine, where theory and therapy interact in quite different ways from the other social sciences. Medicine is clearly composed of two quite distinct forms of knowledge. The one is science-based and progress is made by means of experimental trials, either of drug or of procedure, which provide the objective basis on which to decide whether to launch a new treatment or to modify existing therapies. Theory, research and experiment proceed as they do in the other hard sciences, and advances are made by dint of confronting theory with testing. The other form of knowledge is more subjective in that it concerns the effects of therapy on patients where objective tests are not available – for instance, measuring depression, pain or well-being. Here, the medical profession allows for either the placebo effect or for the achievement of improvement that cannot be measured objectively. It will register such positive outcome but will resist giving it a scientific cause so long as it cannot replicate the effects through randomised trials – its main research method. In other words, medicine makes a clear distinction between the heuristic quality of science-based and non-science-based therapy.

Medical advance, which is cumulative, takes place either through breakthroughs in scientific research or by means of the gathering of evidence to support therapies that may not at first sight appear to be science-based. Here an interesting contrast is that between acupuncture and homeopathy. The first draws on centuries of medical practice in China and has been shown over time to control pain through the application of needles into key nerve centres. It has an objective basis, even if it is not always easy to replicate results. Our original reluctance to accept it was not unconnected to the fact that it was of non-Western origin.[2] The other, though claimed by many to be effective, has no scientific basis and cannot

---

2. And also maybe because of the awareness that the practice is linked to an alien cosmology.

be explained, at least in terms of our present scientific knowledge. Its only justification is a supposed correlation between taking the homeopathic pills and feeling better. Although this might be reason enough to accept it as medicine, medical science rejects its claim to be therapeutically valid since its effect cannot be taken for granted, or guaranteed. It classifies it as placebo, which has its place in medicine.

However, the social sciences cannot call upon the scientific claims of medicine to support their theories. Other than in limited areas of economics, where causalities can be demonstrated, and some experimental psychology, where replication is possible, social sciences are not able to satisfy the most basic requirements of research as applied to the physical sciences. In this way, they fall at the very first hurdle. What they can do is to propose a very basic, quite simplistic, model of social, economic or political change, identify key independent and dependent variables, and study correlations. But since they cannot either hold variables constant or replicate the calculations made in a particular setting, their correlations can be no more than snapshots of particular events or processes at particular times. There is no hard scientific basis for affirming causality or, even less, establishing causal developments over time. The hypotheses offered cannot be tested, or falsified, and they ought to be seen as the 'best possible guesses in the circumstances' rather than as scientific theories.

These remarks are banal and well understood by those working in the field, who do not deny their relevance. But there is a sleight of hand here, which is convenient to both social scientists and policymakers in claiming that the social sciences are 'scientific' – implying thereby that they can carry the same conviction as their sisters studying the physical world. This is an old and much-rehearsed debate, which I will not take up here except to say that my first objection is to the pretence that crunching numbers is the same thing as being scientific. However sophisticated quantification is, and however complex the correlations established, there is no way that the social sciences can advance causal relations to emulate those of the physical sciences. The very meaning of causal explanation, therefore, is distinct.³

So, for instance, what of the theory that recession will depress consumer spending or that an increase in the concentration of unemployed people in separate high-rise housing will cause a rise in criminality? Well, perhaps or probably. A more accurate formulation would be that it is 'likely to cause', since there is no way of demonstrating an automatic cause–effect relation between the two sides of the equation. But this is precisely the point: 'likely to cause' is very different from 'to cause'. And that difference is the difference between non-science and science. At best, the former deals in trends, or tendencies – not causalities. For instance, it is 'probably' the case that a high-rise development with a lot of violent criminality will lead to more car hijacking than other housing developments.

Therefore the claim that theory in the social sciences equates to what it is in the physical sciences is highly misleading. They appear to proceed in the same way: agreeing on axioms, laying out assumptions, justifying the simplifications of the models used, identifying the variables and proposing working hypotheses. But this is where the similarity ends, since the social sciences study human behaviour, which can never be held constant – meaning in effect that the simplifications are greater, the variables more numerous and the hypotheses more complex than they would ever be in the physical sciences. Furthermore, the research required to test the hypotheses can never be anything other than limited and very likely subjective; in most cases it can never be replicated.

---

3. See Gulbenkian Commission, 1996.

This does not mean that such research should not be undertaken but it does imply that there is nothing to be gained, and much to be lost, by claiming that 'theory' in the social sciences can ever be as compelling as it is in the physical sciences. In point of fact, such a definition of theory in the social sciences is liable to give a veneer of 'objectivity', which marks out some 'theories' from others. And because of the supposed similarity with the hard sciences, theories that are quantitative tend to be privileged over those that are based on qualitative research.

The argument is not so much that the meaning of theory in the social sciences is different but that the use of that notion of theory in the study of the conduct of human affairs does have many effects, which we seem too readily to neglect. The first effect is that it provides a scientific gloss on social science research which is not warranted. The best evidence that can be gathered in this area is usually confined to surveys and reviews of previous policies. These are useful, indeed indispensable, but they are, in scientific terms, very crude instruments. Surveys are inherently subjective, even if present techniques enable us to measure public opinion with a fair degree of accuracy. Surveys have (limited) predictive quality when the issues concerned are simple and stark – such as voting intentions. For more complex matters of social, economic or even political significance, it is extremely difficult to produce data that is more than a reflection of possible trends. Public opinion is notoriously fickle and it is beyond the capacity of our analytical tools to anticipate public behaviour in relation to specific changes in, for example, such policies as multiculturalism.

The second effect is that the mantle of science is invoked to justify what are essentially political or ideological decisions. This is useful in many ways. It comforts the view that we live in a post-ideological age and now make policy on good 'objective' grounds. We choose to end public funding of teaching in our universities because 'research' tells us that high fees will not deter applications from the most disadvantaged households. But we have no way of knowing that this is true until the policy has been in place for a while – by which time new research will show that this might not be helpful as theory. Similarly, based on the theory that democracy is a requisite for development, we can impose political conditionalities on aid recipients. Here again, by the time the theory is disproved it will be too late to undo the complicated mechanisms by which we deliver aid to poor countries. On the same register, if we find in international surveys that people 'prefer' democracy to any other political dispensation, are we justified in forcing regime change in countries like Iraq? In all these examples, the 'scientific' argument to validate policy is at best dubious and at worst irrelevant. But it looks better than good old-fashioned ideology.

The third is that it placates our self-image as being 'rational' in what we do and, as Westerners, as being more 'rational' than non-Westerners. In point of fact, looking into the common usage of the concept of 'science' it becomes clear that in everyday parlance 'scientific' is synonymous with 'rational'. The two are used interchangeably. What validates a decision as 'rational' is that it is based on 'objective' – that is, 'scientific' – rather than 'subjective' – that is, 'irrational' – forms of reasoning. This has two consequences. The first is that we provide a seemingly unimpeachable ground for our notion of rationality, since science is meant to be universal. In other words, our rationality is superior not because we say so but because it is based on science. The second is that it enables us to disguise our sense of superiority in 'objective' garb: only when others match our science will their claim to rationality equal ours. This has the immense advantage of refuting the argument that the claims for the superiority of our rationality are due to postcolonial hubris. On the contrary, we can say, the status of our rationality is based on science, which everyone can acquire, and has nothing to do with Western arrogance.

Finally, it provides us with a seemingly objective basis for claiming that our social science theories are not only compelling but also universal. This is of course critical, not just because it helps us validate the claim of the general suitability of our disciplines but also because it makes *our* readings of realities on the ground 'objective'. The more we can convince ourselves, and others, that our theories are 'scientific', the easier it is to ascertain the authority of our interpretations. In particular, it enables us to minimise the cultural variables that may be thought to impinge on people's behaviour in the non-West. Or, rather, it helps to label such cultural variables as being the mark of a non- or pre-rational way of being.

Culture is seen to be an important explanatory element *only* in those cases where modernisation has not yet brought about a more 'rational', 'objective', science-based, framework for agency. This comes close to arguing that the culture of non-Westerners is 'irrational' whereas our own culture is merely an aesthetic refinement in our lives, which are otherwise governed by the exercise of 'scientific reason'. But, if our social theories are universally valid, then they must be of equal relevance to all peoples, whatever their history, traditions and culture. This means that we also use these theories to conceal the fact that we believe our culture to be superior to 'their' culture, which we tend to classify as 'exotic' rather than 'scientific'.[4]

Therefore, if we are to move beyond what are in my view the very serious limitations of current social sciences, we will need to approach the questions with which they deal in a different way. But before we do so it will be useful to consider what is presently on

---

4. See Pomeranz and Topik, 1999.

Interpretations

offer by way of revising the social sciences. A common response to the critique that social theory is not 'scientific' is to explain how it will eventually get there – by which (as any textbook on, say, comparative politics will show) is meant theoretically more sophisticated, better able to use quantitative analytical instruments and increasingly in a position to build on the cumulative advances made in the acquisition of comparative knowledge. But this will not do, except at the margins, precisely because that reasoning is based on the assumption that the social sciences are 'scientific' in the same sense as their physical counterparts.

The other remedy consists in claiming that the steady improvement in our computational power will eventually enable us to test models with numbers of (independent and dependent) variables that are today entirely beyond our capabilities. The more sophisticated our computers, the closer we will come to model real life. But this too is an illusion, for two reasons. First, we can never be sure that we will be able to identify the most significant variables: that exercise will continue to be both historical and subjective. Second, as the attempts at weather forecasting show, the ability to predict remains elusive, even when we do know what the key variables are. Predicting human behaviour would be infinitely more difficult than forecasting the weather.

For this reason it seems futile to make claims on behalf of social theory that cannot possibly be substantiated. If we are to re-examine the nature of our Western rationality, then it is necessary to recast the relationship between theory and thinking. Or, as I discuss below, we will need thinking beyond theory. I will in the remainder of this chapter try to explain what that means in practice. I want here to address the more general context within which I aim to juxtapose theory and thinking. Although this debate may appear somewhat esoteric, it is in fact relatively straightforward.

My argument is twofold: first, social theories are only one, constrained, means of studying human behaviour; second, the claims made for 'theory' in the social sciences act as a deterrent to other possible approaches. Let me elaborate.

When we are confronted with problems, such as the ones discussed above in this book, it is both natural and rational to look for 'solutions' by means of the social sciences. Many of the questions we have about society or individual behaviour can be answered, or at least made clearer, by reference to existing social sciences – economics, political science, sociology, psychology. The difficulty arises when the questions cannot satisfactorily be addressed. Why, for example, do people vote against what appear to be their own interests? Or how is it that, contrary to standard economic theory, above a certain price level the more expensive a luxury item, the more it will sell?

Of course, we can answer these questions but *only* because we locate an explanation outside the existing political or economic theory extant. Thus, in those very simple cases, it is clear that the relevant explanation is given not by the application of the theory but by thinking beyond the theory. In the first instance, for example, some first-generation immigrants might vote for an anti-immigrant party because they resent the newer arrivals. So we come up with the theory that 'self-interest' may be situational. In the second, it is likely that the more expensive an item, the more exclusive it will be, so prompting people who can afford it to outspend each other in order to acquire 'distinction'. Here we can suggest a theory of conspicuous consumption. In other words, when confronted with an uncomplicated question, we realise that the standard theories on offer are inadequate or at least insufficient.

But when the problems are beyond 'commonsensical' comprehension, we are left with having to trust the theories that purport to explain them. If, for instance, we are given an explanation as to why the derivatives market is going to behave in a certain way, most of us have no idea what to think – in part because most of us have no idea what a derivatives market is. Therefore we tend to believe the pronouncements of specialist bank-employed economists who tell us that the market is 'robust' – even though they themselves might know they have no properly scientific way to back up their statements. What is more, many of them have a self-interest in talking the market in the right direction! Or, to take another case, if well-known economists like Jeffrey Sachs tell us that more aid to Africa will mean more development, most of us are likely to believe the pronouncement – in this case, especially because it tallies with our 'gut' instinct that this must be true. Many of us would be surprised, or even shocked, to find out that there is no good theory to back these two assertions. Derivatives markets are no more capable of self-regulation than other markets, and there is no good evidence that more aid will in and of itself generate more development. In other words, expertise in the social sciences is cheap because the 'scientific' aura of the experts endows their statements with a patina of authenticity that is not deserved.

However, my second point – that the claims made for 'theory' in the social sciences act as a deterrent to other possible approaches – is even more important. The prestige of science in our Western societies and the less-than-modest presumptions of the social scientists who advise on policy have conspired to give credence to the 'scientific' authority of the social sciences. This gives them pre-eminence in the interpretation of human affairs, and produces a bias *against* other possible explanations. In other words, the scientific 'discourse' has become hegemonic, banishing other modes of explaining the world to the fringes of 'subjectivity' or the 'irrational'. Within this perspective, rationality is equated with scientific. The very meaning of 'explanation' is limited to what can fit into an apparently clear-cut cause-and-effect mechanism.

Where that mechanism is difficult to identify, great efforts are made to manufacture one in order to give the account the mark of plausibility that is demanded of social science. But in doing so we could be closing other interesting and relevant areas of research, which might be essential to the elucidation of the issue concerned.

Let us return to an earlier example. French politicians, and most of the social scientists who advise them, are wedded to the theory that the problem of the *banlieues* is caused by socio-economic disadvantage. Therefore all efforts to tackle the problems in, say, Marseilles have sought to make good that disadvantage, mostly with state funding to support housing, training, employment and social activities that will channel the energy of disaffected youth into productive directions. Any suggestion that culture might have something to do with the problem is rejected out of hand, chiefly on the grounds that it 'essentialises' people and works to create problems of identity where none existed before. And yet there is little doubt that culture in its many guises is critical.

Three aspects are of importance: one is the 'ghetto culture' within which many of these young people are born and live; another has to do with the culture of identity which troubles them, leaving them unsure as to who they are; and the last concerns the culture of Islam, the religion to which most turn and to which some convert. The very language used by this youth makes it abundantly clear that their lives are probably conditioned by a particular cultural context, which makes integration into the 'normal' world of socio-economic employment and social responsibility very difficult, if not impossible. But, of course, there is no ready theory of culture that would provide a simple cause-and-effect explanation of their predicament, so it is safer to stick to the more easily quantifiable socio-economic indicators – even when actual research shows that a key reason for unemployment is discrimination by way of the applicant's name and address, about which these young people can do nothing.

So, let me now venture onto the difficult terrain of discussing how thinking can be harnessed in directions different from existing social theory.

To think is to theorise

The first step in this enterprise is to return to the distinction between thinking and theory. My claim is that in the West the social sciences have managed to gain such a hold on our perception of the world in which we live that they leave little space for us to think differently. Our notion of rationality, which we value, is rooted in what we like to think of as an 'objective' view of reality. Unlike societies where, for instance, individual and social behaviour is regulated according to religious edicts, ours is one where both freedoms and constraints are drawn from a careful, logical, scientific and research-based consideration of the evidence. We no longer believe in witches. We can order our lives in the ways that we think most 'rationally' justified. But, as I have shown, this implies that we think in a particular way – that is, according to what we believe to be the most 'scientifically' credible arguments. This has worked well in the technical domains but it is clearly much less satisfactory when it comes to the other, more intangible, socio-economic and moral aspects of our existence.

Our belief in the scientific nature of our social theories has now become an impediment to the more open and original form of thinking that we require. So, this is not an argument for or against theory. Rather, it is an argument for thinking outside the boundaries of existing theories. Or, to put it another way, to seek a wider notion of theory. The problem is simple to identify but difficult to address. Just as thought is inchoate until it is put down in writing, so thinking is elusive unless it finds a form of expression that is understandable by all. But the problem is that our minds have been formatted to express our thoughts in ways that conform to the (implicit or explicit) templates of social theory. We think theory even as we are not aware of it. Let me give a few examples.

In the first place, we are overdetermined in what we think and say by the dominant concepts used in the social sciences: class, market, choice, development, trauma, alienation. In other words, we find it difficult to talk about what we observe in terms that are not those proffered by social theory. For example, we all speak today of 'post-traumatic stress disorder', in relation to the widest possible range of events – from war to accident, by way of the witnessing of distressing social events. The ubiquitous nature of the concept helps to condition the ways in which we think about our encounters with the less palatable behaviour of our fellow men and women. But it is by no means certain that the label of post-traumatic stress disorder is equally illuminating about the condition of, say, injured soldiers and the person who has come upon a rape scene late at night. Whereas we might well agree that both have suffered some kind of shock, there is little to be gained by lumping together their experience into this one ostensibly objective description of psychological trauma. A different verbal rendering of the two experiences would probably help in pinpointing better the damage done to the person. And, indeed, it is likely that the treatment of these two different 'patients' ought to be distinct – so it is not clear what added value the concept of post-traumatic stress disorder brings, other than giving an apparently more 'scientific' label to what was known before more prosaically as shock.

In a similar vein, it has been shown that an account of what it means to suffer from depression can be achieved by literary, or artistic, rather than strictly psychological, means.⁵ Although there is nothing wrong with the search for a chemical or neurological cause for depression, it is obvious that we should not neglect those aspects of the alleviation of the condition that could be made possible by literature, music, or art, rather than drugs. It is likely that reflecting upon the dark malady in non-psychological terms – be it through words, images or sounds – might not just enlighten us about the nature of the beast but also allow a freeing of sentiments that could help us to live with it more satisfactorily. Thinking here would mean opening up the experience depression inflicts on the person to an enunciation in words and other forms of expression.⁶ In this instance, as in many others, there may not be an obvious chemical remedy to the condition and the ability subjectively to account for its effects can be a relevant therapy. Learning how to live with depression is not necessarily made easier by focusing only on the medical, rather than personal, nature of the ailment.⁷

In a different register, and to return to earlier examples, we are now conditioned to talk about human rights and democracy not just because they are central aspects of our constitutional commitments but also because we believe they are *universal* 'public goods'. As a result, it has become difficult to discuss the social and political condition of many non-Western countries in any other terms. The questions we ask and the improvements we seek tend to turn around these questions, which have consequences not just for our understanding of these countries but also for the policies we devise, for instance, in relation to development aid. Because we now work with a definition of democracy that tends to encompass a clear

---

5. See Alvarez, 1974.
6. For a presentation of a study looking at the therapeutic benefits of reading for depression, see http://thereader.org.uk/get-into-reading/research; accessed 7 February 2012.
7. Although a scientific approach would want to distinguish between description and explanation, the study of depression might be one in which the two would be synonymous.

notion of human rights, we come to assess the political progress made in non-Western countries by standards that may well not always be appropriate. Instead of trying to measure the extent to which these countries evolve politically to emulate the Western donors, we would often be better advised to try to understand the many possible ways in which political accountability might be enhanced. Perhaps the improvement in human rights will take place as a result of political reforms that are not the mirror image of those that occurred in Europe and North America. And a narrow view of these processes, conditioned by current theories of democratisation, blinds us to crucial evidence of changes that matter for the future.

Finally, the notion that public goods can only be measured in monetary terms, which lies at the heart of economic theory, is now beginning to show its limitations. The current debates about finding a measure of well-being other than GDP has led various governments, including the French, to ask prominent economists like Joseph Stiglitz and Amartya Sen to think how it would be possible to introduce indicators of fulfilment, happiness and contentment. Although economists would contend that these too could be quantified – just as it is possible to quantify ecological markers – that misses the point. The argument here is that we need to begin to *think* about progress and well-being in non-monetary terms – not work on finding a monetary representation of distinct forms of contentment. It is, in some part at least, the overriding constraint of having to give a financial value to public goods that has led to disenchantment with our modernity. And if that is the case, then what is required is the ability to think about economics in totally different terms – terms that may appear to be subjective and incompatible with those used in standard theory-building. However, it is likely that a move in that direction would have serious consequences for economic policy, which is based on the idea that economic growth is necessary to increase well-being and reduce poverty.

The simple point I am trying to make here is that thinking and theory are inextricably linked in ways that condition our ability to reflect on our own state of affairs – and that of the rest of the world. That much is true for everyone, but what is special about the Western mind is the extreme emphasis it places on the rational, meaning scientific, nature of our thought processes. Not only do we have little time for social explanations based on such elusive concepts as, say, culture but we believe firmly that policy can only be evidence-based if it is rooted in quantifiable data.[8] The problem here is not so much that quantifiable data is not useful, since it is, but that there may well be other equally or perhaps more valuable types of evidence. And we do not avail ourselves of it not primarily out of prejudice but because we cannot *think* our way through what it would be. Our minds are conditioned by a belief in the irreconcilable dichotomy between objective and subjective.

For instance, the current definition of poverty based on a percentage of median income focuses attention on pecuniary resources only.[9] And yet we know that poverty is a relative perception, which is informed by a host of social, psychological, mental and personal factors that can radically alter that perception. The ostensibly objective evaluation of poverty is in fact made up of two equally important parts. One is the measure of access to the very basic necessities of life – food, water, shelter, heat, health – and the other is the much more evanescent feeling of deprivation – that is, the lack of those objects or activities that render life more agreeable and that others enjoy. Since it is difficult to assess the latter, it has become more convenient to define poverty in relative

---

8. For a discussion of the place of culture in political theory, see Chabal and Daloz, 2006.
9. A household is considered to be below the poverty line if its income is less than 60 per cent of median household income. 'Deep poverty' is classified as less than 40 per cent of median household income.

income terms. But this is not without consequences. In the first place, it means that the proportion of poor people can never be reduced drastically since it is a moveable default category. Each time median income rises, it affects the level of poverty. Second, therefore, it runs the risk of objectifying a category of people as poor, which attaches stigma to them and may well have unwelcome psychological and social effects on their self-perception and on their behaviour. Instead of alleviating poverty we thereby entrench it.

Thus our thinking about poverty is irredeemably skewed by the concepts and theory with which we work. It may be argued that in a society in which all aspects of life are monetised it would be pointless to devise a measure of poverty that did not have a clear monetary value. After all, it is easier to redress an imbalance if one has a clear sense of how it is quantified. Maybe, but if we were to think in terms of, for instance, well-being, rather than money, then it might appear that there are many types of poverty. It is clear, for instance, that children who do not have access to appropriate schooling are deprived, whatever the income level of their parents. And it is not always the absence of money that impacts on education: the marital situation of the parents, the family's beliefs or religion, the cultural context in which children are brought up, the influences from the country of origin (for recent immigrants), the musical or sporting environment, and so on, are all factors that impinge greatly on the ability of children to benefit from their schooling. And how beneficial education is to their personal development is likely to be the single most important determinant of what they achieve in life, including escaping poverty. A child who receives sterling parental support and lives in an environment where ambition is the norm will in all probability use the local school resources in a more productive way. That child is not as 'poor' as the one who, with the same household financial resources, grows up in a dysfunctional family, where drugs are used and where there is no hope of a better future.

The same is true, but on a larger scale, in non-Western countries. As we have seen, the widespread notion that nomadic peoples are poor and that the best way to alleviate their poverty is to make them live and work in sedentary settlements is almost an article of faith in development circles.[10] This view derives from the economic theory that the material improvement of poor people is best achieved by giving them the opportunity to engage in 'productive' activity. Living with, surviving on and exchanging cattle are not seen by economists as activities with a potential for 'development'. They simply maintain a static way of life, which is liable to crumble when climatic or health conditions begin adversely to affect the cattle. All this is true, but the fact remains that nomadic peoples do not consider themselves to be poor when they live as they see fit, largely because for them wealth is tied to cattle. On the other hand, they do consider themselves poor once they are resettled as 'farmers' – unless they can have cattle, which remains the mark of wealth. This is undoubtedly due to the importance of their culture as nomads, which gives them dignity, but it is also due to the fact that they consider farming a hallmark of poverty. In such circumstances it seems that the theory of economic development is getting in the way of thinking how these nomads might improve their own lives on their own terms.

Nor is it true that cattle-based economies are incapable of developing, as the case of Somaliland demonstrates. And the fact that this instance is virtually unique is not coincidental. Because Somaliland is not recognised as an independent country – the international community refuses to acknowledge its secession from Somalia – it has been left to its own devices by the development

---

10. For a discussion of the case of the Maasai, see Anderson and Broch-Due, 2000.

industry.[11] It receives no foreign aid and, more importantly, suffers no aid conditionalities. Based on past and present experiences, one can easily surmise that, if it were in receipt of development assistance, it would have been put under strong pressure to reform its economy along more orthodox developmental lines. Spared that pressure, the autonomous government of Somaliland has sought to build up an economy that is based on cattle trade with its immediate neighbours, particularly in the Gulf region. In that way it has reconciled a 'traditional' way of life based on a cattle economy with a more modern commercial sector that brings revenues to individuals and the state alike. Is this a model for development? Probably not for all, but it is clearly an example of where 'thinking with the grain' has proved compatible with an indigenous form of development that has brought about a better life. There may well be more than one form of 'development'.

The second way in which theory gets in the way of thinking is linked to the nature of the thought process itself. Theory is useful in that it guides and channels our thinking in a more orderly and productive way than would occur if we were merely daydreaming. It is an instrument that allows us to apply ourselves to a particular task and focus our mental energy on a given set of problems or questions. In science, therefore, there is a clear distinction between what is called applied and fundamental research. The former concentrates on testing and refining the hypotheses with which the scientists work and on finding whether there are practical outcomes to the research that might result in technological innovation and, hence, commercial application. The latter, however, is conceived as a constant reflection on the very nature of science and is driven by the need to push at the boundaries of existing knowledge – that is, effectively, to follow hunches arising from the perceived inadequacies

---

11. See Lewis, 2008.

of existing theories. In the 'hard' sciences, therefore, it is a common and accepted practice to encourage this form of thinking beyond theory. And yet it is unusual and seen as rather unorthodox to suggest that the same could apply to the social sciences.

Perhaps I might illustrate what I mean here by reporting a conversation with a very eminent physicist. He was amused to hear of the social scientists' ever-renewed desire to emulate the hard sciences both because he thought that was not what they should be doing and because he believed that his field, physics, was itself on the verge of a major turn. According to him, the next revolution in the field would not be along the lines of the greater refinement of the theory of 'uncertainty' but, rather, in the development of what one might call a theory of uncertain theories. This would mean that physics would attempt to account not just for the world as we perceive it to be (as, empirically, it is supposed to be 'out there') but for a multiplicity of worlds we cannot perceive and cannot know how to understand but whose (possibly very indirect or merely guessed-at) effects are beginning to be thought to be consequential, and eventually measurable.[12] If true, this would mean that the physicists would now want to evolve methodologically in a direction that is rather closer to what the social sciences ought to be doing!

This detour by way of the physical sciences reveals one of the fundamental limitations of the social sciences as they are practised today in the West. Instead of conceptualising theory as one particular form of thinking, they tend to confine thinking to existing theories. In other words, our approach to the socio-economic and political world is conditioned by a vision that seeks to make sense of reality merely in terms of social theory. I have already explained

---

12. And, indeed, there is now a movement for what is called 'fuzzy', such as fuzzy maths or fuzzy science, which investigates the notion of uncertain theories. For a discussion of 'explanation' in the sciences, see Deutsch, 2011.

how theory overdetermines the categories we use. I want now to look more closely at what this means for the process of thinking about the world of human beings. To repeat, my point is not so much that social science theories are useless – indeed, they are very useful but only in a limited range of applications – but that they ought to be seen as only one of the ways in which we can think about human beings and human agency. The search for more compelling explanations, more plausible accounts, demands that we think beyond existing theories.

What this means is that we must revise our view of theory. Instead of limiting ourselves to a notion drawn from the physical sciences, where the conceptual black box is more easily constructed, we need to see theory as a different enterprise. And that enterprise should be driven by the problems and questions we are trying to elucidate, and not merely by the areas of research most favoured by our various social sciences. In simple terms, we ought to attempt to combine both objective and subjective approaches since what we are after is an account of events, or processes, that are not amenable to straightforward 'scientific' explanation. At the moment this is anathema to many social scientists, who are making the most strenuous efforts to improve their 'scientificity' by ensuring that their *modus operandi* is restricted to the study of objectively defined factors that can be quantified and manipulated mathematically. It is the norm in economics. But this trend is particularly pronounced in political science, where the main American journals now increasingly favour publication of mathematical analyses.[13] But it is also noteworthy in sociology and psychology.

Instead of limiting thinking to what is theoretically acceptable, we should do the reverse; that is, investigate what possible theory might emerge from our thinking. Or, as I put it at the outset,

---

13. See Champney, 1995. For a systematic critique, see Chabal and Daloz, 2006.

recognise that to think is to theorise. In other words, when it comes to the study of human action and behaviour, we ought to allow our thinking to range as far and wide as it will, with as few theoretical preconceptions as possible, in order to approach reality from the most varied number of angles. This implies that we begin to conceive of theory not purely in deductive form but also in *inductive* ones.[14] As is well known, the former instructs that we proceed from theoretical suppositions to be tested whereas the latter operates on the basis that the theoretical architecture needed for analysis will emerge from the nature of the questions under study. Or, to put it differently, an inductive approach provides the leeway by which we can resort to various theories, or none, as we try to account for a particular aspect of human agency. There is nothing original, or controversial, since induction also has its (admittedly more circumscribed) usage in the physical sciences. It is only the artificially narrow conception of science promoted by some of our more theoretically orthodox social scientists which has cast an aspersion on the inductive method.

I illustrate what I mean with two very different examples, both taken from Africa. The first discusses what it means to be an individual; the second touches on the vexed question of corruption. The two are related.

A study of politics in contemporary Africa starts from a well-worn theory of political action that rests on the assumption that people act rationally according to personal preferences and interests. Well, yes they do. However, if the notion of the individual in contemporary Africa is markedly more complicated than that presumed in the theory, then it will be necessary to revise the analysis. And indeed, as I have shown elsewhere, the concept of the individual does encompass a critical collective dimension to what a person is

---

14. For a discussion of induction in political science, see Chabal and Daloz, 2006.

thought to be, which has enormous importance.[15] That notion of the individual includes appurtenance to a series of networks of social interaction, of various importance, that range from family, to kin, village and ethnicity as well as, possibly, the world of the ancestors. Now, this complexity need not have direct causal relevance to, for instance, how people vote – although it may do so – but it may well have more general political implications, which matter greatly. It impinges both on the conception people have of what politics is about and on what possible influence they may have on the behaviour of politicians. Therefore an analysis of electoral politics that sticks to the standard investigation of the causes of voting behaviour may miss entirely the most important explanatory factors.

This notion of the individual is to be conceived within a world in which the person belongs to various networks of reciprocity, which binds him or her to a large number of other people in relations of (more or less equal) interdependence. This means that individuals do not, and cannot, make decisions simply on the basis of their own personal preferences. They must act partly in accordance with the traditions and rules attached to these networks – whether they be kin, village, ethnic or religious. This does not just concern political behaviour; it also affects the economy. Here, individuals are bound by a range of constraints and demands that affect how they can operate as economic actors. They are expected to make decisions and to dispose of their resources according to criteria that include political, social and cultural considerations. So, for instance they may be expected to provide for younger members of their family, to support local religious activities, to contribute to social expenditures such as burials and to redistribute their earnings generously among the members of the close kin networks to which they belong.

---

15. See Chabal, 2009.

These considerations obviously impact on what we call corruption. Here, again, our theories are fairly narrow. They start from a definition that declares as illicit any use of money to influence politics, any use of public resources for private enjoyment or any abuse of official position for the purpose of private gain. But it will quickly be seen that such an approach is much too crude to make sense of what is happening in Africa. And the crudeness of the approach drastically limits both our understanding of financial 'exchanges' on the continent and the relevance of aid conditionalities we, as donors, may want to impose on recipient countries.

Everyone is agreed that a diversion of funds from their intended targets is regrettable but the best way to deal with such a problem is to understand its causes. And in this particular case, its causes are not well conceptualised by the theories extant. Only a more sophisticated qualitative, anthropological-type research can bring to light the myriad economic links that connect people who are bound by ties of reciprocity – ties that are essential to their lives. In effect, then, there are forms of financial transaction that are legitimate, even if they are illicit, and other types of behaviour that are not legitimate and are seen as abusive locally. For example, people might expect politicians to divert public funds for redistribution to their village of origin, whereas they may find unacceptable the payments they have to make to civil servants in order to obtain the identity documents they are required by law to carry.[16]

The point here is to show how a rigid definition of corruption, drawn from that in use in Western countries, and based on a Western normative conception, is likely to be less than useful when studying what is happening in contemporary Africa. Much more productive would be an approach that started with what the people concerned thought about the relations between money and power

---

16. For an enlightening discussion of corruption in Africa, see Blundo and de Sardan, 2006.

in their everyday lives. This would reveal what they believed was legitimate and what was not. It would show that much of what passes for corruption in Western eyes is in fact necessary social transactions that are based on reciprocity and obligation – both of which need also to be understood in their proper context – and are thus not open to discussion. In other words, the concept of corruption would be more useful if it was limited to what the people concerned considered to be unacceptable. Even if some financial transactions are illegal, so long as they are seen as legitimate within the existing socio-political context then it is unlikely that external injunctions from outside donor countries will have the desired effect.

Another theory, which prevails within policy circles, is that corruption is detrimental to development. In a general sense, this is true: it would be better if there was no illicit diversion of funds. But this is not very helpful. A number of studies of the success of the East Asian 'Tigers' have shown that these countries achieved spectacular levels of economic growth *despite* massive corruption. The difference between Africa and East Asia in this regard was not the level of corruption but the uses to which the proceeds of corruption were put. Whereas in Africa, corrupt politicians tended to stash most of their ill-gotten money in banks abroad, in Asia the state forced corrupt politicians and businessmen to invest locally. So, in the latter case the proceeds of corruption were channelled productively, according to clear and well-thought-out investment plans devised and implemented by authoritarian governments. In other words, developmental success stemmed from a number of factors, of which the most important was governmental policy, long-term horizon planning, and a competent administration able to implement state policies.[17]

---

17. For a discussion of the Asian experience, see Khan and Sundaram, 2000.

To theorise is to explain

The above examples show plainly how the way we theorise tends to determine how we explain. Having argued that we need to think outside the box, I now want to discuss more systematically how a different approach to theory might matter. What is always at the forefront of the physical scientists' mind but is often forgotten by social scientists is that theory is merely an instrument, a way of organising knowledge in order to tackle a particular question. Only the students of pure mathematics leave aside practical considerations in order to focus on the refinement and simplification of the abstract questions with which they grapple. A lot of what they do may in due course have practical application but their primary motivation is purely conceptual. They, like musicians, are for the most part concerned with the expression of particular thought processes: the former concerned with the rendering of sound; the latter with the development of formal abstraction and logic. What they do is at the boundary between art and thought, since much of what they achieve is due to intuition or subjectivity. For the rest of us, however, theory is a very concrete business, charged with making our world more intelligible and devising applications that will enable us to act upon it.

The first issue at stake here is the tendency in social and human theory to be more concerned about theorising than about explaining. Although most socials scientists would deny this suggestion, the output of their work usually speaks for itself. For instance, research undertaken by behavioural psychologists persists in setting up experiments to confirm the hypothesis that human beings can be conditioned to do or say certain things under certain circumstances. Yes, but the problem lies in defining such circumstances. Witness the effect of electric shocks when used as torture.[18] And the difficulty arises when the theory behind the experiment is invoked to explain people's actions in the real world, as opposed to the laboratory. The very premiss of behavioural psychologists that further research will ultimately confirm the greater relevance of the theory to human behaviour is flawed, if only because it requires such artificially circumscribed conditions to be observed. What is needed is not more behavioural psychology but other theories about human behaviour, which are not so amenable to replication in the laboratory.

Related to this is the conundrum about rational-choice theory. Although the very assumptions of the theory clearly limit the possible scope of application, there have been consistent attempts to make it more central to the social sciences.[19] Whilst rational-choice theories informed by the Prisoner's Dilemma do have applications in some limited situations where the number of variables can be held constant, their extension to economic or political behaviour is more problematic. The Prisoner's Dilemma is a simple case where two prisoners could maximise the chance of reducing a jail term by 'cooperating' in what they say but in fact, and for perfectly 'rational' reasons, end up 'defecting' – that is, not cooperating – thus ensuring for themselves a longer jail term. The upshot is that the apparently rational wish to minimise one's sentence conflicts with the more agreeable outcome produced by taking into account the other prisoner. Whatever the details of the various forms of the Prisoner's Dilemma, the relevant point here is that the theory is entirely conditioned by its axioms and the assumptions it makes about 'rational' behaviour.

But because the experiments that can be run are liable to very precise mathematical formulation, there has been an inclination on

---

18. Torture might well induce the tortured subject to talk but how likely is it that s/he will speak the truth, as opposed to what the torturer wants to hear?
19. On the limits of the approach, see Boudon, 1998; Chabal and Daloz, 2006.

the part of social scientists concerned about the 'scientificity' of their discipline to construct elaborate economic, political, sociological or psychological theories on the back of rational choice. The results have not been impressive. For example, the extension of the Prisoner's Dilemma to a theory of nuclear deterrence would show that the 'rational' policy for the parties concerned was to engage in an arms race. But any study of the nuclear stand-off during the Cold War would establish that the number of variables that influenced decision-making in each country was so vast as to render meaningless the supposed insights provided by rational-choice theory. The arms race, which can be explained in more prosaic political and ideological terms, ceased when those political factors changed. Whilst there was much work done to try to refine a theory of deterrence based on rational choice, the usefulness of that theory to decision-making declined over time. The Cuban Missile Crisis, for example, can only be properly accounted for by taking into account a vast array of factors, ranging from the military to the psychological, and would have to include a study of the personalities of the main political actors involved. The key to leadership is surely the ability to see beyond the Prisoner's Dilemma.

The extension of rational-choice approaches to deal with the politics of the non-West, for instance, has not brought much added insight. In the main it has resulted in fairly tautological conclusions – for instance, what people do is rational because people behave rationally. Well, yes, that is fine so long as social scientists are able to explain how such 'rationalities' impinge on the behaviour of the people concerned. That is the really difficult work. The greatest failing of rational-choice theory is precisely its inability to take into account different, sometimes contradictory, rationalities.[20] The very

---

20. See Friedman, 1996.

premiss of the theory is the assumption that people act according to a single, dominant, rationality, which is causally significant enough to provide 'a' valid explanation of what they do. In that respect, it is akin to behavioural psychology. But the number of instances where people act according to a single, simple, rationality is both limited and of limited importance. And these tend to be extremes. Yes, faced with a life or death situation, people will 'rationally' opt for the option that will save their lives. Yes, a religious fanatic is likely to behave according to a given, predictable, interpretation of the dogma. But in the majority of cases, finding out 'a' rationality, or more likely a bundle of rationalities, is a much more difficult enterprise, for which rational-choice theory is of reduced value.

Turning to an area that is important in the study of African politics, it has often been argued that ethnicity is the dominant factor. Many political scientists argue that politicians are able to manipulate the 'ethnic' card at will in order to get their way. The assumption, therefore, is that ethnic mobilisation can best be accounted for in terms of the use of identity for political ends. Based on such assumptions, it is relatively simple to explain how people and politicians can switch on and off this form of identity according to their own interests. Viewed in this way, it can be argued that it is 'rational' for people to play, or not, the identity card. But there are two fundamental problems with this approach. The first is the presumption that there is a simple definition of ethnicity – as though it was a matter of 'objective' reality that people were possessed of a single dominant form of identity. The second assumption is that ethnicity is nothing other than a form of identity that can be manipulated by devious politicians. But the truth is far messier and once that is taken into account the usefulness of the rational-choice-theory type of explanation begins to wither. As the more sophisticated studies of the relevance of ethnicity to political action show, there are many competing forms of identity and the key question is to explain which ones become salient under which circumstances.

Once we go beyond the tautological form of reasoning that consists in saying that, since whatever people do is rational, rational-choice theory is the approach of choice to explain what people do, we begin to see that the real work of the social sciences needs to be more refined. Instead of proceeding on the assumption that it is possible to identify and operationalise ethnicity so as to test its political relevance, we need to start from what identity means to the people concerned. Once we do, we come to realise that it is impossible to give a single definition of ethnicity – a complex combination of various forms of identity that come together differently according to circumstances – and very difficult to ascertain whether ethnicity is, or can be, the single cause of particular events. Except in extreme cases, such as the genocide in Rwanda, politics is rarely conducted on the basis of ethnicity alone. In most instances, a particular form of ethnicity becomes politically salient at particular times because of the nature of the politics of the times. So, for instance, in the context of multiparty competition, there is a tendency for politicians and parties to coalesce around simplified forms of identity that can appeal to broad ethnic groups – as has happened in Kenya recently.[21]

The disintegration of the former Yugoslavia and the murderous conflicts in the Russian Caucasus offer different perspectives on ethnicity. In the former, the attempt by Serbia's Milosevic to engineer the dominance of a 'Greater Serbia' led to an orgy of violence between various nationalities, or ethnicities, that had lived together for a long time. The political contest took the form of an ethnic war, which few would have predicted before it happened. However, after the fact, most observers explained what had taken place on the basis

---

21. The 2007 elections were marred by widespread violence. For an enlightening discussion of ethnicity, see Lonsdale, 1994.

of 'centuries-old' ethnic hatred that had supposedly been boiling under the surface for ages. Whereas what we in fact witnessed was the disintegration of an artificially created nation-state that could not survive the collapse of Communism.[22] Violence became ethnic but ethnicity was not the cause of violence. In the Russian Caucasus, the demise of the Soviet empire has brought about a different outcome. The political demands of the various nationalities (Chechen, Ossetian, etc.) that had suffered Soviet oppression were transmuted into a religious war because the Russians responded with force. The result is that today there is a civil war between the 'Islamists', who claim they want to set up an independent Caliphate, and the 'nationalists', who are supported by Moscow. Religion, rather than ethnicity, is now driving the conflict.

The argument here is not that ethnicity is unimportant but that the relevant question for analysis is under what conditions it becomes a driving force in politics. That cannot be answered by rational-choice theory for the simple reason that it proceeds on the assumption of simple causalities that are rarely found. So, the apparently unimpeachable thesis that political action can be explained according to a given theory of rationality rapidly breaks down under the weight of the caveats that have to be introduced in order to make the explanation plausible. When that happens, it becomes clear that the enlightening part of the explanation derives not from the rational-choice causal logic but from the 'thick description' of the various historical, political, social, economic and cultural factors that need to be taken into account in order to provide a convincing account of the events.[23] It is for this reason

---

22. Although it is true that there are no 'natural' nation-states, some are more artificial, and hence less plausible, than others. There is no obvious correlation between artificiality and civil war. In Africa, for example, virtually all countries are artificial and yet there have been few attempts at secession.

23. 'Thick description' is here used in the sense in which Clifford Geertz employed it. What this means is the attempt to describe an event or a process within the appropriate historical, cultural and social context. See Geertz, 1973.

that theories of ethnicity, though still widely used in the social sciences, have brought little added value to the study of those real-life situations where ethnic factors have been important. To the question of whether ethnicity matters, the best answer still remains: it depends on the historical circumstances – which social science theory cannot seriously pretend to predict other than in commonsensical or tautological terms.

Therefore the pursuit of 'better' theory in the social sciences is an undertaking with limited potential. The harder, and more quantitative, a theory becomes, the more detached it has to be from the messiness of the realities of human and social action. As in economics, the areas to which such quantitative theories can be applied are limited. Outside of those processes where it can be shown that individual action has little relevance – like the impact on public finance of a rise in income tax or the effects of a change in the voting system on party configurations – it is not possible plausibly to identify and quantify the variables required for a more accurately sensitive social theory. And the quest for a refinement, or simplification, of the theory can only be at the expense of its heuristic value: the more elegant (in a mathematical sense) a theory of human action is, the less likely it is to add value to our understanding. This is why I argue that the attempts by social scientists to emulate the physical sciences bring about a situation in which, in the end, theory gets in the way of thinking.

The second reason why I contend that theorising constrains how we explain is that it limits the range of questions we ought to be asking about human action. In the physical sciences, that problem is resolved by a constant confrontation with reality: as soon as theories begin to fail the test of experimental replicability or the requirements of prediction, they start losing purchase. In the social sciences, where replicability is impossible (other than in a strictly limited number of cases) there is no 'objective' test to challenge theory. Even when the predictive capacity of a particular theory is shown to be weak – as for instance in the case of the forecast that a minimum wage would (mechanically) increase unemployment – the theory continues to be used. As with most such theories, it might or might not be true depending on circumstances. If an increase in the minimum wage brings into the labour market people who otherwise, and because of social welfare, had no incentive to seek work, then the introduction of such a minimum wage would in fact reduce unemployment. So, the very simple theory that an increase in wages depresses employment is of limited value when the key factors in this instance lie outside the scope of the theory's reach.

The problem is not with the theory *per se* but with the belief that it is capable of offering more than it can deliver. More generally, the difficulty lies with the fact that we are now conditioned to believe that a worthwhile explanation needs to be validated by (social) theory. There are two aspects to this question. The first, and least contentious, is the view that we should think in terms of cause and effect – which is what theory is. What this means is that we should make decisions, and devise policies, on the basis of how we conceptualise particular processes – be they social, political or economic. So, for instance, we speculate that giving free bus passes to people over 60 will reduce congestion in the cities and help retired members of the community to go out more. On that basis we conclude it is worth doing, even if it depresses the revenues of the bus companies and requires public subsidy. Through research we can then find out what effects the policy has had in terms of traffic flows, how much the income of bus companies has reduced and whether pensioners feel a sense of greater well-being as a result. Ultimately, however, we accept that it is a political decision. There is simply no way of measuring, let alone assessing, *all* the possible (tangible and intangible) effects of the policy. So, the only realistic way forward is to focus on one aspect only – for instance, the pensioners' increased well-being. Of course, a different government might well do away with the free bus pass on other grounds, such as the excessive cost of the scheme to the taxpayer!

The second is that we feel the need to proceed according to evidence-based logic. This too can be relatively uncontroversial if what we mean is that we will gather all the information about a particular issue before making a decision. However, it becomes more problematic once we begin to search for the evidence that would 'prove' a particular action is better, because in order to do that we need a theory of causality. How are we to decide, for instance, whether giving public money to associations claiming to represent the 'local community' will contribute to better social relations in a particular city? There are too many variables to take into account and too many imponderables to weigh. What is a community? Is it primarily ethnic, religious, racial, social? Who best represents a community – religious leaders, social activists, local notables? How will the grant be used – for education, recreation, social clubs, religious activities? How can the effects of the funding be measured – crime statistics, mixed marriages, better school results? And yet we know that such grant-giving, which is primarily a political decision, is often justified on the grounds of theory – for instance multiculturalism. That may or may not be true but there is simply no cast-iron 'theory' that can tell us this. In truth, we muddle along according to previous experiences and hunches. But we conceal the subjective nature of the exercise behind pseudo-theoretical arguments.

These two examples of current domestic policies are relatively easy to deconstruct and assess. However, this is not the case when it comes to foreign policy, where we are far less able to measure the relevant factors and the possible consequences of different policies. The dangers of theoretical hubris are far greater. Let me take two examples to illustrate the risks incurred by a naive (or wilful) belief in Western social and political theory.

The first has to do with what is often called regime change. It is the firm belief of Western policymakers that, as per democratic theory, people in the non-Western world are eager to embrace democracy, a political system which all surveys suggest they believe to be better than what is on offer locally. Democratic theory posits not just that democracy is better for non-Western countries but also that the best way to bring about a democratic order is by way of multiparty elections. The theory goes that the successful holding of such elections will over time bring about 'democratisation' – that is, the spread of the democratic 'culture' that will ensure the gradual institutionalisation of democratic politics. There are thus good theoretical grounds underpinning the Western foreign policy seeking to encourage, induce, or even enforce, the 'democratisation' of non-Western polities. Indeed, 'democratisation' has now become a condition for the continued delivery of foreign aid and was the ostensible aim of the West's intervention in countries as far apart as Sierra Leone, Kosovo, Cambodia, Iraq, Libya and Afghanistan.

The dangers, and failures, are many but they come under two broad headings: one has to do with the theory; the other with the application of the theory. A careful examination of democratic theory reveals that there is no solid basis for the proclaimed causalities. As we have seen, it derives from a consideration of the historical experience of Western countries, which resulted in democracy, and the observation that democracy today in the West provides the best combination of political accountability and protection of individual human rights. So, in effect the theory is nothing more than the extension to the rest of the world of the Western experience. Of course, there is nothing wrong with the desire to see the rest of the world benefit from the advantages of a political system that has served the West well, but that is what it is: a desire, not a theory. The problem is that in order to justify that policy we feel obliged to provide a theoretical validation, which is simply not there. Historically, as we have seen, not only is it not the case that in the West democratic politics preceded economic development but it is undoubtedly the case that the reverse is true: economic development was achieved (in Europe and East Asia) by non-democratic authoritarian regimes. Furthermore, there is no good evidence that successful economic development will necessarily lead to Western-style democracy.[24]

In practice, the application of the theory has turned on the organisation of multiparty competitive elections. Gigantic organisational efforts and immense sums of money have been devoted to the preparation and holding of such elections, often in settings (like Sierra Leone, Cambodia or Afghanistan) where this has been very difficult to manage. Leaving aside the enormous technical problems involved in the organisation of such elections, I want to highlight some of the consequences of the exercise. Political mobilisation for competitive elections has often accentuated or actually created deep divisions between constituencies, frequently based on ethnic lines, which have contributed to civil disorder and violence. The need to secure votes has led to massive corruption, ranging from the misuse of funds intended to facilitate voter registration to the buying of votes. In Kenya, for example, the elections engendered grave ethnic tension and unleashed large-scale political violence, much of which was engineered by competing politicians.

Finally, the endorsement by the international community of the election results, even when there are serious doubts about their fairness, confers on the winner a democratic aura that is

---

24. For a relevant discussion of 'democracy' in Africa, see Schaffer, 1998.

rarely deserved. And in many cases, as in Angola for instance, it provides legitimacy to governments that lacked it before the elections. Therefore it is one of the paradoxes of the application of democratic theory that it may ensure the survival of regimes, which are able to use their new 'democratic' authority to practise a form of authoritarian politics that is at odds with democracy. But perhaps the worst is that such debased forms of 'democratisation' discredit democracy in the eyes of the local population, who are not so easily fooled by what has happened. As one perspicacious voter in Zambia once asked: 'can we eat democracy?'[25]

The second example concerns foreign aid. The theory here holds that aid is a transfer of resources from rich to poor countries, which contributes to the well-being of the local population and stimulates development. Indeed, theories of economic development, which are perhaps best put into practice by way of what is today called budget support, demonstrate that cash injections from outside have positive outcomes, boosting investment and savings, both of which are necessary for development. From such reasoning, comforted by the analysis of the experience of the Asian Tigers, there has emerged a policy consensus about both the necessity for and the positive impact of foreign aid.[26] However, the assumptions behind such a theory are such as to invalidate much of what passes for the justification of foreign aid – other than the moral obligation to redistribute resources to the non-West because it is largely made up of poor countries.

The first problem arises from the theory of economic development, which is dubious. It is one thing to assess retrospectively how Western countries developed economically – that is economic history – but it is altogether another to lay out the blueprint of development for the rest of the world. We are well past the time

---
25. See Daloz, 1997.
26. See Sachs, 2005.

when we could believe in the mechanistic theory of the stages-of-economic-growth model proposed by Walter Rostow.[27] Indeed, there is now a fierce debate about the effects of foreign aid, with a number of books arguing that it is nefarious and should be ended.[28] Be that as it may, there is continued belief in Western donor circles that foreign aid is basically a good thing, founded on a version of the trickle-down theory, which holds that monetary transfers to poor countries will eventually benefit their poorer people. This widely held view is almost an article of faith within the aid industry, but what is revealing is precisely the fact that this moral obligation should have to be presented in theoretically convincing terms. In our Western rationality, even charity has to be made more respectable by the use of theory. Unfortunately, the consequences of resorting to theory in this instance are consequential, for they distort our ability to examine the impact of aid with the detached and ultimately more 'scientific' acuity that is required.

The effects of aid are, as we would expect, very diverse. The basic flaw in present theories is that the impact of aid is likely to be dependent on factors that are not often taken into account: for example, the commitment of the recipient country to development policies, the ability of the recipient government to invest in productive areas that are central to development and the capacity of the administration of the recipient countries. These are all factors that were demonstrably crucial in the success of the East Asian Tigers over the last few decades. The logic, therefore, would be that aid should be conditional on these basic attributes, but it is not. Instead, aid is predicated on the needs of the recipient countries – that is, their destitution. But this can have very drastic consequences, which go against the very aims of aid-giving. For example, where aid is in the form of projects, there can develop a negative incentive

---

27. Rostow, 1958. For one critique of Rostow, see Itagaki, 2007.
28. See, among others, Moyo, 2009; Calderisi, 2006.

that consists in trying to ensure that projects keep going, rather than achieve their aims, so that funding lasts longer. In the case of budget support, which is justified on the grounds that donors should treat recipients as 'partners' rather than as mendicants, the misuse of aid can become an obstacle to the agreed aims. Where the intention of recipient governments is to divert aid for patrimonial purposes, budget support becomes a means of obtaining resources that does not depend either on domestic taxation or on the development of productive activities.

Even in the most worthy area of aid, the delivery of assistance to obviate starvation, the effects can be dreadful. For instance, aid to southern Sudan, very largely diverted by the armed forces, contributed (until the peace accord) to the continuation of civil conflict, leading in the end to larger civilian casualties than would otherwise have been the case. And in the eastern Democratic Republic of Congo, emergency assistance to the Hutus who had fled Rwanda in fear of retribution by the Rwanda Patriotic Front government was used by the very Hutu militias responsible for the genocide to regroup and rearm. Therefore, as these last two examples show, emergency aid, designed to keep people from dying, is routinely used in Africa for the pursuit of armed conflict. The deliberate manipulation of starvation in Africa has now become a currency, with which sundry armed groups and militias obtain resources.

This is not to argue that there should be no aid. It is instead to suggest that the use of theory to justify aid policies is often counterproductive, when not downright dangerous. First, the theories concerned are weak because they rest on dubious assumptions and fragile causalities. Second, the purposes to which aid is put are many, not always coherent and sometimes contradictory. There is thus little chance that their success could be anticipated on the basis of *any* theory. A realistic assessment of what has happened in the past – that is, a detailed history of the effects of aid in a particular country or region – would be far more useful. And it is astonishing to discover that in most instances, long-established NGOs, with decades of work in a given country, have virtually no archives and thus no institutional memory of their activities over the years.[29] But there is more. The constant need to refer to theory rather than history in the devising and implementing of aid policy is a very real danger. It is no wonder that some of the effects of aid are kept confidential and certainly never disclosed to the parliaments of donor countries which sanctioned the aid budget in the first place. Who would dare confess that food aid served to buy weapons? It is better to put forward the theory that increased aid will, in due course, spur development.

So, yes, indeed, to theorise is to explain. But it is also to obfuscate.

To explain is to act

The argument so far is that theory impinges greatly on our thinking. Not only do we give more importance to those forms of thinking that claim to be grounded in theory (by which we usually mean 'science'), but we also tend to restrict our thinking to those ways that are 'theoretically sound' – that is, in common parlance, objective rather than subjective. The limitations we thus impose on ourselves are largely invisible since it is our form of thinking, rather than simply the methods we use, that is constrained in this way. And it is the fact that in everyday life we fail to notice that we exercise our minds in this prescribed, and prescriptive, manner – which is an obstacle to rethinking the social or political conundrums we face. In other words, it is not so much the

---
29. Such as NSV, the well-known Dutch NGO. See Brinkman, 2010, which is the *first* attempt to provide a history of SNV.

theories in themselves that are a problem but the impact that such theory-based thinking has on our ability to be creative. If only the theory underpinning the thinking was always made clear, it would be easier to argue with the policy decisions. But since it is not, it becomes difficult to identify the flaws in the thinking and to suggest other avenues of reflection.

There is in this way a real, but obscure, link between theory, thinking and behaviour – both individual and institutional. Our belief in the scientific basis of our thinking – that is, Western rationality – leads us to think that we are more immune than others to the perils of 'subjectivity'. We do things for good, solid, reasons – not on a whim. One of the features of our thinking about others, particularly the non-Western world, is to attribute to them a more subjective – that is, less rational – approach to life, which we take to be one of the main causes of their lack of progress. It is thus not just the fact that the non-Western world is less developed, which is plain for all to see, but the notion that this underdevelopment is, somehow, due to an absence of the type of rationality that marks our own Western societies. The defect here is seen as the limited application of a more 'scientific' approach to the economic, social and political problems with which they grapple, resulting in a reduced capacity to bring about the social and economic changes necessary for modernisation.

But it is not just our behaviour vis-à-vis the non-Western world that is influenced by this type of thinking; it is also our attitude to the problems we face at home. For example, the recent decision in the UK to phase out public funding of university teaching rests on a form of reasoning which reflects a number of theories. One is that students should primarily be seen as individual consumers rather than citizens. As such they decide to *purchase* higher education for personal reasons based on a rational assessment of costs and benefits: they invest in education in order to secure more highly paid employment later. This view is clearly based on standard economic theory, which considers higher education as an individual, rather than a public, good. Therefore the state has no obligation to fund higher education, which should in due course be organised on the model of the market. Universities offer specific goods, which consumers decide to acquire; similarly, the provision of subjects offered in universities is, or ought to be, dictated by consumer demand. But in order to preserve 'fairness', to which Western societies are also committed, various forms of arrangements were put in place by government to ensure that this market-driven approach to higher education does not discriminate against potential students from poorer backgrounds.[30]

What is interesting here is the way in which what is primarily a political (and ideological) decision is cloaked in rational garb, relying as it does on economic theory. Indeed, once it is accepted that the theory of the market should apply to higher education, the debate as to whether it is, or should be considered, a *public* good is flushed out. Yet, what was a momentous decision for British higher education was presented by the coalition (Conservative/Liberal Democrat) government as a 'better' way of organising the university system. The clincher here was not so much that it would save the Exchequer money, which is important in times of budgetary contraction, but that it was a more *rational* way of organising higher education. This reasoning consisted in presenting the change of policy in terms of an 'improvement' in the management of state resources *by way of* the theory of the market. And it worked, not primarily because the theory is sound, as critics have pointed out, but because the recourse to that particular theory endows the policy with an objective, even scientific, quality that chimes with many of

---

30. And for pragmatic reasons, government will also ensure that the reforms do not result in the insufficient provision of scientific and medical teaching. For the rest, however, it is thought that market is best.

our beliefs. But the fact that the UK is the only European country to apply such market-driven policies to higher education shows that despite the supposedly 'good' theory there is no agreement on the matter, even within the West.

Of course, it is the art of politics to find the arguments that will carry conviction domestically, so I am not here neglecting the successful ideological campaign underpinning this change in higher education funding. However, I am interested in the way the resort to theory – here the theory of the market – is seen to bring increased rationality to what is effectively a political decision. Indeed, the theory of the market as applied to the provision of what many consider public goods – education, health, social services – has been a mainstay of British politics since the 1980s. What is intriguing is why it has come to pass for higher education and not (yet?) for the National Health Service, which in other countries is much more privatised. The fact that in Britain government can overturn a long tradition of public funding for higher education but finds it very difficult to do the same for health points to factors that lie outside theory. What this reveals is that the grounds for policy change are not simply rooted in the soundness of the theory but also depend on the extent to which society believes that some goods ought to be public and others not. Despite the efforts of Conservative governments, the bulk of British people refuse to accept that patients can be designated as consumers – hence their opposition to market theory in health.

What this points to is that theory, although it is presented as an *objective* basis for decision-making, is in fact the validation our societies need in order to justify policy decisions that are political, hence *subjective*. For politicians it is a convenient way of limiting discussion of the political basis of their policies, but for society as a whole it is a sign of the narrow range of thinking we allow ourselves. So, the interesting question is why attachment to health care in Britain is so subjective whereas the attitude to higher education has now become so cold and calculating. The obvious answer has to do with history and culture, two factors that our social sciences tend to neglect. The first is that the introduction of the NHS after the Second World War was historically a complete break with the limited, and private, health provisions available before. It was in effect a revolution, presenting those who had hitherto not had access to proper medical care with a public good they thought they would never get. The culture of the individual's relation to health provisions was thus changed for good and the attachment to the NHS became almost visceral. Whether such a revolution would have occurred without the war is a moot point.

The history of education is quite distinct. The expansion of the university system, and thus the widespread availability of higher education, is a product of the 1960s. From a narrow elite privilege, university education became the aspiration of a large number. And the economic expansion taking place at the time made a university degree a particularly desirable qualification. But the idea that higher education was, like health, a public good never prevailed in the UK. Although university access was democratised and the proportion of young people who could aspire to higher education increased dramatically, the elitist image did not disappear. The large number of meritocratic grammar schools made it possible for pupils from modest backgrounds to go to university. Since higher education was free and grants were made available, these pupils could avail themselves of higher education. But the majority of students outside the private education sector ('public' schools) did not expect to benefit from higher education and did not aspire to university. The divide found in secondary schooling was replicated at the higher level: university was for 'toffs' or 'swots'.[31]

---

31. For a summary discussion of the history of university access, see the History and Policy report: www.historyandpolicy.org/papers/policy-paper-61.html; accessed 10 February 2012.

Therefore, it is culture rather than economic theory that makes the present discourse of a 'market' in higher education palatable to the majority.

And it is history and culture, rather than the application of theory, which explain the difference in attitude in the UK towards health and education. So it is in the USA, where attitudes towards a market system in education and health are very different. There, too, the choices made are justified in terms of an economic doctrine that claims greater efficiency and where individuals are conceptualised as consumers, rather than students and patients. In this way, the USA can assert itself as a more economically 'rational' society since it allows greater leeway to the market, which is far less constrained by notions of public goods requiring state funding. Viewed from Europe that claim to greater 'rationality' is debatable: Europeans see through the political motives that lie at the heart of the application of market theory to health and education. And there is a wide range of opinions on this question within Western Europe itself, in which notions of public good and state funding for health and education differ. These differences point to the fact that 'rationality' in this respect seems to be in the eye of the beholder. We see the lack of rationality, indeed the ideological bent, in the behaviour of others but we continue to claim that we are entirely 'rational' ourselves.

But this difference between Western countries is as nothing compared to that between West and non-West. As we have seen already, the assumption in the West is that we order things, people and society more rationally. We conceive our modernity as being more amenable to the exercise of objective thinking and to the deployment of a more scientifically sound approach to solving the problems we face. The grounds on which we consider ourselves superior in this respect have to do with the proper application of the theories we have devised to explain how our societies work and how technology can be harnessed to increase our well-being. This prompts us to think that our ways have universal application, regardless of the differences in history, culture, religion and philosophy that may exist between the West and the rest. And although there is nowadays a certain reluctance to assert this 'superiority' overtly, our utter belief in the ultimate supremacy of our civilisation affects the ways we relate to the non-West in most areas.

I illustrate this proposition with two very different examples from Africa: one concerns the production of rice; the other has to do with gender issues.

The issue over rice production in West Africa is whether a more modern approach would result in higher yields, and thus greater income and security for producers. The lessons of the Green Revolution elsewhere were that the use of certain types of rice, the application of more targeted inputs such as fertilisers, and the wet rather than dry method of cultivation would bring significant advantages. The theoretical validity of this argument was backed by solid scientific evidence and was not to be doubted. But it required a complete change to existing production patterns in West Africa, which were seen as archaic and incapable of change. However, what was left out of the equation were factors that lay outside the theory – namely, funding and risk. This radical change in rice production would require large-scale funding, which local governments could not afford, over long periods. It would also demand the introduction of new, genetically modified, seeds that were expensive. Moreover, it would hinge on the ability of producers to sell their rice at sufficiently high prices. The move to new seeds, fertiliser-dependent and wet-rice methods would thus involve enormous risks for the farmers, who (like all agriculturalists in precarious circumstances) were highly risk-averse.[32]

---

32. See Richards, 1986.

Whatever the merit of the new and more productive approach, the scheme could not succeed for reasons having little to do with the lack of 'rationality' of the producers. And in the event, they were right to be dubious of the momentous changes proposed, since events vindicated them. Indeed, it soon emerged that the changes in production would result in more expensive rice and that in those conditions an increased output was not a sufficient advantage. If domestically produced rice became more expensive, consumers would buy less of it. The problem was not the amount produced but the price at which it was sold. Since in the meantime, and largely on the recommendations of the World Bank and the IMF, African countries were forced to reduce tariffs and open their markets, the price of imported rice from Asia fell. Soon, imported rice was significantly cheaper than its local competitor. The result was the collapse of local rice production, which brought about the bankruptcy of domestic producers. Those who had stuck to the 'traditional' methods lost less than those who had converted to the modernist 'religion'. Today, the production of rice in West Africa has virtually ceased, leaving these countries at the mercy of the world market. That outcome is welcomed by market theorists, who point to the fact that rice is now cheaper to consumers. However, the cost to the countries concerned of the end of domestic production is yet to be fully appreciated.

The lesson here is in the meaning of rationality, or rather the clash of rationalities. The argument that the superior rationality is that which meets the criterion of higher production and lower costs is flawed because it ignores context. If, as present orthodoxy dictates, African countries are to allow free trade and remove tariff protection, then it is not to their advantage to engage in any form of agricultural production that will raise the price of domestic food. If, on the other hand, the theory of the market is discarded and African countries are allowed to behave as the

West did when it developed, then tariffs should be increased so as to protect domestic production. Only if such protection obtained would it make sense for farmers to take the risk of changing centuries of agricultural method, which had stood the test of time and allowed them to eat and to sell their surpluses. So, the fact that these African countries suffer aid conditionalities they cannot escape puts them at the mercy of the contradictions produced by two apparently watertight Western rationalities: the technical and the economic.

The question over gender issues concerns reproduction and the number of children. The concern over the plight of women in Africa is justified. They bear many children. They are usually responsible for agricultural work in the rural areas and income-generating activities in the cities. They must cook and feed their families. They usually oversee the education of the children, providing for their material needs and ensuring they go to school. And when illness strikes, they are more often than not the main providers and carers. With some exceptions, their condition is thus more arduous than that of the men. It is with these problems in mind that many Western NGOs seek to ameliorate the plight of women. Their reasoning is usually that this would require empowering women, so they could have the material means and the social leeway to reduce the number of children and make more demands on their menfolk. The corollary to this claim for greater empowerment is a programme of female emancipation by way of the introduction of legislation that would give them more protection and, especially, more rights.

Here, again, the rationality of such policy advice is on the face of it unimpeachable. And yet Western NGOs are often confronted with deep reluctance on the part of the women they seek to help. Their apparently admirable universal aims appear to the locals as 'irrational', in the sense that they do not believe it is going to help them. Their argument is that they need more support for what they do, rather than a social revolution enabling them to do less and to demand more of men. Their reasoning is that the problem is not the social structure but the lack of resources. They fear that any attempt to impose a 'feminist' agenda will be counterproductive. It will destabilise the family unit, upset social relations and antagonise men, who are likely to be even less amenable to change when so challenged. Since in the end their responsibilities will still have to be discharged, and in particular children will still have to be looked after, the result of any programme of female emancipation will achieve the opposite, making their lives even more difficult.

This clash of rationalities also affects Western campaigns to reduce the number of children, on the ground that the large number of offspring hits women disproportionately hard. But, as is now well known, the main reason for having numerous children is poverty, insecurity and a lack of education. For people whose lives are economically and socially precarious, children provide both manpower and social security since they can get resources for the family and, later, care for ageing parents. It is thus perfectly rational to have more, rather than fewer, children. Here, too, women argue that what is needed is not a campaign to limit the number of births, but an increase (through education or employment) in their revenues and thereby their security. Of course, China provides an example of the effects of a coercive policy to limit a couple's offspring to one – on economic grounds rather than out of concern for women's rights. But leaving aside that case, the rationality for having children hinges on a number of reasons, which are not necessarily addressed by the ostensibly more 'rational' arguments of Western NGOs or supporters of women's rights. The conclusion, which is hardly surprising, is that women's rights cannot be dissociated from overall societal changes at the local level, and that the application of Western norms does not always make sense to the women concerned.[33]

Taken separately, these examples are not overly striking, and most analysts in the West are aware of the dangers of projecting simplified visions of how to 'improve' the Third World onto very different non-Western areas. But perhaps the most contentious issue in this respect is the relationship between rationality and power. The argument that Western rationality is demonstrably superior — whether it is in the application of technology or the defence of human rights — cannot so easily be dissociated from the fact that the West has been the dominant political and military force since the nineteenth century. As such it has been in the position to impose a vision of the world in keeping with its beliefs and values. So, the perception of its rationality by the non-West has been influenced by the reality of the forceful imposition of world domination. Whilst the non-West was able quickly to understand the value of modern science and adopt its technology, which it could adapt to its own ends, it was less taken by the economic, social and political theories that came along with it. Nor could it fail to note that the West was selective in how it applied the theories it considered most relevant. The imposition of Western (economic, social and political) 'ways' to the non-West seemed decidedly one-sided, when not entirely driven by double standards.

The theory of the free market was fine if it meant removing the protection of Indian weavers so as to provide an outlet for British manufacturers. Electoral democracy was better so long as it was not applied by the French to its departmental 'citizens' in Algeria. The protection of civil rights was sterling so long as it did not provide the colonised with the means to challenge colonial domination. Social security provisions and legal protection were powerful

---

33. For a discussion of women's rights in Africa, see the African Women's Rights Observatory: http://awro.uneca.org; accessed 19 October 2011.

means of reducing poverty and helplessness but they were not to be extended to colonial subjects, who were deemed to come under native jurisdiction. The point is clear: the application of Western rationality in these areas of human activity was inevitably linked to the domination of the West over the non-West. In this way it stood to be seen as a means of asserting Western supremacy, rather than as a more 'rational' way of organising society and improving people's well-being. The colonised could acknowledge, and envy, the attraction of the Western way of life as displayed in the images of the metropolis. But they were aware that it was built on the exploitation of the colonies. For this reason, the anti-colonial movement could not but question the superiority of Western social theory.

In effect, the assertion of the superiority of Western (economic, social and political) theories rested on two pillars: the evident Western domination of the world and the rejection of non-Western rationalities as inferior, or less 'advanced'. Inevitably, the two became entwined. Non-Westerners who pined for Western modernity were quick to associate it with the superiority of Western forms of thinking. Non-Westerners who sought to remove the Western yoke were equally quick to dismiss these forms of thinking. This created a divide within non-Western societies that continues today to affect the relations between West and non-West, just as it impinges on the thinking of immigrants in Western societies. In other words, the relevance and attractiveness of Western theories has been, and continues to be, assessed in terms of the relations of power between West and non-West. There is nothing surprising about this but it ought to make us wary about approaching the question of Western rationality without proper reference to the political context within which it is being considered. This is as true today as it was in colonial times.

What this means is that the appreciation of the superiority of Western social theory rests on a position of political and economic dominance and not, as is usually claimed, simply on the fact that it is inherently more 'rational'. An interesting example of the complexity of this issue is that of human rights – to which I return in the epilogue. On the face of it, there can be few instances of the desirability of a theory of individual rights and protection than the Universal Declaration of Human Rights (UDHR), proclaimed by the UN in 1948, based on the vision of the best agenda for the safeguard and emancipation of all peoples. Its very premiss is that the Charter provides a statement of what are *universal* human rights, which are thus relevant and applicable to all – Western and non-Western alike. Although there is little in the Declaration that is not admirable, its relevance to the non-West has long been debated. Whilst many, especially in the West, see it as the most significant advance in the protection of human rights, many in the non-West question its validity.[34] Not because they are against the notion of human rights *per se* but on the grounds that these are Western norms, which do not convey either the importance of local differences or the reality of how rights and obligations are contextually related in each distinct setting.[35]

The debate about the universal application of the UDHR has been vitiated by issues of politics and identity, both in the West and elsewhere. And the question of whether there can be such a thing as a universal notion of human rights has divided people across the world. Those who support such universality base their argument on the fundamental equality of all human beings. Those who declare that there can be no such universal accord claim that local history, customs, values and rationalities ought to form the foundations of a relevant charter of human rights in each specific setting. They claim that the imposition of the UDHR regardless of local conditions is merely an attempt to fashion all societies in the

---
34. See, for instance, de Bary, 1998; Donnelly, 1989.
35. For an important discussion of human rights in context, see Vincent, 1986.

Western mould. There can be no common ground between the two positions and there is no good way of 'proving' that one is more 'right' than the other. The difficulty does not lie so much in the disagreement on principle but in the politics of human rights.

The UDHR, which many in the non-West see as enshrining *Western* values, has assumed universal validity by dint of its UN pedigree. It has thus acquired an authority which it is difficult to contest. But the politics of extending these human rights to the entire world runs into the opposition of those who dispute their universal application and those who feel that it is a threat to their identity and way of life. So, too crude or insistent demands that all countries implement the UDHR, however desirable this in theory might be, runs the risk of being counterproductive since it can readily be painted as Western neo-imperialism. Both in and outside the West, there has thus emerged a view that in order to combat neo-imperialism, it is necessary to reject this Western vision of human rights. It is obvious in the attitude of China vis-à-vis international critique – and was amply demonstrated in its reaction to the award of the 2010 Nobel Peace Prize to Liu Xiaobo.[36]

But, more interestingly, the view is also to be found among those in the West who reject the individualist notion of human rights and those who profess cultural relativism. The first (for instance, some environmentalists and many religiously inclined groups) argue that there can be no individual human rights that are not in accordance with collective, or communal, rights. In this they rejoin those who reject the assumption that the only meaningful constitutive unit of society is the discrete individual. They favour the subordination of individual to more societal rights. The latter assert that there can be no *universal* human rights and that respect must be given to the ways in which every society defines and guarantees *its* human

---

36. Since Liu Xiaobo was in prison, he was obviously not allowed to travel. The Chinese authorities also prevented anyone else from receiving the award on his behalf.

rights. For this reason, they refuse to condemn practices that are at odds with the UDHR on the grounds that it is not for Westerners to tell others how best to live their lives. Of course, they face the critique from non-Westerners who support the UDHR and who contend that cultural relativism is *also* a theory from the West: who are those Westerners to tell non-Westerners they do not need the full panoply of human and rights enjoyed in Western countries?

The point here is not to adjudicate between these various positions but to suggest that our thinking is often clouded by conflicting approaches and theories. The notion that human rights are universal makes sense from our Western standpoint but may not be so convincing when seen from a different perspective. Others can point to 'their' vision of what constitutes human rights and claim that these too ought to have universal application. There is no good 'rational' answer to this challenge. The problem would not arise, however, were it not for the fact that we in the West are convinced that our definition of human rights is both the most 'advanced' and of universal relevance. We pursue the protection of these rights with missionary zeal, using foreign aid as a political tool. It is for this reason that opposition to the West's approach to human rights comes from countries like China, which can resist aid conditionality because they enjoy strong economic power of their own. And it is a reasonable assumption that many other countries agree with China rather than with the West.

These few examples show that underlying our (domestic and foreign) policies there is a clear link between theory, thinking and behaviour. In itself, this is not a particularly new or original observation. What is of greater interest, however, is the fact that this link is usually invisible, or subterranean, so that it escapes our notice. We take the merit of our 'rationality' for granted: it appears to us obvious or common sense. We fail to think about, or even to see, the assumptions that underpin our standpoint. This failure is not especially Western, of course. All powerful nations tend to interpret the world according to their own rationality. But since the West has been dominant for the last few centuries, the projection of its rationality upon the globe is of some significance. Indeed, we readily mistake the display of our power for the validity of our thinking, and hence the righteousness of our actions. And it is only recently that the challenge coming from China – and to some extent from political Islam – has led to a reassessment of our perspectives on the economic and political world in which we live.

To act is to think (again)

If we are to open up our way of thinking or, as I prefer to put it, think beyond theory, we need to engage in some serious reappraisal. It is less a question of claiming that we need to discard our social theories than to suggest that we need to approach theory in a different way. Before I turn to my approach, I want to mention what has been labelled 'Southern Theory'.[37] The attempt to consider theory from the perspective of those societies that have been the 'victim' of imperialism and colonialism is important. But the question arises as to whether a non-'southerner' is able to rethink the notion of theory from a non-Western perspective. An interesting attempt is to be found in Euben's book, which sets out to explain Islamic political thought from its local perspective in Egypt.[38] One of the key findings of this book is that Islamic thought is not, as is often believed, frozen in time. On the contrary, it is of its time – meaning thereby that it is modern. And it points to a more fruitful reading of those Muslim thinkers who sought to find a theoretical response to the challenge of the West. But I

---

37. See here, among many, Connell, 2007; Burke, 2007.
38. See Euben, 1999.

now turn to my own approach, which involves tackling several key issues that are usually neglected in our social sciences. And I do so from the experience of having attempted to analyse politics in Africa from a non-Western standpoint.[39]

I proceed in four steps. The first is to reconsider what 'science' can mean for the analysis of human affairs. The second is to build into any models we might put forward the inevitable subjectivities within which they are conceptualised. The third is to make explicit the limits of the theories in question, taking particular care to highlight the constraints under which they labour. The last is to stress the extent to which theories in the social sciences are determined by the language used in order to analyse and interpret the questions we ask ourselves. The medium of social theory is linguistic, not mathematical. I discuss these in turn.

(1) Much of the confusion about the role of theory stems from the fact that we operate on the assumption that the social sciences are indeed 'scientific'. Now, there is nothing wrong in the application of the notion of science to the study of human society *so long as* we are clear about what we mean by 'scientific'. The problem is that this is never discussed explicitly. Social scientists operate on the assumption they know that what they do, or rather what they aspire to do, is as 'scientific' as what chemists, biologists or physicists do. They may have different difficulties but the ambition is the same: to increase knowledge of society and human affairs by applying the principles of the 'scientific' approach. And even when social scientists are wary of proclaiming the 'hardness' of their work, the implicit definition of the word 'science' they use is the one that comes from the physical sciences. This, I think, is due to a combination of two factors, which have come to interact, often without our being aware of it.

---

39. See Chabal, 2009.

The first is that, since the nineteenth century, there has been a systematic attempt by those who consider themselves the descendants of the founders of the social sciences (Marx, Durkheim, Weber, Freud, etc.) to extend the principles of the physical sciences to human affairs. The aim has been to move beyond common sense and tradition by laying down the methods that make it possible to approach social questions in a more analytical fashion. The nineteenth century was a time when the belief in the systematisation of knowledge was at its peak and there seemed to be no limit to the ability of scholars to theorise social processes. The second factor is that we live today in a world that is in thrall to science and technology. We may have our doubts about some scientific experiments and we readily criticise scientific hubris, but we tend to assess the merit of arguments and policies largely on the basis of their scientific – that is objective – quality. We want to know what the evidence is. For instance, we seek to establish once and for all whether there are scientific grounds for differences in intelligence or whether thought processes can be broken down into neurological components. We still debate whether nature or nurture is responsible for our behaviour.

But, as I have argued throughout the book, it has now become clear that this unquestioning faith in the scientific basis of our knowledge of human affairs is no longer satisfactory. This has become visible among those who are wary of social and political policies – environmentalists, for example. Their critique of science is not just about the effects of growth *à tout prix* but also about the theories we employ. For instance, Green parties suggest that we should calculate the cost of pollution, or of reprocessing our rubbish – that is, in effect, that we should provide a different economic justification for a change of policy. That is fine as far as it goes, and everyone is now converting to 'being green'. But it does not address the more fundamental issue of whether our way of life is adequately conceptualised by way of a cost–benefit analysis. The harder questions about the future will likely involve a way of discussing our well-being in terms that will not easily be encapsulated by economic theory, or indeed represented in financial terms. For example, the present increase in mental ill health, of which depression is only one expression, could suggest that we may have (perhaps unconsciously) become dissatisfied with the material – that is, quantifiable – measure of the quality of our life. Hence the turn back towards religion, or spirituality.

The common response given by social scientists to this critique is that the nature of their scientific enterprise is indeed different from that of the physical sciences but that it is about redefining the nature of our enquiries rather than abandoning their aims.[40] What this usually means is that the social sciences must employ a mix of quantitative and qualitative methods in order to carry out research. So, for example, where statistical and regression analyses are possible, they should be used. Where they are not, then a more anthropological approach to the collection of evidence is appropriate. However, such a stance fails to acknowledge that the problem with the social sciences is not primarily the methods they use but the assumptions they make about theory. It is the theory that should determine the methods – as is indeed the case in the physical sciences – not the reverse. The methods are only as good as the theories to which they relate. Therefore the key issue for the social sciences is whether the theories proposed are capable of advancing our knowledge. Since, with some exceptions (where meaningful statistical analysis and experiments are possible), these theories are not capable of being tested (as in the hard sciences), we need to reconsider in what ways they are actually 'scientific'.

---

40. For revealing discussion, see Kagan, 2009; Shapiro, 2007.

The measure of the scientific approach in the social sciences, as famously formulated by Karl Popper, is falsifiability or refutability – meaning that a proposition can be shown to be false by experiment or observation.[41] I do not intend here to go into the intricate detail of Popper's own theory but would merely want to point out that his approach derives from, and consists in, the application of the methods of physical sciences to the study of human affairs. The focus on method, once again, fails to address the specific nature of the analysis of society, where the point of the exercise is not to determine once and for all whether behaviour can be shown to accord with some theory but to understand why human beings behave as they do in historically contextualised societies. From that point of view, therefore, the test of falsifiability is well-nigh irrelevant, since it is likely to be met by few, if any, theories of human behaviour. In such circumstances, the search for better theory is a dead end, which not only diverts attention from more relevant research but also confines thinking to the narrow range of questions that might be amenable to such 'scientific' testing.[42]

Because of this, it seems to me that the most useful criterion of what 'science' might mean in the social sciences would be *plausibility* – and not either testability or predictability. Thinking in terms of plausibility changes both the meaning of theory and the claims that can usefully be made on behalf of the social sciences.

Indeed, starting from the notion of plausibility implies right away the recognition that any theory is contextual and restores history to the centre of analysis. The first consequence of such a standpoint, therefore, is that the more ahistorical a theory is, the less plausible it will be. Of course, this is in complete opposition to what theory is in the hard sciences, since the point there

---

41. Popper, 2002.
42. Popper's student Paul Feyerabend wrote a pungent criticism of his teacher's theory. See Feyerabend, 1993.

is precisely to propose theories that are not contingent. In the social sciences, however, the role of proper contextualisation is absolutely critical: insight, or knowledge, depends on the ability to propose an analysis that explicitly connects context and action. It follows from this that the ever expanding ahistorical industry of theory-making in the social sciences is a dead end – as is amply demonstrated, for example, by the attempts to offer mathematical models in political science.[43] In fact, it can safely be said that such mathematical modelling is likely to provide less valuable insights than straightforward narrative accounts of the phenomena under analysis. Furthermore, it is also likely to fail the test of plausibility, in that the proxies used in the calculations are bound to be overly general and thus to provide only vague, or tautological, answers to the questions posed.[44]

The test of plausibility also implies that theories need to be assessed not on their presumed logical excellence but on their suitability to the case study. In other words, it is not sufficient to claim that a particular theory, for instance on voter behaviour in US cities in the 1920s, which has been found to work well in that particular setting, will be relevant to another setting, in a different context. Its relevance would have to be demonstrated in, for example, the case of African cities in the 1980s. This entails proceeding in an *inductive* rather than deductive manner, which here means testing the plausibility of the theory *in situ* before concluding it is relevant to the case study. At the very least it involves avoiding the use of a theory before it can be shown through preliminary research on the ground that it is more likely than not to provide added-value insight. This, as I have written elsewhere, is pretty much the

---

43. For a critique of comparative politics, see Chabal and Daloz, 2006.
44. A proxy in statistical and regression analysis is a factor, or 'variable', that is both quantifiable and that stands in lieu of the process being analysed. For example, voting participation can be used as a proxy for support for democracy.

opposite of how theories of comparative politics are deployed today by research students when they go on their field research.[45]

The test of plausibility also means that the social sciences need to measure what they do in terms that make sense not just to social scientists but to the people who are the object of the research. At the risk of stating the blindingly obvious, it seems to me important that social scientists should take the trouble to find out whether their findings chime with local interpretations. Of course, this does not mean that one would expect the local people to agree with the conclusions of the research in question since it could reveal issues that are new, shocking or unpalatable. However, these findings should make some sense locally. For instance, stating as some researchers do that the people of a particular African country are in their majority favourable to 'democracy' is probably so vague as to be meaningless. This is particularly so if it is obvious, as many observers can testify, that the people surveyed have no idea what 'democracy' means other than in terms that may have little to do with the notion imported from the West.[46] Comforting ourselves with the idea that the desirability of 'democracy' is increasing all the time in Africa is likely not just to mislead us but to make us miss other more important political processes at work.

Finally, the test of plausibility is a constant reminder that social scientists largely deal in intangibles – which is pretty much the opposite from their colleagues in the physical sciences. And part of the problem in the social sciences is that the 'scientific' label is a way of obscuring the fact that the acquisition of knowledge and the production of insights are far from straightforward. 'Doing' social sciences is not just a matter of applying the right method but of asking oneself how the method is likely to help interpret the questions at hand. Acknowledging from the outset that we are

---

45. Chabal and Daloz, 2006.
46. For a relevant case study, see Schaffer, 1998.

dealing with intangibles would help us to frame the questions, test the theories, and devise the methodologies from a more realistic perspective. Freed from the ostensibly 'scientific' yoke derived from the hard sciences, the social sciences would find themselves at greater liberty to explore how best to address the questions that really matter and suggest policies that might actually be relevant. Plausibility, rather than certainty, would be a far more realistic and user-friendly way of trying to make sense of human affairs than the desiccated reductionism of theory-driven quantitative social science.

(2) Beyond applying the test of plausibility, it is imperative for the social sciences to build into any models they might propose the inevitable 'subjectivities' within which they are conceptualised. What this means in concrete terms is that in the study of human affairs and society the question of *standpoint* is critical. This, again, contrasts radically with the situation in the physical sciences where either the question of perspective is agreed in principle as part of the axiomatic premiss of the theory or it is simply not relevant. Indeed, this is what makes possible replication, which lies at the heart of scientific experiment: any researcher starting from the same agreed standpoint ought to be able to run the equivalent experiment and, thus, to confirm or disprove the results found by others. This is how fraudulent research is exposed, wherever it is carried out. The same applies to medical experimentation, making it possible both to build up a large base of comparable data and to assess the impact of treatment in any part of the world.

However, this is not the case in the social sciences. Although most social scientists, with the exception of anthropologists, rarely address the matter of 'subjectivities', it is of course fundamental to an appreciation of the potential 'scientific' nature of their discipline. Indeed, if the question of standpoint is critical and if research in the social sciences must take into account the perspective of the researcher, then it is quite clear that there is little chance of emulating the hard sciences. We must accept that our theories cannot in any meaningful sense be as 'scientific' as theirs. Instead, we must think in different terms, which imply confronting the matter of subjectivity head on. My contention is that, unless this is made explicit, the validity of the findings is vitiated at source. Conversely, incorporating subjectivities increases the plausibility of the interpretations and of the insights achieved.

What I call subjectivities covers the range of issues that impinge on the choice of the research topic, the nature of the theories selected, the kind of evidence generated and the type of interpretation offered. I discuss the first three here and return to the issue of interpretation later in the chapter.

In the first place, then, it is necessary to make plain who the researchers are and why they are conducting this particular enquiry. For better or worse, the identity, motivations and qualifications of the researcher are relevant factors in their work; it is pointless and often counterproductive to ignore this factor. The research done on, for instance, 'community relations' in Britain or France will necessarily be affected by the identity, affiliations, religion and role in society of those who propose to ask the questions. This is plainly a fact of life, which need not be a problem so long as it is made explicit and the possible biases that this might engender are taken into account. Similarly, the purpose of the research will matter greatly. To continue with the same example, if it is a matter of looking to shore up 'security' in society, then the nature of the enquiry, and its results, will differ from those achieved by a researcher who tries to understand why young people are unemployed. Equally, research carried out by a government sociologist will not likely generate the same evidence as that done by a researcher who has grown up locally and is believed to have the best interests of 'his' community at heart. There cannot be 'objective' research in this respect.

This much seems obvious enough, but the question of subjectivities is equally relevant to ostensibly more 'scientific' areas, such as economics. Above and beyond the collection of statistics, difficult as that can be, there are few areas of economics where subjectivities are not significant. Even econometrics, which is by definition quantitative, depends on the working assumptions that are fed into the models. The notion of 'risk', for instance, is not an immutable given; it is clearly historically and contextually defined. The concept of marginal cost derives from the definition of 'cost', which need not be limited to a computable figure: how, for instance, does one measure the marginal cost of having to stand on a commuter train in the morning? Or, for that matter, how does one define 'full employment' – on which there has always been debate? Even as well rehearsed a difference in perspective as that between Keynesians and monetarists has an impact on the ways in which economic dynamics are conceived, since both the starting point and standpoint of analysis differ. As for forecasting, despite the blessed self-assurance of the economists interviewed on television, it is obvious that what is provided is at best a combination of well-informed common sense and guesswork.

What matters, therefore, is not so much the identity of the social scientists – although their professional self-interest is by no means irrelevant – as their theoretical standpoint and their working hypotheses. There is nothing to be lost, and indeed much to be gained, by stating clearly why some theories are employed and, more importantly, what assumptions need to be made in order to apply them. However, social scientists are reluctant to do so both because they would like to believe that their theories are universal and because they believe that such openness might undermine their work. And, indeed, a mandatory discussion of the assumptions on which theories of human affairs are based would reveal the extent to which they are 'subjective'. But what is seen as a weakness by those who view themselves as social *scientists* could, in my view, be turned into an advantage, and this for two reasons. It would make more obvious the link between the theory and the question asked and it would exonerate the researcher from the impossibly burdensome weight of having to pretend that the findings are generalisable; or, even more, that they are universally valid.

If, in what I have labelled an inductive approach, the theory is shown to have been validated as relevant by preliminary research *in situ*, then the 'subjective' nature of the choice will be seen to be an asset rather than a liability. I give two examples. A wellworn social theory in France is that the threat to cut child benefit to parents who do not ensure their children go to school can be effective – as indeed it has been among, for instance, unemployed communities of North African migrants. However, this appears not to be true among Gypsies – which social workers explain by the fact that they are more concerned to use their children for their own 'economic' activities than to receive child benefit.[47] And education is not high on their list of priorities. Hence the need to adapt theory to reality. The second example comes from Africa, where democratic theory tells us that the more frequently elections are held, the more a 'democratic culture' emerges. But in instances such as Mozambique and Angola the reverse seems to be the case: whereas the first multiparty election showed strong support for the opposition, this support evaporated over time even as discontent was growing. Here, it is probably the case that the failure of elections to deliver meaningful political reform induces people either to become apathetic (and abstain) or to renew their trust in the patrimonial system offered by the previous single-party

---

47. Information gathered during discussions with social workers in France, who wished to remain anonymous.

dispensation. Paradoxically, therefore, multiparty elections become a means of legitimising single-party rule.[48]

The question of subjectivity also applies to the kind of evidence social scientists seek out. Here, again, it is often the case that what is prized most is what is labelled 'hard' evidence – by which is meant statistical or quantitative. Most social science research relies on surveys, which are then manipulated in the search for correlations and, if possible, causalities. This bias towards quantification overdetermines the type of data that is gathered in three important ways. The first is that the search for evidence is obviously limited to what is most easily quantifiable. The second is that it has to be statistically based, which implies that attention must be devoted to the quality of sampling and the quantification of the responses. Finally, the research relies on the use of the best possible proxies, since it is rarely possible to find the precise quantitative data that will be liable to statistical manipulation. This would not be a problem if it were limited to the type of research that is best suited to statistical interpretation, but such is not the case for the majority of questions that social science addresses.

As should be clear by now, the analysis of most of the issues I have discussed in the book are not amenable to simple statistical treatment. Even where quantitative evidence may be useful, it can only be usefully interpreted within the relevant historical and contingent context. For instance, the evidence that the number of young women converting to Islam in Britain and France is increasing is of little help when it comes to understanding why this is happening. Similarly, the fact that in Brazil and Africa a growing number of people are turning towards Pentecostal churches will do little to explain why so many should devote a high proportion of their meagre income to supporting ministers who are growing

---

48. For a recent assessment of democracy in Africa, see Mustapha and Whitfield, 2009.

rich amidst poverty. We might suggest any number of reasons for explaining these two phenomena, but the evidence on which it will be possible to say something plausible, and meaningful, will not come from the quantitative data. It will entail a different sort of enquiry, centred on cultural, social and psychological factors, the relative importance of which we cannot ascertain by theory until we undertake the kind of anthropological research needed.

But since qualitative research is more onerous and time-consuming than its quantitative counterpart, social scientists are loath to go down that road. Not only does statistical evidence appear more 'solid' than the narratives generated by anthropological research but it is also easier to handle since it does not require the same type of knowledge of the local setting or of its history. The common criticism of qualitative research is that it is too parochial and that it precludes comparison. In-depth history or anthropology, it is argued, does not make possible the type of statistical inference or correlations needed. Too detailed an account of a particular question obscures the possible trends and changes that are taking place and that can usefully be compared with what is happening elsewhere. But this is a spurious dichotomy. It is possible to do comparative qualitative research without spending years immersed in the localities in question. The quality of the evidence gathered depends largely on the relevance of the questions asked, and not primarily on the exhaustiveness of that evidence. For instance, it is possible to gather meaningful data on what factors affect local elections in different parts of the world without a detailed knowledge of kinship systems in every setting. The key here is to find out which questions it is worthwhile to ask locally rather than arriving *in situ* with a preset questionnaire on the grounds that it is required to generate proper comparative analysis. The reverse is in fact the case: it is the relevance of the questions asked locally that will enable the comparison to be meaningful.

(3) The third caveat would be to make explicit the limits of the theories in question, taking particular care to highlight the constraints under which they labour. Above and beyond the impact of the subjectivities attached to social science research, we should be much more up-front about what theories can achieve. Instead of relying on the implicit model of conceptualisation prevalent in the physical sciences, we need to recast the role of theory from the perspective of the subject matter – that is, human affairs. If, as I have suggested, we are constrained by history and context and if we are to work according to the test of plausibility, then theory itself is going to be both contingent and open-ended. It will be contingent because it will not be able to formulate assumptions and hypotheses that are not linked to the historical and geographical environment within which the social scientists do research. It will be open-ended because it will not be possible to claim that theories remain valid over time: they are likely to change according to circumstances. Beyond some agreeable generalities, a theory of citizenship in nineteenth-century Britain, for example, is probably of little value to nineteenth-century China or, for that matter, twenty-first-century Africa.

But the notion that theory might be contingent is not one that social scientists favour, both because it appears to demean their enterprise and because it offends our modern scientific mind. And yet an acceptance of the fact that theories in the social sciences are, as it were, moveable feasts would be liberating. The end of the compulsion to formulate conceptualisations that are supposed to be universally true, which is seen to be essential to comparative analysis, would make it far more likely that the theories deployed were more relevant and more enlightening. It would also allow for a much more concentrated focus on what is specific to the settings under study. This might mean that we would have to work with different 'theories' of ostensibly similar phenomena, but this ought not to be an issue if we remind ourselves that comparisons should be built from the bottom up – that is, from the nature of the evidence – rather than from the top down – that is, according to the dictates of an allegedly universally valid 'science' of human action.

For example, returning to the question of the nature of democracy in today's world, it would undoubtedly be more enlightening to attempt to provide an accurate description of the different cases than to try to ascertain how they fit into the parameters of contemporary (Western) democratic *theory*. The objection here is that if we do not know what we need to compare, we will never be in a position to explain how different the cases are. But if we bear in mind that the purpose of comparison is to provide *meaningful* distinctions, which actually add to our understanding of what the differences imply, then it is clear that the objection does not stand. Moreover, there is no reason why we cannot find categories of analysis that make it possible to compare processes. In a comparative study of democracy, it is less important to gauge whether the procedures in places in, say, Sweden and Nigeria are similar than it is, for instance, to explain how legitimacy, representation and accountability operate in the two countries.[49] Whatever the differences in democratic practices between the two, comparison is possible precisely because the use of these three concepts can be shown to be relevant to both. What they help to make sense of is what I would call the processes of political accountability – processes which are indeed integral to the functioning of democracy. Whether as a result of the study we are able to say whether Nigeria is 'democratic' is in the end less important than to be able to explain how political accountability operates in that country.

---

49. For a discussion of the comparison between Sweden and Nigeria, see Chabal and Daloz, 2006.

Or, to take another very topical issue, it is possible to say something meaningful about corruption without having recourse to a *single* theory. Most current attempts to study corruption comparatively involve the presentation of a theory built on a simple definition of the phenomenon and a list of its (negative) consequences.[50] This is both too simplistic and too normative. Unfortunately, it is a fact of life that what is considered corrupt in one setting might not be so in another. Moreover, it is clear that what is blatantly illegal according to the local judicial norms may not be considered *illegitimate* within the prevailing political culture. If that is the case, and if we want to understand the nature and effects of corruption, then we will need to build a theory of what is illegitimate and what is not. Here, a comparison between Nigeria and Indonesia might reveal that the difference between the two is not so much the amount of corruption, which is huge in both, but the fact that in Indonesia the fruits of corruption have largely been channelled back into productive investment whereas in the case of Nigeria they have primarily gone in the direction of Swiss banks. This conclusion, if accurate, would be far more enlightening about the effects of corruption and the degree of economic progress in both countries than a straightforward (and largely normative) ranking of corruption would allow.

But recognising the limits of theory in the social sciences would have far greater significance than these examples suggest. It would entail a reconsideration of our approach to the study of human affairs, which would force a different way of asking questions and framing answers. Going back to an issue we have taken up at regular intervals in this book, we might want to consider, for example, whether we are approaching the question of the conversion of young women to Islam from the wrong angle. We have so

---

50. For a standard study of corruption, see Johnston, 2005.

far offered general sociological theories: both French and British social scientists have suggested that we are faced with a search for spirituality or identity within increasingly secular and intolerant Western societies. There is probable truth to this hypothesis but it is only one aspect of the question. Perhaps we ought to look at this issue differently. Could it be that it is the standpoint of observer, rather than the subject, which has changed?

There have always been conversions to non-Christian religions (including Islam) in Europe, but today Western societies have become hypersensitive to this question. After all, there has been a steady stream of conversion to Buddhism since the 1960s – with the appearance in our cities of saffron-robed converts. And yet this has largely passed unnoticed. Why? I do not have 'the' answer but research on that phenomenon might be worth exploring, not just because it would help explain today's anxieties about Islam but also because it would reveal something worthwhile, and comparative, about our perception of religious conversion in present circumstances. Here too, therefore, paying attention to subjectivities would probably add insight. General theories about secularism may not be of much use.

Or, returning to the question of poverty in the West, could it be that our theories are now a constraint on fresh thinking? I have already explained how our definition of poverty locks us into a vicious circle since, as it is presently calculated, it cannot by definition be eradicated. But still we continue to work with theories that are supposed to lessen the burden of poverty. This is convenient for the better off since such theories propose remedies that will have little impact on their social or material standing: a marginal redistribution of resources by way of taxation does not threaten the existing social edifice. But another approach might make a difference. If, instead of focusing on poverty, we concentrated attention on opportunity, then there would be scope for much more drastic reforms. We already have evidence of how education is one of the single most important factors in the achievement of a decent (or 'non-poor') way of life. Therefore we might want to propose that all children should be offered the same type and quality of education. Since this would obviously entail the abolition of the private education sector and the ruthless enforcement of school places according to need rather than privilege, it is not a popular theory. But the example of Finland, where such a system is in place, strongly suggests that such a systematic concern with equality of education offered not only produces the best results (as measured by tests) but also contributes to a society in which opportunities for advancement are more widely available than almost anywhere else in Europe.[51]

Of course, these are political decisions, which lie beyond the reach of social science. But it would be more productive if social scientists openly acknowledged the limits of their theories and worked harder to provide the variety of perspectives that would offer the policymakers a greater range of choices. After all, it is precisely the determination of scientists and activists alike that has brought about the rise of Green parties and has moved environmental issues to the top of the agenda. But dealing with such long-standing questions as poverty, corruption or democracy is more difficult because in most instances we have well-established socio-economic theories which lie at the core of our disciplines and weigh heavily on any attempt we might make to effect paradigmatic shifts. Moreover, unlike in the hard sciences, there are no obvious experimental or mathematical tests that would easily confirm the obsolescence of our theories. For instance, we still hold Adam Smith's classical economic theory as essentially valid whereas in physics we now know both what the limits of Newtonian theory

---

51. On the benefits of equality, see Wilkinson and Pickett, 2010.

are and how to overcome those when necessary. In this respect, it is probably the case that to conceptualise people merely as 'rational' discrete individual consumers is probably no longer tenable. But because we have no better economic theory, we continue to confine our analysis to the refinement of the concept of consumer rather than search for a notion that would provide more insight into people's economic decisions.

As already mentioned, there is today much interesting work done in economic psychology that is directly relevant to contemporary analysis. Even politicians are beginning to pay attention – for example in relation to the 'nudge' theory, which has recently caught the attention of some Western governments, including the British.[52] However, this work would have measurably more impact if the social theory framework within which it is done had evolved more radically in the direction suggested above. The application of the test of plausibility and the overt acknowledgement of the importance of subjectivities would undoubtedly open up more space for rethinking the theories we use to explain common problems and the policies we offer to deal with them. One example is the theory that there is a (psychological or social) profile to would-be home-grown terrorists. In other words, there must be an identifiable social or psychological theory highlighting the factors that turn people into terrorists – factors that might be alleviated by well-targeted social policy. So we go on a chase. But what if there is no identifiable profile and that such a search is a waste of time? Perhaps the only plausible response to terrorism is good old-fashioned intelligence.

(4) The last stipulation would be to stress that theories in the social sciences cannot be dissociated from the language used to formulate

---

52. See Thaler and Sunstein, 2008.

them. Again, this is completely unlike the physical sciences, where a universal mathematical language enables the expression of a theory, the exposition of the methods and the presentation of the results in what might be termed neutral, or at least not context-dependent, language. Such cannot be the case in the study of human affairs, except where the theories apply only to statistical data. But even here, as I have suggested already, there are two key caveats. One is that the discussion of the assumptions behind the use of the particular statistics will demand some explanation, or justification, which will rest in large part on how it is formulated within a given context. The other is that the statistics are likely to be a limited, or even crude, reflection of the reality under study, the interpretation of which will require the use of careful language. In every case, then, the use of language is critical.

Therefore the very fact that social science theory is tied to language, if only because meaningful interpretation depends on it, invalidates the pretension of some social scientists to emulate their colleagues in the physical sciences. And the search for the quantitative, or mathematical, holy grail is not just futile but distracts attention from the contribution social science can make to knowledge. For example, the correlation between the proportion of free school meals and test results might be relevant but its interpretation rests on the narrative offered to explain in which way it is relevant. One needs first to explain that free school meals stands here as a proxy for poverty at home. Second, one needs to discuss the assumption that poverty at home is likely (and likely is the operative word here) to result in worse school performance. Finally, one needs to assess whether poor nutrition is a factor or not. Since the comparative results reveal significant differences between schools, any worthwhile explanation of the importance of the use of that proxy will have to make clear under what conditions it matters. Some schools obviously are better at achieving good results than others – to such an extent that a few compare well with those that have very few school-meal students. So the conclusion is likely to be that this particular indicator is context-dependent and its relevance is likely to vary greatly according to, say, school leadership. Clearly, then, a simple table of figures correlating the proxy with school results would be far less enlightening than the rich narrative interpretation that should go with it.

But the importance of language to social science goes far beyond such examples. It touches on three key areas, which are at the heart of what our disciplines aim to do. The first is that the very conceptualisation of what it is that the social sciences do rests on language: we could not, for example, study alienation until such a concept had emerged. The second is that the formulation of our theories, such as they are, is also conditioned by language: Marx's proposition that the members of social classes can suffer 'false consciousnesses' could not be made until the notions of class and consciousness had arisen. The last is that both the organisation and the interpretation of our research are entirely dependent on language: studying human rights in Somalia is impossible unless we expound precisely what that means, including in Somali, and how we will be able to explain our results. I discuss all three briefly.

The recognition that language is critical to what the social sciences are about is probably the single most important step in rethinking our approach to the study of human affairs. It involves two radical steps, which social scientists are loath to take. One is to accept that social 'sciences' are not either universal or 'timeless' but of their time: history- and context-dependent disciplines. Their claim of 'scientificity' cannot exempt them from the obligation to work into their theories the relevance of historical knowledge and current events. For instance, and as I mentioned before, the notions of war trauma and now 'post-traumatic stress disorder' only came about because of a new consciousness of the nature of psychological damage in conflicts, starting with the First World War. The other is to accept that the formulation of theories, hypotheses and the conceptualisation of the issues at stake are all dependent on the language that is, or can be, used for that purpose. For example, the theory of 'irrational' consumer behaviour, based on the identification of what is called 'impulse buying', has not been formulated primarily *because* economic psychologists have 'discovered' a new phenomenon.[53] It has been made possible by the widespread acknowledgement of a form of behaviour which has been *labelled* as 'impulse' driven. In other words, it is the emergence of that concept which has made possible the formulation of the theory.

Indeed, it is this very dynamic that drives the social sciences. Far from being the case that social 'scientists' uncover new phenomena, which they seek to conceptualise, it is the evolution of the language we use to define, identify, explain or justify what we do that drives the search for explanation. To be 'scientific' in this context is to be attuned to the changes in language, which are the first indicators of mutations in our perceptions and behaviour. But it is also to recognise that the language itself provides the matrix within which the social sciences work and evolve. In other words, our theoretical thinking reflects not just the evolution of society but the development of the language we use to make sense of what is happening in society.

A striking example is the recent buzz of interest in the notion of 'fairness' – as popularised by the Cameron government in the United Kingdom. The standard interpretation of that development is that this was a compromise policy between Conservatives and Liberal Democrats, who also stress fairness in their literature. But a more realistic interpretation is that the concept had become more

---

53. See Ariely, 2008.

fashionable in Europe, where the old notions of equality, which the Labour Party 'owned', had lost purchase. Western societies from the end of the twentieth century seem to have come to terms with the fact that equality was impossible and largely meaningless. What mattered now was that society should be 'fair' – even if the meaning of the notion was eminently vague. The French Socialist Party issued a clarion call for a 'caring society', even using the English word!

The fact that no one is sure what fairness means is itself an indication that it is the change of language that is triggering reflections in social theory rather than the reverse. Indeed, nothing has fundamentally changed in Western societies since the notion of 'fairness' has come into fashion. But the word itself is redirecting our attention to what some like to think of as a 'new phenomenon'. Similarly, we now accept that there is such a thing as 'child hyperactivity', which is often treated with drugs. Yet, here too, this supposed medical condition only became identifiable after the notion of being 'hyperactive' gained a foothold. Until then, it was thought 'normal' that some children should appear to be more physically active, more unruly as it were, than others. Just as it was thought common that some children would appear to be more 'moody', quiet or reflective. Now, the perception that many children are 'ill' in that their behaviour is excessively frantic has found expression in the concept of 'hyperactivity'. Whether the diagnosis is accurate depends less on the tests that are carried out to measure the condition than on the firm belief that this type of behaviour is now beyond the pale – that is, 'abnormal'. But is the use of drugs the best way to address what is now seen as an 'objectively' identified ailment?

On a different but related register, the events of 9/11 have given rise to the notion of fundamentalist Islamic terrorism. But the definition of that supposed new threat – political Islam – only came about because of the convergence of two linguistic threads.⁵⁴ One is the emergence of the notion that fundamentalism, Christian as well as Muslim, could be virulent in modern, and not just in 'traditional', society. Indeed, the Christian fundamentalists are more politically active, and possibly more violent, in the USA now than they were thirty years ago. So the meaning of the existing word changed radically. It is no longer a leftover from the past but has become a present danger. The other is the impact of a notion that has been labelled 'Occidentalism' – that is, the idea that non-Westerners (and particularly Muslims) entertain a distorted, perhaps primitive, idea of what the West means, and against which they are willing to commit violence.⁵⁵ This overturned a long-standing consensus that non-Westerners were not only admiring of the West but that they *all* aspired to become more Western. So, the very meaning of the word 'West' came to change also.

Finally, social sciences are almost entirely dependent on language when it comes to the interpretation of the evidence, even when there is statistical support to the research. Indeed, it is not the raw data that matters but the words used to explain it. Or, to put it another way, statistics can be interpreted in more than one way, thus making the language used to explain their relevance absolutely critical. And since language evolves over time, the interpretation of social science research is bound to differ according to period and circumstances. One interesting social science question concerns the prevalence of and the reasons for suicide – which was the topic of a ground-breaking theory by Émile Durkheim, a father of sociology.⁵⁶ That apparently simple question, which seems amenable to statistical inference, is in fact very tricky. First, how can one study suicide in settings where it means vastly different

---

54. Volpi, 2010.
55. See Carrier, 1995; Buruma and Margalit, 2004.
56. Durkheim, 1997.

things, or is not recognised at all? In such circumstances, how can one trust the data on suicide collected at different times and in different countries? Above and beyond the standard difficulty of finding reliable data, there is a prior question about language, especially in societies where suicide is 'forbidden', and therefore where there is no word for it. Conversely, societies where suicide is taken to be a common, if regrettable, fact of life are likely to register more causes of death as suicide.[57]

But beyond the collection of raw data on suicide, the interpretation of the reasons for the act is likely to prove difficult and language-bound. If at one time 'melancholy' might have been adduced as one of the main causes, it is clear that now the word has lost any practical meaning in our Western societies. Today, a likely reason might be labelled 'alienation', which is rather a different concept from 'anomie', as proposed by Durkheim. On the other hand, we tend to focus today on concepts such as 'peer pressure' or 'copycat', which are often given as the main reasons for teenage suicide. But clearly these could not have been given as reasons until such concepts had been formulated. Moreover, the choice of words is not incidental or inconsequential: it reflects our attempt to frame explanations in terms that are consonant with the society in which we live. And this is of course a positive development since what we want our social sciences to do is to interpret social and political events, or processes, in ways that make sense to us – that is, in the present circumstances in which we live.

However, it does confirm that the social sciences cannot aspire to a status above the language they use to formulate their theories and offer interpretation. Once this is accepted, it becomes easier to see how it might be possible to think beyond theory, or, in journalistic parlance, to think outside the box. Instead of working

---

57. For a study of suicide from a literary perspective, see Alvarez, 1974.

on the assumption that social sciences can become more 'scientific', more like the physical sciences, we need to see how best to deploy the instruments they provide us within the historical and contingent context in which we operate. We need to work with, rather than against, language because the evolution of language itself is one of the most important indicators of actual or potential social and political change. With some caveats, the same applies to economics – or at least to a large part of what economists do. Language is both the medium and the measure of interpretation in the social sciences.

EPILOGUE

Three questions

THE LANGUAGE of Western rationality defines its scope and makes plain its limits. Whilst social scientists have been keen to identify those aspects of Western thought that mark it as supreme, the very words they use to define this rationality have exposed the assumptions they make when asserting the superiority of the West over the non-West.

Western rationality is characterised by two key assumptions: the claim to *universality* and the presumption of *modernity*. The first is seen to confer upon Western social and political thought the attributes that make it the template of worldwide reason. The second is the belief that there is a close correlation between Western rationality and modernity. In other words, Western rationality is both of universal validity and a mark of modernity: Westernisation and modernisation are directly correlated. What we need to tease out, therefore, are the implications of such assumptions both in the West and in the non-West.

So, I should like to close this book with a discussion of the postcolonial critique of these Western presumptions.[1] Its main

---

1. See here Chakrabarty, 2000.

objection is aimed at the assumption that modernisation equates to Westernisation; or, to put it differently, that it is Western rationality which makes it possible to assert the universal superiority of the West's system of reasoning. The postcolonial critique rejects the assumption that Western rationality is the ultimate form of reason, which allows for the best, if not the only, way of explaining the world. It thus disputes the claim that modernity is only possible by way of Westernisation. It argues that Western rationality appears to be superior only because it is the West that has imposed, by force when necessary, a system of thought that has served it well.

One reply to this postcolonial critique has been the acknowledgement that we now all live in a hybrid environment, which is influenced by Western and non-Western forms of modernity.[2] This recognition that Western thought is also the outcome of the encounter between West and non-West makes possible a form of modernity in which both bring their rationality. Theories of hybridity allow for a more congenial approach to this question, but the notion of hybridity does not do away with the assumption that West is best.[3] It merely pays homage to the fact that present-day modernity is far more diverse than is allowed by existing Western theories of social and political thought. For example, it accepts that there may be different ways to democratise but it continues to assume that Western forms of democracy will repay the best political and economic dividends. That is why the postcolonial critique of hybridity rejects what it sees as a sleight of hand: hybridity is a minimal concession to the non-West but in effect it is nothing but a continued belief in the Western claims of superiority.[4]

---

2. Edward Said was perhaps the first postcolonial critic to intimate the relevance of hybridity. See Said, 1978, 1993.
3. For a discussion of hybridity, see Hannerz, 1992, 1996; Burke, 2007.
4. Although Homi Bhabha, a strong critic of Western rationality, was in favour of the notion of hybridity. See Bhabha, 1994.

In order to explain more clearly what these different claims consist of, I propose to look in some detail at the non-Western critique of three important concepts of Western social and political theories I have already touched upon: secularism, human rights and sovereignty. This is of interest because all three of them have been subjected to astringent debates in the recent past, many of which challenge the Western vision of its own rationality.

Secularism

As we have seen, the argument here is that the hallmark of modernity is the form of Western secularism that has led to the separation between Church and State and to the private exercise of one's individual faith. The claim is that it was this particular form of secularism that made possible modern scientific rationality. Indeed, it was the Western ways of *secularisation* that secured the dominance of the man-made social and political arrangements in which the modern individual escaped the diktat of religion and was granted the freedom to live in society in the ways she or he chose. This generated a theory of Western secularisation that, in time, began to be seen as the mark of a freer and more attractive form of modernity. Casting the West as the pinnacle of modernity, this theory came to equate secularism with a superior type of social and political arrangement between rational critical thought and faith, to which all should aspire.

The critique of these assumptions of superiority rests on two powerful arguments: one historical, the other conceptual. The first contends that what passes for universal secularism is in fact nothing other than the historical path followed by the West. In other words, secularism happens to be the way in which the West evolved social and political arrangements that led in due course to the separation between Church and State, between religious and secular forms of social intercourse, thus freeing the individual from the constraints of religion. To claim that this is the only type of modernity that can ensure freedom of thought and agency is to legitimise the Western way of 'dealing' with religion. But in truth, the critique avers, this is nothing other than the attempt to grant universal significance to what is a validation by the Christian West of *its* path to modernity.[5]

Returning to what has been a consistent thread in the book – our discussion of the role of Islam in Western societies – this critique objects to the West's claim that only *its* kind of secularisation is the peak of modernity. Arguing against the West's definition of secularism, the critique shows that the current separation of religion and politics is the display of the West's bias in favour of *its* form of secularism. In what has sometimes been described as secular fundamentalism – perhaps best embodied by French social and political thought – the critique claims that such Western assumptions end up casting aside all attempts by Western Muslims to find their own path of secularisation.[6] In doing so it rejects all other ways in which religion and politics might be organised. Conceptually, therefore, redefining secularisation as a more general process of modernisation, this critique argues that what is defined as secularism in Western thought is merely the Western variant of this process of secularisation.[7] In other words, it ought to be seen as the 'ideology' of the West's attempt to delineate the difference between secular and non-secular societies. The critique is in three parts.

The first is that present-day definitions of secularism are in fact the extrapolation of the process from a 'Christian West', which leaves out what has happened in the non-Christian, or

---

5. See Asad, 1993.
6. See Iqtidar, 2011.
7. For one recent example of such argument, see Iqtidar, 2011.

non-Western, rest of the world. It is the historical dominance of this Christian West over the rest, by way of imperial and colonial control, that has made possible this conceptual domination. And it is this domination that has led the West to see *its* current social and political theory as universal. So, the debate here is about cause and effect. Is secularism the means to a more 'enlightened' social and political dispensation or is it merely the outcome of the historical battle between Church and State in Europe?

The second is that secularism ought to be defined according to what it does rather than what it is. In this view, secularism is merely the outcome of a *Western* process of modernisation, by which religion is separated from politics. This second critique seeks to puncture the pretension of the Western argument that there is only one way to modernise. If secularism in the West is defined by this particular form of modernisation, it behoves the West to seek to understand the non-Western experience of the development of the relation between religion and politics, rather than assume that the one is incompatible with the other. Indeed, this process of modernisation may take different forms, as it did in Turkey under Atatürk. And the experience of what has been dubbed the 'modernity of piety' in countries such as Egypt or Pakistan, which may appear to the West as the 're-traditionalisation' of Muslim societies, is in fact the reverse – that is, the modernisation of the religious experience. What matters in the end is the ways in which this modernisation takes place.[8] Modernity, therefore, is varied and may accommodate a religious experience that is wholly different from that of the Christian West.

Third, this process of secularisation is made possible by a form of individual agency which differs from that of the West. Religion is incorporated into a vision of modernity that favours

---

8. See Mahmood, 2005.

the conscious decisions by individuals to claim for themselves a form of social and political practice based on the shared religious beliefs of their community. It is this argument that underpins the view that the process of Muslim secularisation in the West, although at odds with prevailing norms, ought to be given the space that is required for the exercise of Muslim 'agency'. And it is this argument that lies at the heart of the vision of a European Muslim for whom religion and politics cannot be separated. The attempt by the West to legislate on what are acceptable symbols of Islam (by way of the woman's Muslim garb or the construction of minarets) is a sign of a failure of imagination and of the recourse to an intolerant position, which only fans the flame of Islamophobia. Western political thought now stands undermined by a narrow interpretation of secularism, exposing the limits of its (Western) rationality, which has no good theory to account for such (non-Western) demands within its concept of modernity.

Human rights

A similar problem arises when it comes to the West's promotion of human rights.[9] The claim that human rights are both universal and a proof of modernity is contested by those who see such an assumption as the means for the West to try to enforce *its* singular regime of civil rights. The postcolonial critique argues that such a concept of human rights is based on the extension to the non-West of the Western notion of *individual*, which may not be shared by the non-West. And, it claims, the call to protect individual human rights can thus be interpreted as a means to castigate those societies in which they fail to obtain. Here, again, it appears that the debate about the nature and role of human rights is a debate about the

---

9. See Griffin, 2008.

West's rationality. The West is not able to countenance, or make allowance for, political and social arrangements that do not place its own notion of individual human rights at the centre of the 'modern', meaning 'civilised', way of life.[10]

Although there is disagreement about the origins of the present notion of human rights, it is clear that it issues both from the post-war UN Declaration of Human Rights and the move in the 1970s to construct a theory of international relations that reflected the growing primacy of this concept of rights.[11] The upshot of this change in the way the West would now interact with the non-West exposed the limits of Western rationality. It entrenched a vision of the world in which the West's view of itself as the protector of human rights now gave it the right to define what that meant and how best to enforce it. But, as we have seen, it was the challenge posed by the practices of the non-West in the West, particularly by Western Muslims, that triggered the most radical questioning of the notion of human rights. Even if the West was able to understand why non-Western societies might not subscribe to its notion of human rights, it would not accept the (re)introduction of these non-Western practices into Western societies.

What is at play here, then, is not merely a question of definition; it is a debate about the superiority of the West's protection of individual rights. But it is also a debate about the superiority of the democratic liberal agenda over the notion of 'collective' rights, which was the mainstay of the socialist agenda. Even if the West, in the guise of cultural relativism, was prepared to admit that non-Western practices were acceptable *in situ*, it would not countenance them in its own midst. And it was indeed the realisation that some Western citizens of non-Western descent continued to abide by norms such as polygamy, the wearing of

---

10. For a discussion of the notion of human rights, see Beitz, 2009.
11. See Moyn, 2010.

the *burqa*, forced marriages, or even genital mutilation, which has led to the banning of such practices. In other words, it was the internal challenge by citizens of non-Western origins that struck at the heart of the West's vision of itself as the land of individual civil and human rights.

The West now cast itself as the judge and jury. It extended its protection of these rights to the non-Western world, thereby redesigning its relations not just with its own citizens but with the citizens of the rest of the world.[12] What was at stake, therefore, was a new theory of rights, operating as the gateway to 'civilised modernity'. Whilst the postcolonial critique of this position readily accepted the desirability of human rights in general, it rejected the Western imposition of its criteria on the ground that non-Western societies had different norms. In other words, it rejected the idea that there was just one way of defining human rights. Furthermore, it pointed out that the human rights agenda served primarily to condemn the non-West. As is often pointed out, the International Criminal Court (ICC) has challenged the behaviour of non-'Western' – primarily African – politicians whilst exonerating Western heads of state whose violation of human rights outside their own constituencies was blatant, as was amply demonstrated by the military intervention in Iraq.[13]

But it is the second objection that is more telling. Returning to the question of Western Islam, which we have discussed at length in the body of this book, there is clearly incompatibility with some of the demands made upon the West by Western Muslims. The now notorious remark made by Tariq Ramadan to President Sarkozy in 2003 about the stoning of women, a comment that was surely unwise, was primarily an argument against the West's right to adjudicate on the nature of individual rights in societies that

---
12. See Forsythe, 2000.
13. For an enlightening discussion of what he calls 'atrocity crimes', see Scheffer, 2011.

differed markedly from the West. Ramadan said that personally he was against stoning but what mattered was to have a 'moratorium' in Muslim countries so that there could be a debate that would result in a change in the law allowing the stoning of women for 'adultery'.[14] Much as it appeared desirable to ban such an appalling practice, Sarkozy's reaction made for a convenient way to rule out of court those constituencies that did not subscribe to the protection of women's rights as defined by the West.

Starting from the view that the safeguarding of individual rights trumps all other criteria for civilised living, the West has elevated the notion of the protection of the *individual* to the acme of human rights. What is at issue is not just the concept of right but the definition of the individual, which, as we have seen, rests on a restricted view of the make-up of modern society. The focus on the individual rules out any compromise with those who claim that they take their cue from the community of which they are a part and which defines them as persons. In other words, there is no place in the West for those who view themselves primarily in communal terms. As we have seen, therefore, there is no place for Muslims who claim that their identity and their relation to the 'other' are determined by the demands of a transnational *ummah*, which may not readily accord with the West's social and political arrangements placing the protection of *individual* rights at its constitutional apex.

But in imposing such restrictions, the postcolonial critique maintains, the West's approach to human rights is an impediment to the expression of the collective rights of the Muslims.[15] The demand for a Western Islam that gives proper protection to those who see themselves as Muslims first and Europeans second is thus ruled out. The argument, therefore, is one of balance, and

---

14. For a searing critique of Ramadan, see Fourest, 2008.
15. See Ramadan, 2004.

the primacy given to human rights as defined by the West has now tilted that balance firmly in favour of those who advocate a resolutely individualist theory of rights. We shall see below how this has impacted on the question of sovereignty. Here I want to highlight the consequences of a stance that has no place for a more community-based notion of rights.

The conceptualisation of human rights that is now projected onto the 'other', whether in Western societies or abroad, derives from a three-pronged notion of rights. The first stands firmly behind the primacy of the individual in modern societies. What matters above all is a notion of rights that protects the individual from the 'tyranny' of the community. The second amounts to a projection of this notion to the rest of the world, implying thereby that the process of modernisation demands the liberation of the individual from the 'shackles' of the community. In effect, again, modernisation means Westernisation. Third, therefore, the present notion of human rights serves to mark a distance between those societies that are more or less 'modern' in terms of whether they uphold the human rights of the individual.

What this means is that the change in Western theory from a notion of rights to that of *individual* human rights, as has occurred since the 1970s, places a new obstacle in the way of those who conceive modernity differently. Indeed, it is the stress on the individual nature of such rights that marks out the Western concept of human rights today. So, for instance, it is not sufficient to call for the right of formerly colonised societies to be free from poverty; human rights are now meant to protect the individual from the consequences of poverty. Therefore the claim by some in the non-West that they need to be accepted on their own, different and more communitarian terms if they are to accord their behaviour with the demands of their beliefs cannot be accommodated within this Western theory of human rights.

The consequence of the narrowing of the concept of human rights, which now privileges the individual, is the claim by the West that this approach has universal validity. The upshot is a return to a teleology of development that had been challenged by the formerly colonised world after decolonisation. At that time, the assumption of the modernity of Westernisation was uncontested, but the end of colonial rule brought about a reaction against this continuation of colonial ideology by other means. The extension of this reaction to the diasporas living in the colonial metropolis, which at first went unnoticed, now marks out those who refuse to accept the pre-eminence of the individual as defined by the Western rules of identity that have become enshrined in a legal order claiming universal validity.

Here, too, it is plain to see, the shift from the protection of social, political and economic 'rights' to the protection of *individual* human rights has provoked a reaction from those who suffered most from the absence of such protection in the former colonies. It points to the hypocrisy of the West, which now finds it convenient to change the criteria of modernity to suit its new theory of rights. Hence the dispute turns less around the desirability of such protection as around the Western imposition of this new dispensation on the rest of the world, which is thus relegated to a less advanced stage of modernity, of 'civilisation'.

The most concrete move made in this direction was the creation of the International Criminal Court (ICC) in 2002. The ICC, which operates under the aegis of the UN, is tasked with sanctioning all those, chiefly politicians, who are held responsible for the most extreme violation of human rights (notably, crimes against humanity and genocide) and have thereby made themselves liable to arrest and prosecution. However, the fact that a number of countries – including the United States – have failed to ratify the ICC gives comfort to those who contend that this tribunal is a legal imposition on the non-West by a West that sees itself as being above the fray.

The main justification for this new theory of the sanctity of human rights has been the recognition of the brutality of a number of regimes against their own people and the growing importance of non-state actors in international politics. The argument is that too many non-Western governments hide their deeds behind the Westphalian principle that keeps them safe from outside interference.[16] However, the prosecution by the Special Court for Sierra Leone of the Liberian politician Charles Taylor, for his involvement in Sierra Leone's murderous civil war, is emblematic of this trend. Although he had been duly elected president of Liberia in elections sanctioned by the 'international community', following a number of years during which he operated as a warlord, he was deemed by the West to have lost the protection of sovereignty on account of his misdeeds. The message was clear: no one, not even a head of state, is safe from having to account for domestic policies that clash with the protection of individual human rights.

But here, too, this new dispensation may have reached its limits, as is clear in the case of Omar al-Bashir, the current president of Sudan, who has been indicted by the ICC for his government's actions in Darfur. Al-Bashir has received widespread support from his African colleagues and other non-Western governments in his refusal to acknowledge the ICC's writ. Short of Western military intervention in Sudan, for which there is no appetite, the case against the Sudanese president is unlikely to succeed, at least in the short run. After all, Sudan is a major oil-producing country able to sell to China and thus evade Western sanctions. The example of Sudan exposes the duplicity of the

---

16. As previously explained, Westphalia refers to the treaties signed in 1648 to mark the end of the Thirty Years War. The Westphalian principles refer to the system of international relations built on the sovereignty of individual states and a system of diplomacy that only recognised state actors.

West, which can simultaneously claim that the Darfur conflict amounts to genocide and yet refrain from intervention on good realist grounds. The obligation placed on the West to intervene in cases such as genocide is ignored because Sudan is too important to Western economic and geopolitical interests. Because of this, the ICC indictment of the head of state can be seen as a fig leaf, with no prospect of success, a soothing of the West's conscience now caught in the bind of the new post-Westphalian theory of sovereignty.

Sovereignty

The West's emphasis on the protection of human rights, which has influenced its approach to the non-West, has led to a shift in its foreign policy. It has brought about a duty of responsibility upon the West, whereby it ought to help sustain human rights throughout the world. Indeed, recent Western incursions in countries like Afghanistan have often been justified on the grounds that human rights were being trampled. And the decision by NATO to engage in Libya was justified by the need to prevent the regime from abusing its power and deny the civilian population its civil and human rights. The greater prominence now given to the protection of human rights – however ill defined they might be – has led to an important shift in the theory of International Relations (IR), which has changed the concept of sovereignty.[17]

Standard theories of IR were based on two fundamental principles. The first was the assumption that relations between international actors were effectively relations between states and not regimes. Indeed, diplomacy continues by and large to follow this ground rule. The second was that the sovereignty of states was

---

17. One of the first, and one of the most influential, arguments in that direction was Vincent, 1986. For a systematic overview, see Hobson, 2012.

inviolable, regardless of the policies pursued by their governments. This theory of IR is based on the Westphalian principle of the sanctity of state sovereignty. Although this remains the mainstay of realist theories of IR, there has now developed an alternative approach which places the protection of human rights at the centre of the relations between West and non-West. And new IR theories have emerged to justify this shift away from the Westphalian standpoint and towards the doctrine of Responsibility to Protect (RtoP).[18]

The concern since the mid-1970s to protect human rights has brought about a change in the West's approach to the question of sovereignty. A series of events that cast doubt upon the primacy of the Westphalian principle paved the way to theories of intervention that effectively violated the principle of state sovereignty. It was the Biafra conflict in the mid-1960s, which led to the creation of the very influential NGO – Médecins sans Frontières – that marked the beginning of the awareness that the protection of individual rights should be placed above the principle of state sovereignty. Since then, there has been a rapid development of IR theories to give justification to a new theory of sovereignty sanctioning Western intervention in the internal affairs of another state – regardless of its invocation of the right of sovereignty.[19]

The West's unilateral move to adopt a different approach to the sanctity of sovereignty has put the non-West on the defensive. Since it quickly became apparent that this new approach to sovereignty applied mostly to the previously colonised world or more generally to the South, it was perceived as yet another criterion imposed by the West to sanction action against the non-West. Indeed, the

---

18. See Falk, 1981. The concept of Responsibility to Protect is a UN initiative that stresses that governments have a duty to protect its population and explicitly states that foreign intervention is justified as a last resort if governments engage in crimes against humanity, genocide, war crimes or ethnic cleansing.
19. See Halliday, 1994.

postcolonial critique has stressed that it was less the result of a commitment to human rights *per se* – after all, the Westphalian principle continues to regulate relations between Western states – than a means by which to claim the universality of the Western standpoint as applied to the non-West.[20] Here, too, the critique points to the duplicity of this shift, which implicitly redefined the notion of modernity. As a result, the non-West could no longer claim to be modern, or civilised, so long as it failed to allocate to the protection of human rights the same priority as was now defined by the West.

This move away from realist theories of international relations made possible the right of intervention in the affairs of countries whose regimes were adjudged to have abused human rights.[21] But this right of intervention called into question the sovereignty of the state. Whatever its merit – for it is now recognised that there might well be a need to protect citizens from their government – it is clear that this doctrine of intervention has radically changed the meaning of sovereignty and has endorsed a de facto Western foreign policy of regime change. The fact that the UN continues largely to operate on the basis of the Wesphalian principle reminds us that this new Western emphasis on the protection of human rights is controversial. It has not been approved by many in the non-West or by some of the key members of the Security Council (Russia, China), who reject the right of the West to set itself up as judge and jury on the question. However, the increasing number of cases where there appears to be a need to protect civilians from their own governments has begun to inflect UN policies. And in a number of cases (such as Kosovo or Iraq) the West is willing to act without UN endorsement.

---

20. See Anghie, 2004.
21. See Crawford, 2002.

This new approach to sovereignty, which sanctioned the right of intervention, is clearly seen by its critics as a way of exercising control over those who are in no position to resist. Since there is no universally recognised doctrine of intervention, this shift is perceived by those who stand to lose most as an abuse of power on an international scale. And since there can be no clear-cut agreement as to when the right of intervention might be invoked, it is left to a Western 'coalition of the willing' to impose it over those who are deemed to have breached the recognised protection of human rights. The debate about the limits of this approach brings to light the limits of Western rationality. The argument is that sovereignty should now be defined according to criteria of morality set by the West, but which are supposed to be both universally valid and the mark of a 'civilised' modernity. Here again the West faces fresh charges of double standards. However admirable this devotion to the protection of human rights appears to be in the West, it comes against those who argue that it is not for the West to redefine the Westphalian concept of sovereignty that has prevailed for so long.

The point here is not so much that this change in the concept of sovereignty is illegitimate but that its *imposition* on the non-West marks it out as an abuse of power on the part of those who are in a position to police the world.[22] Because of this, the debate is vitiated from the very beginning, drifting from the merit of a particular case (such as the 'genocide' in Darfur) to an argument about the universality of a notion of human rights that can override the Westphalian principle. The position of China, an international actor that cannot be bullied so easily by the West, reinforces the opposition to this change in the definition of sovereignty, thus lending greater weight to those who argue that the matter of civil and human rights is not for the West to decide. It must be left to

---

22. For a critique of the Western notion of sovereignty, see Anghie, 2004.

the discretion of states that have different historical origins and who approach the issue of individual rights and sovereignty according to their own criteria. This is an argument the West cannot counter without resorting to a new theory of sovereignty that is not universally recognised – in part because it is obvious that the West itself does not accord its behaviour with the claims it makes for a more normative approach to international relations.

The recourse to a different theory of sovereignty, with an emphasis on individual human rights, has become more common in recent years. This is due to two main developments. The first is that the work of the ICC is becoming increasingly legitimate, even if it has met with a chorus of protests from those who think they suffer disproportionately from it. The recognition that even heads of state must justify their conduct before the Court has given greater impetus to the de facto definition of what is 'wrong'. The second is the insistence by the West that foreign relations must now incorporate an ethical dimension. The key argument here is that of accountability. The Western approach insists on the fact that all politicians must abide by notions of accountability such as are included in the new human rights policy dispensation. But since there is very little consensus on what that may entail and since the West appears to exonerate itself from such obligation,[23] the West is seen to counter the Chinese, and other non-Western states, on eminently subjective grounds. The case of Sudan, therefore, is characteristic of the difficulty that hampers the West's claim to follow its new theory of intervention. The West fails to intervene in Sudan but it also fails to prevent China from developing strong economic links with that country.

The West's intrusion in Libya was a test case of this new theory of intervention. The UN endorsed limited NATO attacks

---

23. It is unlikely that Tony Blair and George Bush Jr will ever be brought to book for having invaded Iraq without UN approval.

on Colonel Gaddafi's forces, which were responsible for violence against civilians. Libya's sovereignty was thus curtailed by the new criteria of accountability that now attached to the West's intervention. And since NATO intervention in the Libyan conflict clearly went far beyond the protection of civilians – after all, it destroyed all heavy weapons, thus making it possible for the rebels to advance – it showed how its notionally admirable aims were implemented ruthlessly, leading to numerous casualties among civilians. But it also showed the West's double standards, as it clearly applies this new doctrine of intervention selectively. For instance, the West is not about to attack China in order to protect civilians in Tibet.[24]

A quick survey of Western intervention in Africa brings to light the contradictions of this policy change. The most clear-cut case for intervention was the 1994 Rwanda genocide – defined as such by the UN and therefore subject to the new policy that demanded intervention. In Rwanda, there was even a UN force on the ground but it was devoid of the number of troops deemed necessary. Nevertheless, the attitude of the West, within and outside the UN, meant there was little impetus on the part of the major Western powers to intervene militarily. The USA in particular was traumatised by the earlier killing of US troops in Mogadishu and did not want to get stuck in the Rwanda 'quagmire'. In any event, the situation on the ground would have made it impossible for NATO to mount the sort of air sorties it later committed to Libya. Following the killing of Belgian (UN) troops the UN withdrew entirely, against the advice of the local UN commander. And the killing continued apace.

Similarly, the decision to leave Somalia to its own internal struggles suggests that intervention in that country would be

---

24. For this reason it seemed odd that China and Russia should agree to Resolution 1973 on Libya when both had hitherto been reluctant to sanction intervention to secure human rights.

too costly to the West. Not only would it pit the UN against a growing Muslim fundamentalist movement but it would also involve the deployment of a large number of troops. Thus Western governments have limited their intervention to making declarations about the dangers of al-Shabaab and to support the troops from other African countries tasked with bringing order and especially peace to the country.[25] The protracted nature of the conflict shows that there is very little scope for a compromise between the West and al-Shabaab. Therefore, UN intervention is confined to the protection of the 'official' Somali government in Mogadishu and (through NGOs) to help finance the running of the refugee camps across the border in Kenya.

The discussion of these three important questions – secularism, human rights and the right to intervention – brings to light the contradictions inherent in the West's approach to domestic and international affairs. On the one hand, there is clearly a commitment to what is seen as more 'civilised' behaviour – hence the insistence on the superiority of a secular dispensation and the protection of human rights in a modern setting. On the other hand, the West's approach marks out the way in which it deals with other states – hence the priority on human rights as the bulwark of this more 'civilised' living. However, the changes in domestic and international policies brought about by these new principles cannot but be seen as yet another way in which the West seeks to claim superiority over the rest of the world. And the priority given to human rights and secularism redefines the West's relationship with the non-West.

But this stance will not remain unchallenged by other polities, like China, which claim that there is more than one way of achiev-

---

25. The al-Shabaab movement consists of extremist Muslims who claim links with al-Qaeda and who enforce extreme 'Muslim' justice in the areas they control.

ing 'civilised' living. Similarly, the western Muslim stance on how it is possible to live one's faith unhindered will continue to come up against the West's notion of secularism. These challenges are not leftovers from a distant and 'traditional' past; they are rational and 'modern' responses to the attitude and behaviour of the West. More importantly still they present challenges that set the West's *present* rationality against rationalities more in keeping with local history and culture. In time these challenges will undoubtedly require a more serious reconsideration by the West of its rationality than it has so far been willing to entertain.

The end of conceit is upon us. Western rationality must be rethought.

Bibliography

Abel, T. 1970. *The Foundation of Sociological Theory.* New York: Random House.
Abélès, M., and H.-P. Jendy (eds). 1997. *Anthropologie du politique.* Paris: Armand Colin.
Abrams, P. 1982. *Historical Sociology.* Ithaca NY: Cornell University Press.
Ahmed, A. 1992. *Postmodernism and Islam: Predicament and Promise.* London: Routledge.
Aho, J. 1999. *This Thing of Darkness: A Sociology of the Enemy.* Seattle WA: University of Washington Press.
Aldcroft, D., and A. Sutcliffe (eds). 1999. *Europe in the International Economy 1500–2000.* Cheltenham: Edward Elgar. 1999.
Alexander, J. 2003. *The Meanings of Social Life: A Cultural Sociology.* Oxford: Oxford University Press.
Alexander, J., and S. Seidman (eds). 1991. *Culture and Society: Contemporary Debates.* Cambridge: Cambridge University Press.
Alexander, J., P. Smith and M. Norton (eds). 2011. *Interpreting Clifford Geertz: Cultural Investigations in the Social Sciences.* New York: Palgrave Macmillan.
Allen, R., et al. 2005. *Living Standards in the Past: New Perspectives on Well-Being in Asia and Europe.* Oxford: Oxford University Press.
Almond, G. 1996. 'Political Science: The History of the Discipline'. In R. Goodin and H. Klingeman (eds), *A New Handbook of Political Science.* Oxford: Oxford University Press.
Alvarez, A. 1974. *The Savage God: A Study of Suicide.* Harmondsworth: Penguin.

Bibliography

Amin, S. 1990. *Delinking: Towards a Polycentric World.* London: Zed Books.
Amsden, A. 2001. *The Rise of the Rest: Challenges to the West from Late Industrializing Economies.* Oxford: Oxford University Press.
Amselle, J.-L. 1990. *Logiques métisses: anthropologie de l'identité en Afrique et ailleurs.* Paris: Payot.
Amselle, J.-L. 1996. *Vers un multiculturalisme français: l'empire de la coutume.* Paris: Aubier.
Anchor, R. 1967. *The Enlightenment Tradition.* New York: Harper & Row.
Anderson, B. 2006. *Imagined Communities: Reflections on the Origin and Spread of Nationalism.* London: Verso,
Anderson, D., and V. Broch-Due (eds). 2000. *The Poor Are Not Us: Poverty and Pastoralism in Eastern Africa.* London: James Currey.
Anghie, A. 2004. *Imperialism: Sovereignty and the Making of International Law.* Cambridge: Cambridge University Press.
Ansari, H. 2004. *'The Infidel Within': The History of Muslims in Britain from 1800 to the Present.* London: Hurst.
Appadurai, A. 1996. *Modernity at Large: Cultural Dimensions of Globalization.* Minneapolis: University of Minnesota Press.
Appadurai, A. 2006. *Fear of Small Numbers: An Essay on the Geography of Anger.* Durham NC: Duke University Press.
Appiah, K.A. 2005. *The Ethics of Identity.* Princeton NJ: Princeton University Press.
Appiah, K.A. 2006. *Cosmopolitanism: Ethics in a World of Strangers.* Princeton NJ: Princeton University Press.
Appleby, J. 2010. *The Relentless Revolution: A History of Capitalism.* New York: W.W. Norton.
Archer, M. 1995. *Realist Social Theory: The Morphogenetic Approach.* Cambridge: Cambridge University Press.
Archer, M. 1996. *Culture and Agency: The Place of Culture in Social Theory.* Cambridge: Cambridge University Press.
Arendt, H. 1968. *Between Past and Future.* Harmondsworth: Penguin.
Ariely, D. 2008. *Predictably Irrational: The Hidden Forces That Shape Our Decisions.* New York: HarperCollins.
Armstrong, K. 2001. *The Battle for God.* New York: Ballantine Books.
Armstrong, K. 2009. *The Case for God: What Religion Means.* London: Bodley Head.
Arndt, H. 1987. *Economic Development: The History of an Idea.* Chicago: Chicago University Press.
Arrighi, G. 1994. *The Long Twentieth Century.* London: Verso.
Arrighi, G., et al. 2003. *The Resurgence of East Asia.* London: Routledge.
Arrow, K. 1951. *Social Choice and Individual Values.* New York: Wiley.

Asad, T. 1973. *Anthropology and the Colonial Encounter*. Atlantic Highlands NJ: Humanities Press.
Asad, T. 1993. *Genealogies of Religion: Discipline and Reasons of Power in Christianity and Islam*. Baltimore MD: Johns Hopkins University Press.
Ashcroft, B., et al. 2002. *The Empire Writes Back: Theory and Practice in Postcolonial Literatures*. London: Routledge.
Audi, R. 1998. *Epistemology: A Contemporary Introduction to the Theory of Knowledge*. London: Routledge.
Avineri, S., and A. de Shalit (eds). 1992. *Communitarianism and Individualism*. Oxford: Oxford University Press.
Badie, B. 1986. *Les deux États: pouvoir et société en Occident et en terre d'Islam*. Paris: Fayard.
Bairoch, P. 1997. *Victoires et déboires: histoire économique et sociale du monde du XVIe siècle à nos jours*. Paris: Gallimard.
Baker, K. 1990. *Inventing the French Revolution: Essays on French Political Culture in the Eighteenth Century*. Cambridge: Cambridge University Press.
Baker, K., and P. Hanns Reill (eds). 2001. *What's Left of Enlightenment? A Postmodern Question*. Stanford CA: Stanford University Press.
Baldwin, D. (ed.). 1993. *Neorealism and Neoliberalism: The Contemporary Debate*. Princeton NJ: Princeton University Press.
Baldwin, P. 2004. 'Comparing and Generalizing: Why All History is Comparative, yet No History is Sociology'. In D. Cohen and M. O'Connor (eds), *Comparison and History: Europe in Cross-national Perspective*. New York: Routledge.
Banerjee, A., and E. Duflo. 2011. *Poor Economics: A Radical Rethinking of the Way to Fight Global Poverty*. New York: Public Affairs.
Barnard, A. 2000. *History and Theory in Anthropology*. Cambridge: Cambridge University Press.
Barnes, B. 1974. *Scientific Knowledge and Sociological Theory*. London: Routledge & Kegan Paul.
Barnes, B. 1981. *T.S. Kuhn and Social Science*. London: Macmillan.
Barr, M. 2011. *Who's Afraid of China? The Challenge of Chinese Soft Power*. London: Zed Books.
Barry, A., T. Osborne and N. Rose (eds). 1996. *Foucault and Political Reason*. London: UCL Press.
Bassey, N. 2012. *To Cook a Continent: Destructive Extraction and the Climate Crisis in Africa*. Cape Town: Pambazuka Press.
Bates, R. (ed.). 1988. *Towards a Political Economy of Development: A Rational Choice Approach*. Berkeley and Los Angeles: University of California Press.
Bates, R., V.Y. Mudimbe and J. O'Barr (eds). 1993. *Africa and the Disciplines*. Chicago: Chicago University Press.

Bibliography 339

Bauman, G. 1999. *The Multicultural Riddle: Rethinking National, Ethnic and Religious Identities*. London: Routledge.
Bauman, Z. 1978. *Hermeneutics and Social Science: Approaches to Understanding*. London: Hutchinson.
Bayly, C.A. 2004. *The Birth of the Modern World, 1780–1914*. Oxford: Blackwell.
Bayly, C.S. 1998. *Origins of Nationality in South Asia: Patriotism and Ethical Government in the Making of Modern India*. Oxford: Oxford University Press.
Beattie, J. 1964. *Other Cultures*. London: Routledge & Kegan Paul.
Becker, G. 1976. *The Economic Approach to Human Behaviour*. Chicago: University of Chicago Press.
Beitz, C. 1979. *Political Theory and International Relations*. Princeton NJ: Princeton University Press.
Beitz, C. 2009. *The Idea of Human Rights*. Oxford: Oxford University Press.
Bell, D. 1976. *The Cultural Contradictions of Capitalism*. New York: Basic Books.
Bellah, R. 1985. *Tokugawa Religion: The Cultural Roots of Modern Japan*, 2nd edn. New York: Simon & Schuster.
Bendix, R. 1962. *Max Weber. An Intellectual Portrait*. New York: Doubleday.
Benedict, R. 1946. *The Chrysanthemum and the Sword: Patterns of Japanese Culture*. Boston MA: Houghton Mifflin.
Benn, S., and G. Mortimore (eds). 1976. *Rationality and the Social Sciences*. London: Routledge & Kegan Paul.
Ben-Rafael, E., and Y. Sternberg (eds). 2005. *Comparing Modernities*. Leiden: Brill.
Bentley, J. 1993. *Old World Encounters: Cross-cultural Contacts and Exchanges in Pre-modern Times*. Oxford: Oxford University Press.
Berger, P., and M. Hsiao (eds). 1988. *In Search of an East Asian Model*. New Brunswick NJ: Transaction.
Berlin, I. 2002. *Liberty*. Oxford: Oxford University Press.
Bernal, M. 1987. *Black Athena: The Afroasiatic Roots of Classical Culture*. New Brunswick NJ: Rutgers University Press.
Berry, P., and A. Wernick (eds). 1992. *Shadow of Spirit: Postmodernism and Religion*. New York: Routledge.
Bhabha, H. 1994. *The Location of Culture*. London: Routledge.
Biernacki, R. 1995. *The Fabrication of Labor: Germany and Britain, 1640–1914*. Berkeley and Los Angeles: University of California Press.
Bin Wong, R. 1997. *China Transformed: Historical Change and the Limits of European Experience*. Ithaca NY: Cornell University Press.
Blackburn, R. 1997. *The Making of New World Slavery: From the Baroque to the

Modern, 1492–1800. London: Verso.
Blalock, H. (ed.). 1972. *Causal Models in the Social Sciences*. London: Macmillan.
Blaug, M. 1980. *The Methodology of Economics*. Cambridge: Cambridge University Press.
Blaut, J. 1993. *The Colonizer's Model of the World: Geographical Diffusionism and Eurocentric History*. New York: Guilford Press.
Blaut, J. 2000. *Eight Eurocentric Historians*. New York: Guilford Press.
Bloemraad, I. 2006. *Becoming a Citizen: Incorporating Immigrants and Refugees in the United States and Canada*. Berkeley and Los Angeles: University of California Press.
Blundo, G., and J.-P. Olivier de Sardan. 2006. *Everyday Corruption and the State: Citizens and Public Officials in Africa*. London: Zed Books.
Blyth, M. 2002. *Great Transformations: Economic Ideas and Political Change in the Twentieth Century*. Cambridge: Cambridge University Press.
Bohman, J. 1991. *New Philosophy of Social Science: Problems of Indeterminacy*. Cambridge: Polity Press.
Bonnell, V., and L. Hunt (eds). 1999. *Beyond the Cultural Turn: New Directions in the Study of Society and Culture*. Berkeley and Los Angeles: University of California Press.
Boone, C. 2003. *Political Topographies of the African State: Territorial Authority and Institutional Choice*. Cambridge: Cambridge University Press.
Boudon, R. 1986. *Theories of Social Change: A Critical Appraisal*. Berkeley and Los Angeles: University of California Press.
Boudon, R. 1998. 'Limitations of Rational Choice Theory', *American Journal of Sociology*, vol. 104, no. 3.
Bourdieu, P. 1979. *Algeria 1960: The Disenchantment of the World*. Cambridge: Cambridge University Press.
Bourdieu, P. 1993. *The Field of Cultural Production*. Cambridge: Polity.
Bowen, J., and R. Petersen (eds). 1999. *Critical Comparisons in Politics and Culture*. Cambridge: Cambridge University Press.
Braudel, F. 1979. *Civilization and Capitalism. 15th–18th Century*. 3 vols. London: HarperCollins.
Bray, F. 2000. *Technology and Society in Ming China*. Washington DC: American Historical Association.
Braybrooke, D. 1987. *Philosophy of Social Science*. Englewood Cliffs NJ: Prentice-Hall.
Brinkman, I. 2010. *Bricks, Mortar and Capacity Building: A Socio-cultural History of SNV Netherlands Development Organisation*. Leiden: Brill.
Brook, T., and G. Blue (eds). 1999. *China and Modern Capitalism*. Cambridge: Cambridge University Press.

Brooks, D. 2011. *The Social Animal*. London: Short Books.
Brown, C. 1995. *Serpents in the Sand: Essays on the Nonlinear Nature of Politics and Human Destiny*. Ann Arbor MI: University of Michigan Press.
Brown, S. (ed.). 1979. *Philosophical Disputes in the Social Sciences*. Brighton: Harvester.
Bryant, J. 2006. 'The West and the Rest Reunited: Debating Capitalist Origins, European Colonialism and the Advent of Modernity'. *Canadian Journal of Sociology*, vol. 31, no. 4.
Bryman, A. 1988. *Quantity and Quality in Social Research*. London: Routledge.
Bryman, A. 1995. *Critical Social Theory: Culture, History and the Challenge of Difference*. Oxford: Blackwell.
Burbank, J., and F. Cooper. 2010. *Empires in World History: Power and the Politics of Difference*. Princeton NJ: Princeton University Press.
Burke, K., and P. Reill (eds). 2001. *What's Left of Enlightenment? A Postmodern Question*. Stanford CA: Stanford University Press.
Burke, P. 1985. *Vico*. Oxford: Oxford University Press.
Burke, P. 2000. *A Social History of Knowledge*. Cambridge: Polity Press.
Burke, P. 2005. *History and Social Theory*. Cambridge: Polity Press.
Burke, P. 2007. *Cultural Hybridity*. Cambridge: Polity Press.
Burke, P., and M.-L. Pallares-Burke. *Gilberto Freyre: Social Theory in the Tropics*. Oxford: Peter Lang.
Burnell, P. 2011. *Promoting Democracy Abroad: Policy and Performance*. New Brunswick NJ: Transaction.
Buruma, I., and A. Margalit. 2004. *Occidentalism: A Short History of Anti-Westernism*. London: Atlantic Books.
Buur, L., and H. Kyed. (eds) 2007. *State Recognition and Democratization in Sub-Saharan Africa: A New Dawn for Traditional Authorities?* New York: Palgrave Macmillan.
Cabrera, M. 2005. *Postsocial History: An Introduction*. Lanham MD: Lexington Books.
Cain, P., and M. Harrison. 2001. *Imperialism. Critical Concepts in Historical Studies*. London: Taylor & Francis.
Calderisi, R. 2006. *The Trouble with Africa: Why Foreign Aid Isn't Working*. New York: Palgrave Macmillan.
Calhoun, C. 1995. *Critical Social Theory: Culture, History and the Challenge of Difference*. Oxford: Blackwell.
Carrier, J. 1995. *Occidentalism: Images of the West*. Oxford: Clarendon Press.
Carrithers, M., et al. 1985. *The Category of the Person: Anthropology, Philosophy, History*. Cambridge: Cambridge University Press.

Cavell, S. 1979. *The Claim of Reason*. Oxford: Oxford University Press.
Chabal, P. 1992. *Power in Africa: An Essay in Political Interpretation*. London: Macmillan.
Chabal, P. 1996. 'The African Crisis: Context and Interpretation'. In Terence Ranger and Richard Werbner (eds), *Postcolonial Identities in Africa*. London: Zed Books.
Chabal, P. 2009. *Africa: The Politics of Suffering and Smiling*. London: Zed Books.
Chabal, P., and J.-P. Daloz. 1999. *Africa Works: Disorder as Political Instrument*. Oxford: James Currey.
Chabal, P., and J.-P. Daloz. 2006. *Culture Troubles: Politics and the Interpretation of Meaning*. Chicago: Chicago University Press.
Chakrabarty, D. 2000. *Provincializing Europe: Postcolonial Thought and Historical Difference*. Princeton NJ: Princeton University Press.
Champney, L. 1995. *Introduction to Quantitative Political Science*. New York: HarperCollins.
Chan, S. 2009. *The End of Certainty*. London: Zed Books.
Charlesworth, J.C. 1962. *The Limits of Behavioralism in Political Science*. Philadelphia PA: American Academy of Political and Social Science.
Chase-Dunn, C., and T. Hall. 1997. *Rise and Demise: Comparing World Systems*. London: Routledge.
Chatham House. 2011. *Right Response: Understanding and Countering Populist Extremism in Europe*. A report by Matthew Goodwin. London: Chatham House.
Chatterjee, P. 1993. *The Nation and Its Fragments: Colonial and Postcolonial Histories*. Princeton NJ: Princeton University Press.
Chaudhuri, K. 1990. *Asia before Europe*. Cambridge: Cambridge University Press.
Chérif, M. 2006. *L'Islam et l'Occident: rencontre avec Jacques Derrida*. Paris: Odile Jacob.
Clarke, L., and L. Lange. 1979. *The Sexism of Social and Political Theory: Women and Reproduction from Plato to Nietzsche*. Toronto: Toronto University Press.
Clifford, J. 1988. *The Predicament of Culture: Twentieth-century Ethnography, Literature and Art*. Boston MA: Harvard University Press.
Cohen, S., and J. Bradford DeLong. 2010. *The End of Influence: What Happens When Other Countries Have the Money*. New York: Basic Books.
Cole, M., and S. Scribner. 1974. *Culture and Thought: A Psychological Introduction*. New York: Wiley.
Coller, I. 2010. *Arab France: Islam and the Making of Modern Europe, 1798–1831*. Berkeley and Los Angeles: University of California Press.

Collier, P. 2008a. *The Bottom Billion: Why the Poorest Countries are Failing and What Can Be Done About It.* Oxford: Oxford University Press.

Collier, P. 2008b. 'Backbone, Berman, and Buruma: A Debate that Actually Matters'. *World Affairs*, Winter.

Collins, R. 1986. *Weberian Sociological Theory.* Cambridge: Cambridge University Press.

Comaroff, J., and J. Comaroff (eds). 1993. *Modernity and Its Malcontents: Ritual and Power in Postcolonial Africa.* Chicago: University of Chicago Press.

Connell, R. 2007. *Southern Theory: Social Science and the Global Dynamics of Knowledge.* Cambridge: Polity Press.

Cook, T., and C. Reichardt (eds). 1979. *Qualitative and Quantitative Methods in Evaluation Research.* New York: Sage.

Cooper, F. 2005. *Colonialism in Question: Theory, Knowledge, History.* Berkeley and Los Angeles: University of California Press.

Cooper, F., and R. Packard (eds). 1997. *International Development and the Social Sciences: Essays on the History and Politics of Knowledge.* Berkeley and Los Angeles: University of California Press.

Costello, P. 1993. *World Historians and Their Goals.* De Kalb IL: Northern Illinois University Press.

Cramer, C. 2006. *Civil War is Not a Stupid Thing: Accounting for Violence in Developing Countries.* London: Hurst.

Crawford, N. 2002. *Ethics, Decolonization, and Humanitarian Intervention.* Cambridge: Cambridge University Press.

Crick, B. 1960. *The American Science of Politics: Its Origins and Conditions.* Berkeley and Los Angeles: University of California Press.

Crick, M. 1976. *Explorations in Language and Meaning: Towards a Semantic Anthropology.* London: Malaby Press.

Crook, R., and J. Manor. 1998. *Democracy and Decentralization in South Asia and West Africa: Participation, Accountability and Performance.* Cambridge: Cambridge University Press.

Crosby, A.W. 1986. *Ecological Imperialism: The Biological Expansion of Europe 900–1900.* Cambridge: Cambridge University Press.

Crouzet, F. 2001. *A History of the European Economy 1000–2000.* Charlottesville VA: University of Virginia Press.

Curtin, P. 1984. *Cross-Cultural Trade in World History.* Cambridge: Cambridge University Press.

D'Andrade, R. 1995. *The Development of Cognitive Anthropology.* Cambridge: Cambridge University Press.

Dallmayr, F. 1996. *Beyond Orientalism: Essays on Cross-cultural Encounters.* Albany NY: State University of New York Press.

Daloz, J.-P. 1997. '"Can we eat democracy?" Perceptions de la "démocratisation" zambienne dans un quartier populaire de Lusaka'. In J.-P. Daloz and P. Quantin (eds), *Transitions démocratiques africaines: dynamiques et contraintes*. Paris: Karthala.

Darwin, J. 2007. *After Tamerlane: The Global History of Empire*. Harmondsworth: Penguin.

Dasgupta, P. 2007. *Economics*. Oxford: Oxford University Press.

Dawkins, R. 2006. *The God Delusion*. Boston MA: Houghton Mifflin.

de Bary, W. 1998. *Asian Values and Human Rights: A Confucian Communitarian Perspective*. Cambridge MA: Harvard University Press.

de Certeau, M. 1974. *La culture au pluriel*. Paris: Union Générale d'Editions.

de Certeau, M. 1975. *L'écriture de l'histoire*. Paris: Gallimard.

de Vries, J. 1994. 'The Industrial Revolution and the Industrious Revolution'. *Journal of Economic History* 54.

Déloye, Y. 1997. *Sociologie historique du politique*. Paris: La Découverte.

Deng, Gang, 1993. *Development versus Stagnation: Technological Continuity and Agricultural Progress in Pre-modern China*. Westport CT: Greenwood Press.

Deng, Gang, 1997. *Chinese Maritime Activities and Socioeconomic Development c. 2100 B.C.–1900 A.D.* Westport CT: Greenwood Press.

Denzin, N. 1997. *Interpretative Ethnography: Ethnographic Practices for the Twenty-first Century*. London: Sage.

Derrida, J. 1976. *Of Grammatology*. Baltimore MD: Johns Hopkins University Press.

Detienne, M. 2003. *Comment être autochtone?* Paris: Seuil.

Deutsch, D. 2011. *The Beginning of Infinity: Explanations that Transform the World*. London: Allen Lane.

Devji, F. 2005. *Landscapes of the Jihad: Militancy, Morality and Modernity*. London: Hurst.

di Leonardo. M. 1998. *Exotics at Home: Anthropologies, Others and American Modernity*. Chicago: University of Chicago Press.

Dirks, N. (ed.). 1992. *Colonialism and Culture*. Ann Arbor: University of Michigan Press.

Donham, D. 1990. *History, Power, Ideology: Central Issues in Marxism and Anthropology*. Cambridge: Cambridge University Press.

Donnelly, J. 1989. *Universal Human Rights in Theory and Practice*. Ithaca NY: Cornell University Press.

Douglas, M. (ed.). 1973. *Rules and Meanings: The Anthropology of Everyday Knowledge*. Harmondsworth: Penguin.

Douglas, M. 1975. *Implicit Meanings: Essays in Anthropology*. London: Routledge & Kegan Paul.

Douglas, M. 2007. *Thinking in Circles*. New Haven CT: Yale University Press.

Bibliography 345

Dowding, K., and D. King (eds). 1995. *Preferences, Institutions and Rational Choice*. Oxford: Oxford University Press.
Duchesne, R. 2004. 'On the Rise of the West. Researching Kenneth Pomeranz's Great Divergence'. *Review of Radical Political Economics* 36.
Dumont, R. 1985. *Essais sur l'individualisme: une perspective anthropologique sur l'idéologie moderne*, 2nd edn. Paris: Seuil.
Dunleavy, P. 1991. *Democracy, Bureaucracy and Public Choice: Economic Explanations in Political Science*. Hemel Hempstead: Harvester Wheatsheaf.
Durkheim, E. 1997. *Suicide: A Study in Sociology*. New York: Free Press.
Eagleton, T. 2009. *Reason, Faith and Revolution: Reflections on the God Debate*. New Haven CT: Yale University Press.
Ekbladh, D. 2010. *The Great American Mission: Modernization and the Construction of an American World Order*. Princeton NJ: Princeton University Press.
Eliasoph, N. 2000. *Avoiding Politics*. Cambridge: Cambridge University Press.
Elman, B. 2001. *From Philosophy to Philology: Intellectual and Social Aspects of Change in Late Imperial China*. Los Angeles: UCLA Asian Pacific Monograph Series.
Elster, J. 1983. *Sour Grapes: Studies in the Subversion of Rationality*. Cambridge: Cambridge University Press.
Elster, J. (ed.). 1986. *Rational Choice*. Oxford: Blackwell.
Elvin, M. 1973. *The Pattern of the Chinese Past*. Stanford CA: Stanford University Press.
Elvin, M. 1996. *Another History: Essays on China from a European Perspective*. Sydney: Wild Peony Press.
Epstein, L. 2000. *Freedom and Growth: The Rise of States and Markets in Europe 1350–1750*. London: Routledge.
Escobar, A. 1995. *Encountering Development: The Making and Unmaking of the Third World*. Princeton NJ: Princeton University Press.
Euben, R. 1999. *Enemy in the Mirror: Islamic Fundamentalism and the Limits of Modern Rationalism*. Princeton NJ: Princeton University Press.
Evans, R. 1997. *In Defense of History*. New York: W.W. Norton.
Evans-Prichard, E. 1965. *Theories of Primitive Religion*. Oxford: Clarendon Press.
Eze, E.C. 2008. *Reason: Rationality in a World of Cultural Conflict and Racism*. Durham NC: Duke University Press.
Fabian, J. 1983. *Time and the Other: How Anthropology Makes its Object*. New York: Columbia University Press.
Falk, R. 1981. *Human Rights and State Sovereignty*. New York: Holmes & Meier.
Featherstone, M. (ed.). 1990. *Global Culture: Nationalism, Globalization and*

Modernity. London: Sage.
Ferguson, J. 2006. *Global Shadows: Africa in the Neoliberal World Order*. Durham NC: Duke University Press.
Ferguson, N. 2011. *Civilization: The West and the Rest*. London: Allen Lane.
Feyerabend, P. 1993. *Against Method: Outline of an Anarchistic Theory of Knowledge*, 3rd edn. London: Verso.
Finnegan, R., and R. Horton (eds). 1973. *Modes of Thought: Essays on Thinking in Western and Non-Western Societies*. London: Faber & Faber.
Firth, R. (ed.). 1970. *Man and Culture*. New York: Humanities Press.
Fisher, D. 2011. *Morality and War: Can War Be Justified in the Twenty-first Century?* Oxford: Oxford University Press.
Fiske, D., and R. Shweder (eds). 1986. *Metatheory in Social Science: Pluralisms and Subjectivities*. Chicago: Chicago University Press.
Fodor, J. 1979. *The Language of Thought*. Cambridge MA: Harvard University Press.
Forsythe, D. 2000. *Human Rights in International Relations*. Cambridge: Cambridge University Press.
Foucault, M. 1969. *L'archéologie du savoir*. Paris: Gallimard.
Foucault, M. 2002. *The Archaeology of Knowledge*. London. Routledge.
Foucault, M. 2003. *The Essential Foucault*. Ed. P. Rabinow and N. Rose. New York: Free Press.
Fourest, C. 2008. *Brother Tariq: The Doublespeak of Tariq Ramadan*. New York: Encounter Books.
Frazer, E. (ed.). 1993. *The Politics of Community: A Feminist Critique*. New York: Harvester Wheatsheaf.
Friedberg, A. 2011. *A Contest for Supremacy: China, America, and the Struggle for Mastery in Asia*. New York: W.W. Norton.
Friedman, J. (ed.). 1996. *The Rational Choice Controversy: Economic Models of Politics Reconsidered*. New Haven CT: Yale University Press.
Frost, M. 1986. *Towards a Normative Theory of International Relations*. Cambridge: Cambridge University Press.
Fukuyama, F. 1992. *The End of History and the Last Man*. New York: Free Press.
Fukuyama, F. 1995. *Trust: The Social Virtues and the Creation of Prosperity*. New York: Free Press.
Fukuyama, F. 2011. *The Origins of Political Order: From Prehuman Times to the French Revolution*. London: Profile Books.
Furet, F. 1995. *Revolutionary France, 1770–1880*. Oxford: Oxford University Press.
Gadamer, H.-G. 1976. *Philosophical Hermeneutics*. Berkeley and Los Angeles: University of California Press.

Gadamer, H.-G. 1992. *Truth and Method*. New York: Crossroad Publishing.
Gamble, A., D. Marsh and T. Tant (eds). 1999. *Marxism and Social Science*. London: Macmillan.
Gay, P. 1969. *The Enlightenment: An Interpretation*. New York: Knopf.
Geertz, C. 1973. *The Interpretation of Cultures*. New York: Basic Books.
Geertz, C. 2000. *Available Light: Anthropological Reflections on Philosophical Topics*. Princeton NJ: Princeton University Press.
Gell, S. 1995. 'Legality and Ethnicity: Marriage among the South Asians of Bedford'. *Critique of Anthropology*, vol. 14, no. 4 (December).
Gellner, E. 1973. *Cause and Meaning in the Social Sciences*. London: Routledge & Kegan Paul.
Gellner, E. 1984. *Rationality and the Social Sciences*. Cambridge: Cambridge University Press.
Gellner, E. 1992. *Postmodernism, Reason and Religion*. London: Routledge.
Gellner, E. 1992. *Reason and Culture: The Historic Role of Rationality and Rationalism*. Oxford: Blackwell.
Gerges, F. 2011. *The Rise and Fall of Al-Qaeda*. Oxford: Oxford University Press.
Geschiere, P. 1997. *The Modernity of Witchcraft: Politics and the Occult in Postcolonial Africa*. Charlottesville VA: University of Virginia Press.
Geschiere, P. 2009. *The Perils of Belonging: Autochthony, Citizenship and Exclusion in Africa and Europe*. Chicago: University of Chicago Press.
Gest, J. 2010. *Apart: Alienated and Engaged Muslims in the West*. London: Hurst.
Giddens, A. 1979. *Central Problems in Social Theory*. London: Macmillan.
Giere, R. 1979. *Understanding Scientific Reasoning*. New York: Holt, Rinehart & Winston.
Gilovitch, T. 1991. *How We Know What Isn't So: The Fallibility of Human Reason in Everyday Life*. New York: Free Press.
Gilroy, P. 2005. *Postcolonial Melancholia*. New York: Columbia University Press.
Gingrich, A. (ed.). 2002. *Anthropology by Comparison*. London: Routledge.
Gintis, H. 2000. *Game Theory Evolving*. Princeton NJ: Princeton University Press.
Gladwell, M. 2001. *The Tipping Point*. London: Abacus.
Gladwell, M. 2006. *Blink: The Power of Thinking without Thinking*. Harmondsworth: Penguin.
Goffmann, E. 1959. *The Presentation of Self in Everyday Life*. Garden City NJ: Anchor Books.
Goldstone, J. 1998. 'The Problem of the "Early Modern" World'. *Journal of the Economic and Social History of the Orient*, vol. 41, no. 3.

Goldstone, J. 2002. 'Efflorescence and Economic Growth in World History: Rethinking the "Rise of the West" and the Industrial Revolution'. *Journal of World History* 13 (Fall).
Goldstone, J. 2008. *Why Europe? The Rise of the West in World History*. New York: McGraw-Hill.
Goody, J. 1996. *The East in the West*. Cambridge: Cambridge University Press.
Goody, J. 2006. *The Theft of History*. Cambridge: Cambridge University Press.
Grafstein, R. 1999. *Choice-Free Rationality: A Positive Theory of Political Behaviour*. Ann Arbor MI: University of Michigan Press.
Grandy, R. 1973. 'Reference, Meaning and Belief'. *Journal of Philosophy* 70.
Graubard, S. (ed.). 1986. *Norden: The Passion for Equality*. Oslo: Norwegian University Press.
Gray, C. 1997. *Postmodern War: The New Politics of Conflict*. New York: Guilford Press.
Griffin, J. 2008. *On Human Rights*. New York: Oxford University Press.
Gulbenkian Commission. 1996. *Open the Social Sciences: Report of the Gulbenkian Commission on the Restructuring of the Social Sciences*. Stanford CA: Stanford University Press.
Gunder Frank, A. 1998. *ReOrient: Global Economy in the Asian Age*. Berkeley and Los Angeles: University of California Press.
Gutmann, A. (ed.). 1994. *Multiculturalism*. Princeton NJ: Princeton University Press.
Haan, N., et al. (eds). 1983. *Social Science as Moral Enquiry*. New York: Columbia University Press.
Habermas, J. 1972. *Knowledge and Human Interest*. London: Heinemann.
Habermas, J. 1987. *The Philosophical Discourse of Modernity*. Cambridge: Polity Press.
Hafez, K. 2010. *Radicalism and Political Reform in the Islamic and Western Worlds*. Cambridge: Cambridge University Press.
Hahm, P.C. 1987. *The Korean Tradition and Law*. Seoul: Royal Asiatic Society, Korean Branch.
Halfpenny, P., and P. McMylor (eds). 1994. *Positivist Sociology and Its Critics*. London: Unwin Hyman.
Halliday, F. 1994. *Rethinking International Relations*. London: Macmillan.
Hallpike, C. 1979. *The Foundations of Primitive Thought*. Oxford: Clarendon Press.
Hanlon, J. 1991. *Mozambique: Who Calls the Shots?* Oxford: James Currey.
Hanlon, J. 2009. *Do Bicycles Equal Development in Mozambique?* London: James Currey.

Hannerz, U. 1992. *Cultural Complexity: Studies in the Social Organization of Meaning*. New York: Columbia University Press.

Hannerz, U. 1996. *Transnational Connections*. London: Routledge.

Hansen, S., J. Mesøy and T. Kardas (eds). 2009. *The Borders of Islam: Exploring Samuel Huntington's Faultlines from Al-Andalus to Virtual Ummah*. London: Hurst.

Harris, J. 1992. *Essays on Industry and Technology in the Eighteenth Century*. Aldershot: Variorum.

Harris, M. 1989. *Our Kind: Who We Are, Where We Came From, and Where We Are Going*. New York: Harper & Row.

Harrison, L.E. 1992. *Who Prospers? How Cultural Values Shape Economic and Political Success*. New York: Basic Books.

Harvey, D. 1989. *The Condition of Postmodernity: An Enquiry into the Origins of Cultural Change*. Oxford: Blackwell.

Hausman, D. 1991. *The Separate and Inexact Science of Economics*. Cambridge: Cambridge University Press.

Hawthorn, G. 1987. *Enlightenment and Despair: A History of Sociology*. Cambridge: Cambridge University Press.

Hawthorn, G. 1991. *Plausible Worlds: Possibility and Understanding in History and the Social Sciences*. Cambridge: Cambridge University Press.

Heffer, S. 1989. *Like the Roman: The Life of Enoch Powell*. London: Harper Collins.

Held, D., et al. 1999. *Global Transformations: Politics, Economics and Culture*. Stanford CA: Stanford University Press.

Hellevik, G. 1984. *Introduction to Causal Analysis*. London: Allen & Unwin.

Hempel, C. 1965. *Aspects of Scientific Explanation and Other Essays in the Philosophy of Science*. New York: Free Press.

Henriques, J., et al. (eds). 1998. *Changing the Subject: Psychology, Social Regulation and Subjectivity*. London: Routledge.

Hindess, B. 1988. *Choice, Rationality and Social Theory*. London: Unwin Hyman.

Hobsbawm, E., and T. Ranger (eds). 1983. *The Invention of Tradition*. Cambridge: Cambridge University Press.

Hobson, J. 2004. *The Eastern Origins of Western Civilization*. Cambridge: Cambridge University Press.

Hobson, J. 2012. *The Eurocentric Conception of World Politics*. Cambridge: Cambridge University Press.

Hodgson, M. 1993. *Rethinking World History: Essays on Europe, Islam and World History*. Cambridge: Cambridge University Press.

Hollinger, D. 1995. *Postethnic America: Beyond Multiculturalism*. New York: Basic Books.

Hollis, M. 1977. *Models of Man: Philosophical Thoughts on Social Action.* Cambridge: Cambridge University Press.
Hollis, M. 1994. *The Philosophy of Social Science: An Introduction.* Cambridge: Cambridge University Press.
Hollis, M., and S. Lukes. (eds). 1982. *Rationality and Relativism.* Oxford: Blackwell.
Hookway, C., and P. Pettit (eds). 1978. *Action and Interpretation: Studies in the Philosophy of the Social Sciences.* Cambridge: Cambridge University Press.
Horton, R. 1967. 'African Traditional Thought and Western Science'. *Africa* 38.
Horton, R. 1982. 'Tradition and Modernity Revisited'. In M. Hollis and S. Lukes (eds), *Rationality and Relativism.* Oxford: Blackwell.
Horton, R., and R. Finnegan (eds). 1973. *Modes of Thought: Essays on Thinking in Western and Non-Western Societies.* London: Faber.
Hoselitz, B. 1960. *Theories of Economic Growth.* New York: Free Press.
Hountondji, P. 1976. *Sur la 'philosophie africaine': critique de l'ethnophilosophie.* Paris: Maspéro.
Howland, D., and L. White. 2008. *The State of Sovereignty: Territories, Laws, Populations.* Indianapolis: Indiana University Press.
Huertas, T. 2010. *Crisis: Cause, Containment and Cure.* London: Palgrave.
Huff, D. 1991. *How to Lie with Statistics.* Harmondsworth: Penguin.
Hull, D. 1988. *Science as a Process: An Evolutionary Account of the Social and Conceptual Development of Science.* Chicago: University of Chicago Press.
Hunt, L. 1984. *Politics, Culture and Class in the French Revolution.* Berkeley and Los Angeles: University of California Press.
Hunt, L. (ed.). 1989. *The New Cultural History.* Berkeley and Los Angeles: University of California Press.
Huntington, S. 1996. *The Clash of Civilizations and the Remaking of the World Order.* New York: Simon & Schuster.
Huntington, S. 2004. *Who Are We? The Challenges to America's National Identity.* New York: Simon & Schuster.
Ikels, C. 1996. *The Return of the God of Wealth: The Transition to a Market Economy in Urban China.* Stanford CA: Stanford University Press.
Inkeles, A. and D. Smith. 1974. *Becoming Modern: Individual Change in Six Developing Countries.* London: Heinemann.
Iqtidar, H. 2011. *Secularising Islamists? Jamaat-e-Islami and Jamaat-ud-Dawa in Pakistan.* Chicago: University of Chicago Press.
Itagaki, Y. 2007. 'Criticism of Rostow's Stage Approach: The Concepts of Stage, System and Type'. *The Developing Economies*, vol. 1, no. 1.
Jackson, M., and I. Karp (eds). 1990. *Personhood and Agency: The Experience*

of Self and Other in African Cultures. Washington DC: Smithsonian Institution Press.

Jameson, F. 1991. *Postmodernism, or, The Cultural Logic of Late Capitalism*. Durham NC: Duke University Press.

Johnston, M. 2005. *Syndromes of Corruption: Wealth, Power and Democracy*. Cambridge: Cambridge University Press.

Jones, E. 1988. *Growth Recurring: Economic Change in World History*. Oxford: Oxford University Press.

Jones, E. 2006. *Cultures Merging: A Historical and Economic Critique of Culture*. Princeton NJ: Princeton University Press.

Joyce, P. 1991. *Visions of the People: Industrial England and the Question of Class, 1848–1914*. Cambridge: Cambridge University Press.

Jullien, F. 2009. *Les transformations silencieuses*. Paris: Grasset.

Jung, D. 2011. *Orientalists, Islamists and the Global Public Sphere: A Genealogy of the Modern Essentialist Image of Islam*. Sheffield: Equinox.

Kaarsholm, P. (ed.). 2006. *Violence, Political Culture and Development in Africa*. Oxford: James Currey.

Kagan, J. 2009. *The Three Cultures: Natural Sciences, Social Sciences and the Humanities in the 21st Century*. Cambridge: Cambridge University Press.

Kahn, J. 1995. *Culture, Multiculture, Postculture*. London: Sage.

Kang, D. 2010. *East Asia before the West: Five Centuries of Trade and Tribute*. New York: Columbia University Press.

Kaviraj, S. 2005. 'An Outline of a Revisionist Theory of Modernity'. *European Journal of Sociology*, vol. 46, no. 3.

Kaviraj, S., and S. Khilnani (eds). 2001. *Civil Society: History and Possibilities*. Cambridge: Cambridge University Press.

Kegley, C. (ed.). 1995. *Controversies in International Relations Theory: Realism and the Neoliberal Challenge*. New York: St Martin's Press.

Kelley, D. 1970. *Foundations of Modern Historical Scholarship*. New York: Columbia University Press.

Kepel, G. 1997. *Allah in the West: Islamic Movements in America and Europe*. Cambridge: Polity Press.

Kepel, G. 2004. *The War for Muslim Minds: Islam and the West*. Cambridge MA and London: Belknap Press.

Kersten, C. 2011. *Cosmopolitans and Heretics: New Muslim Intellectuals and the Study of Islam*. London: Hurst.

Khan, M., and J. Kwame Sundaram (eds). 2000. *Rents, Rent-Seeking and Economic Development: Theory and Evidence in Asia*. Cambridge: Cambridge University Press.

Kiel, L.D., and E. Elliott (eds). 1996. *Chaos Theory in the Social Sciences: Foundations and Applications*. Ann Arbor MI: University of Michigan Press.

Kindleberger, C. 1996. *World Economic Primacy 1500–1900*. Oxford: Oxford University Press.
King, S. 2010. *Losing Control: The Emerging Threats to Western Prosperity*. New Haven CT: Yale University Press.
Klein, J.T. 2005. *Humanities, Culture and Interdisciplinarity*. Albany NY: State University of New York Press.
Knorr, K. 1976. 'Policy-Makers Use of Social Science Knowledge: Symbolic or Instrumental?' Research Memorandum No. 103. Vienna: Institute for Advanced Studies.
Knorr, K. 1981. *The Manufacture of Knowledge: An Essay on the Constructivist and Contextual Nature of Science*. Oxford: Pergamon Press.
Kobak, A. 1998. *Isabelle: The Life of Isabelle Eberhardt*. London: Chatto & Windus.
Krimerman, L. 1969. *The Nature and Scope of the Social Sciences: A Critical Anthology*. New York: Appleton–Century–Crofts.
Kuhn, T. 1962. *Structure of Scientific Revolutions*. Chicago: Chicago University Press.
Laclau, E. 2005. *On Populist Reason*. London: Verso.
Lacorne, D. 1997. *Crise de l'identité américaine: du melting-pot au multiculturalisme*. Paris: Fayard.
Laing, R.D. 1960. *The Divided Self: An Existential Study in Sanity and Madness*. Harmondsworth: Penguin.
Laing, R.D. 1961. *The Self and Others*. London: Tavistock Publications.
Lakatos, I. 1978. *The Methodology of Scientific Research Programmes*. Cambridge: Cambridge University Press.
Lamont, M., and L. Thévenot (eds). 2000. *Rethinking Comparative Cultural Sociology*. Cambridge: Cambridge University Press.
Landes, D. 1998. *The Wealth and Poverty of Nations: Why Some Are So Rich and Some Are So Poor*. New York: W.W. Norton.
Lash, S., and J. Friedman (eds). 1992. *Modernity and Identity*. Oxford: Blackwell.
Latouche, S. 2006. *Le pari de la décroissance*. Paris: Fayard.
Latour, B. 1991. *Nous n'avons jamais été modernes: essai d'anthropologie symétrique*. Paris: La Découverte.
Lawson, S. 2006. *Culture and Context in World Politics*. Basingstoke: Palgrave Macmillan.
Lebow, R. 2008. *A Cultural Theory of International Relations*. Cambridge: Cambridge University Press.
Lebow, R. 2010. *Why Nations Fight: Past and Future Motives for War*. Cambridge: Cambridge University Press.
Lee, J. and Wang Feng. 2002. *One Quarter of Humanity: Malthusian Mythologies*

and Chinese Realities. Cambridge MA: Harvard University Press.
Lee, K.B. 1984. *A New History of Korea*. Cambridge MA: Harvard University Press.
Lehmann, H., and G. Roth (eds). 1993. *Weber's Protestant Ethic: Origins, Evidence, Contexts*. Cambridge: Cambridge University Press.
Lévi-Strauss, C. 1970. *Tristes Tropiques*. New York: Atheneum.
Levitt, S., and S. Dubner. 2005. *Freakononomics*. London: William Morrow.
Lévy-Bruhl, L. 1910. *Les fonctions mentales dans les sociétés inférieures*. Paris: Alcan.
Lévy-Bruhl, L. 1975. *The Notebooks of Lévy-Bruhl*. Trans. P. Rivière. Oxford: Blackwell.
Lewis, G. 1980. *Day of Shining Red: An Essay on Understanding Ritual*. Cambridge: Cambridge University Press.
Lewis, I. 2008. *Understanding Somalia and Somaliland: Culture, History and Society*. London: Hurst.
Lichbach, M., and A. Zuckerman (eds). 1997. *Comparative Politics: Rationality, Culture and Structure*. Cambridge: Cambridge University Press.
Lieberman, V. (ed.). 1999. *Beyond Binary Histories: Re-imagining Eurasia to c.1830*. Ann Arbor MI: University of Michigan Press.
Little, D. 1991. *Varieties of Social Explanation: An Introduction to the Philosophy of Science*. Boulder CO: Westview Press.
Lloyd, B., and J. Gay. (eds). 1981. *Universals of Human Thought: Some African Evidence*. Cambridge: Cambridge University Press.
Lloyd, C. 1986. *Explanation in Social History*. Oxford: Blackwell.
Lonsdale, J. 1994. 'Moral Ethnicity and Political Tribalism'. In P. Kaarsholm and J. Hultin (eds), *Inventions and Boundaries: Historical and Anthropological Approaches to the Study of Ethnicity and Nationalism*. Papers from the Researcher Training Course held at Sandbjerg Manor, 23–29 May 1993. Roskilde: IDS Roskilde University.
Lukes, S. 1977. *Essays in Social Theory*. London: Macmillan.
Lupia, A., and M. McCubbins. 1998. *The Democratic Dilemma: Can Citizens Learn What They Need to Know?* Cambridge: Cambridge University Press.
Lyotard, J.-F. 1984. *The Postmodern Condition: A Report on Knowledge*. Minneapolis MN: University of Minnesota Press.
MacDonald, G., and P. Pettit. 1981. *Semantics and the Social Science*. London: Routledge & Kegan Paul.
Macfarlane, A. 2000. *The Riddle of the Modern World: Of Liberty, Wealth and Equality*. Basingstoke: Palgrave Macmillan.
MacGilvray, E. 2011. *The Invention of Market Freedom*. Cambridge: Cambridge University Press.
MacIntyre, A. 1970. 'Is Understanding Religion Compatible with Believing?'

In B. Wilson (ed.), *Rationality*. Oxford: Blackwell.
MacIntyre, A. 1984. *After Virtue*. Notre Dame IN: University of Notre Dame Press.
MacIntyre, A. 1988. *Whose Justice? Which Rationality?* Notre Dame IN: University of Notre Dame Press.
Mahmood, S. 2005. *Politics of Piety: The Islamic Revival and the Feminist Subject*. Princeton NJ: Princeton University Press.
Makdisi, G. 1990. *The Rise of Humanism in Classical Islam and the Christian West*. Edinburgh: Edinburgh University Press.
Malloch Brown, M. 2011. *The Unfinished Global Revolution*. Harmondsworth: Penguin.
Mamdani, M. 2009. *Saviors and Survivors: Darfur, Politics, and the War on Terror*. New York: Pantheon Books.
Mandelbaum, M. 1987. *Purpose and Necessity in Social Theory*. Baltimore MD: Johns Hopkins University Press.
Mannheim, K. 1936. *Ideology and Utopia: An Introduction to the Sociology of Knowledge*. New York: Harvest Books.
Marie, A. (ed.). 1997. *L'Afrique des individus*. Paris: Karthala.
Marquand, D. 2011. *The End of the West: The Once and Future Europe*. Princeton NJ: Princeton University Press.
Martin, M., and L.C. McIntyre (eds). 1994. *Readings in the Philosophy of Social Science*. Cambridge MA: MIT Press.
Masolo, D.A. 2010. *Self and Community in a Changing World*. Indianapolis: Indiana University Press.
Mayall, J. 1990. *Nationalism and International Society*. Cambridge: Cambridge University Press.
Mayer, A. 1991. *Islam and Human Rights: Tradition and Politics*. London: Pinter.
Mazlish, B. 2006. *The New Global History*. London: Routledge.
Mbembe, A. 2000. *De la postcolonie: essai sur l'imagination politique dans l'Afrique contemporaine*. Paris: Karthala.
McCarthy, T. 1991. *Ideals and Illusions: On Reconstruction and Deconstruction in Contemporary Critical Theory*. Cambridge MA: MIT Press.
Meijer, R. (ed.). 2009. *Global Salafism: Islam's New Religious Movement*. London: Hurst.
Meillassoux, C. 1981. *Maidens, Meal and Money: Capitalism and the Domestic Community*. Cambridge: Cambridge University Press.
Melucci, A. 1996. *The Playing Self: Person and Meaning in the Planetary Society*. Cambridge: Cambridge University Press.
Merton, R. 1968 [1949]. *Social Theory and Social Structure*, 3rd edn. New York: Free Press.

Meyer, B., and P. Geschiere (eds). 1999. *Globalization and Identity: Dialectic of Flow and Closure*. Oxford: Blackwell.

Milanovic, M. 2011. *Extraterritorial Application of Human Rights Treaties: Law, Principles, and Policy*. Oxford and New York: Oxford University Press.

Miller, D. 1998. *Material Cultures: Why Some Things Matter*. Chicago: University of Chicago Press.

Miller, R. 2010. *Globalizing Justice: The Ethics of Poverty and Power*. Oxford: Oxford University Press.

Mishler, W., and D. Pollack. 2003. 'On Culture. Thick and Thin: Toward a Neo-Cultural Synthesis'. In D. Pollack et al. (eds), *Political Culture in Post Communist Europe*. Aldershot: Ashgate.

Mohr, L. 1996. *The Causes of Human Behavior: Implications for Theory and Method in the Social Sciences*. Ann Arbor MI: University of Michigan Press.

Mokyr, J. 1990. *The Lever of Riches: Technological Creativity and Economic Progress*. Oxford: Oxford University Press.

Moore, H., and T. Sanders (eds). 2001. *Magical Interpretation, Material Realities: Modernity, Witchcraft and the Occult in Postcolonial Africa*. London: Routledge.

Morris, I. 2010. *Why the West Rules – for Now: The Patterns of History and What They Reveal about the Future*. London: Profile Books.

Morton, R. 1999. *Methods and Models*. Cambridge: Cambridge University Press.

Morton, R., and K. Williams. 2010. *Experimental Political Science and the Study of Causality*. Cambridge: Cambridge University Press.

Moyn, S. 2010. *The Last Utopia: Human Rights in History*. Cambridge MA and London: Belknap Press.

Moyo, D. 2009. *Dead Aid: Why Aid Is Not Working and How There is Another Way for Africa*. London: Allen Lane.

Mueller, D. 2009. *Reason, Religion and Democracy*. Cambridge: Cambridge University Press.

Munkler, H. 2007. *Empires: The Logic of World Domination from Ancient Rome to the United States*. Cambridge: Polity Press.

Mustapha, A.R., and L. Whitfield (eds). 2009. *Turning Points in African Democracy*. Woodbridge: James Currey.

Muthu, S. 2003. *Enlightenment against Empire*. Princeton NJ: Princeton University Press.

Myrdal, G. 1970. *Objectivity in Social Science*. London: Duckworth.

Needham, R. 1972. *Belief, Language and Experience*. Oxford: Blackwell.

Nicholson, M. 1989. *Formal Theories in International Relations*. Cambridge: Cambridge University Press.

Nietzsche, F. 1956. *The Birth of Tragedy*. New York: Anchor Press.

Nisbet, R. 1980. *History of the Idea of Progress*. New York: Basic Books.
Noiriel, G. 2007. *A quoi sert l'identité nationale?* Paris: Agone.
Nora, P. (ed.). 1992. *Les lieux de mémoire*. Paris: Gallimard.
North, D. 1990. *Institutions, Institutional Change and Economic Performance*. Cambridge: Cambridge University Press.
Nugent, P. 2004. *African since Independence: A Comparative History*. New York: Palgrave Macmillan.
Nyamjoh, F. 2006. *Insiders and Outsiders: Citizenship and Xenophobia in Contemporary Southern Africa*. London: Zed Books.
Nye, J. 2011. *The Future of Power*. New York: Public Affairs.
O'Brien, K. 1997. *Narratives of Enlightenment: Cosmopolitan History from Voltaire to Gibbon*. Cambridge: Cambridge University Press.
O'Brien, P. 2001. 'Metanarratives in Global Histories of Material Progress'. *International History Review*, vol. 23, no. 2 (June).
O'Brien, P. 2006. 'Historiographical Traditions and Modern Imperatives for the Restoration of Global History'. *Journal of Global History*, vol. 1, no. 1.
O'Hear, A. (ed.). 1996. *Verstehen and Humane Understanding*. Cambridge: Cambridge University Press.
O'Rourke, K., and J. Williamson. 2001. *Globalization and History: The Evolution of a Nineteenth-century Atlantic Economy*. Cambridge MA: MIT Press.
Olivier de Sardan, J.-P. 1992. 'Occultism and the Ethnographic "I": The Exoticizing of Magic from Durkheim to "Postmodern" Anthropology'. *Critique of Anthropology*, vol. 12, no. 1.
Olivier de Sardan, J.-P. 1999. 'A Moral Economy of Corruption'. *Journal of Modern African Studies*, vol. 37, no. 1.
Olson, M. 1965. *The Logic of Collective Action: Public Goods and the Theory of Groups*. Cambridge MA: Harvard University Press.
Ong, A. 2006. *Neoliberalism as Exception: Mutations in Citizenship and Sovereignty*. Durham NC: Duke University Press.
Ordeshook, P. 1986. *Game Theory and Political Theory*. Cambridge: Cambridge University Press.
Pacey, A. 1991. *Technology in World Civilization: A Thousand-year History*. Cambridge MA: MIT Press.
Pagden, A. 1996. 'The Rise and Decline of Intellectual History'. *Intellectual News* 1.
Pahuja, S. 2011. *Decolonising International Law: Development, Economic Growth and the Politics of Universality*. Cambridge: Cambridge University Press.
Pandey, G. 2006. *Routine Violence: Nations, Fragments, Histories*. Stanford CA: Stanford University Press.
Papineau, D. 1978. *For Science in the Social Sciences*. London: Macmillan.
Parsons, T. 1937. *The Structure of Social Action*. Glencoe IL: Free Press.

Parsons, T. 1951. *The Social System*. Glencoe IL: Free Press.
Pateman, C. 1989. *The Disorder of Women: Democracy, Feminism and Political Theory*. Cambridge: Polity Press.
Paxman, J. 1999. *The English: A Portrait of a People*. Harmondsworth: Penguin.
Paxton, R. 2005. *The Anatomy of Fascism*. Harmondsworth: Penguin Books.
Phillips, A. (ed.). 1998. *Feminism and Politics*. Oxford: Oxford University Press.
Phillips, T., and M. Phillips. 2009. *Windrush: The Irresistible Rise of Multi-racial Britain*. London: HarperCollins.
Pierson, C. 1986. *Marxist Theory and Democratic Politics*. Cambridge: Polity Press.
Polanyi, K. 1944. *The Great Transformation: The Political and Economic Origins of Our Time*. Boston MA: Beacon Press.
Pollock, S. 2005. *The Ends of Man at the End of Premodernity*. Amsterdam: Royal Netherlands Academy of Arts and Sciences.
Pollock, S., H. Bhabha and D. Chakrabarty (eds). 2002. *Cosmopolitanism*. Durham NC: Duke University Press.
Pomeranz, K. 2000. *The Great Divergence: China. Europe and the Making of the Modern World Economy*. Princeton NJ: Princeton University Press.
Pomeranz, K., and S. Topik. 1999. *The World that Trade Created: Culture, Society and the World Economy. 1400 to the Present*. London: M.E. Sharpe.
Popper, K. 2002. *Conjectures and Refutations: The Growth of Scientific Knowledge*, 2nd edn. London: Routledge.
Putnam, H. 1978. *Meaning and the Moral Sciences*. London: Methuen.
Putnam, H. 1981. *Reason, Truth and History*. Cambridge: Cambridge University Press.
Rachman, G. 2010. *Zero-Sum World*. London: Atlantic Books.
Ragin, C. 2000. *Fuzzy-Set Social Science*. Chicago: University of Chicago Press.
Ramadan, T. 1999. *To Be a European Muslim*. Markfield: Islamic Foundation.
Ramadan, T. 2003. *Islam, the West and Challenges of Modernity*. Markfield: Islamic Foundation.
Ramadan, T. 2004. *Western Muslims and the Future of Islam*. New York: Oxford University Press.
Ramadan, T. 2010. *The Quest for Meaning: Developing a Philosophy of Pluralism*. London: Allen Lane.
Randall, V., and G. Waylen (eds). 1998. *Gender, Politics and the State*. London: Routledge.
Reddy, W. 1987. *Money and Liberty in Modern Europe: A Critique of Historical Understanding*. Cambridge: Cambridge University Press.

Reinalda, B. 2011. *The Ashgate Research Companion to Non-State Actors*. Farnham: Ashgate.

Reinhart, C., and K. Rogoff. 2009. *This Time is Different: Eight Centuries of Financial Folly*. Princeton NJ: Princeton University Press.

Richards, J. 1997. Early Modern India and World History. *Journal of World History*, vol. 8, no. 2.

Richards, P. 1986. *Coping with Hunger: Hazard and Experiment in a West African Rice Farming System*. London: UCL Press.

Richards, P. (ed.). 2005. *No Peace No War: An Anthropology of Contemporary Armed Conflicts*. Oxford: James Currey.

Richter, M. 1995. *The History of Political and Social Concepts: A Critical Introduction*. Oxford: Oxford University Press.

Rittberger, V. 1993. *Regime Theory and International Relations*. Oxford: Oxford University Press.

Robert, A.-C. 2004. *L'Afrique au secours de l'Occident*. Paris: Éditions de l'Atelier.

Robinson, J. 1969. *The Economics of Imperfect Competition*, 2nd edn. London: Macmillan.

Rodgers, D. 2011. *Age of Fracture*. Cambridge MA: Harvard University Press.

Rorty, R. 1998. *Truth and Progress*. Cambridge: Cambridge University Press.

Rosenau, J. 1992. *Post-Modernism and the Social Sciences: Insights, Inroads and Intrusions*. Princeton NJ: Princeton University Press.

Rosenberg, A. 2000. *Philosophy of Science: A Contemporary Introduction*. London: Routledge.

Ross, M.H. 2007. *Cultural Contestation in Ethnic Conflict*. Cambridge: Cambridge University Press.

Rostow, W. 1958. *The Stages of Economic Growth*. Cambridge: Cambridge University Press.

Rostow, W. 1990. *Theorists of Economic Growth from David Hume to the Present*. Oxford: Oxford University Press.

Roy, O. 1994. *The Failure of Political Islam*. London: I.B. Tauris.

Roy, O. 2004. *Globalised Islam: The Search for a New Ummah*. London: Hurst.

Roy, O. 2010. *Holy Ignorance: When Religion and Culture Part Ways*. London: Hurst.

Runciman, D. 2006. *The Politics of Good Intentions: History, Fear and Hypocrisy in the New World Order*. Princeton NJ: Princeton University Press.

Ruthven, M. 2004. *Fundamentalism: The Search for Meaning*. Oxford: Oxford University Press.

Ryan, A. 1970. *The Philosophy of the Social Sciences*. New York: Random House.

Sachs, J. 2005. *The End of Poverty: How We Can Make It Happen in Our Lifetime.* Harmondsworth: Penguin.
Sahlins, M. 2008. *The Western Illusion of Human Nature.* Chicago: Chicago University Press.
Said, E. 1978. *Orientalism.* New York: Pantheon.
Said, E. 1993. *Culture and Imperialism.* London: Chatto & Windus.
Salmon, W. 1984. *Scientific Explanation and the Causal Structure of the World.* Princeton NJ: Princeton University Press.
Samuelsson, K. 1061. *Religion and Economic Action.* London: Heinemann.
Sandel, M. 1986. *Liberalism and the Limits of Justice.* Cambridge: Cambridge University Press.
Sanderson, S. 1999. *Social Transformations: A General Theory of Historical Development.* London: Rowman & Littlefield.
Sarrazin, T. 2010. *Deutschland schafft sich ab: wie wir unser Land aufs Spiel setzen.* Munich: Deutsche Verlag-Anstalt.
Sassen, S. 2008. *Territory, Authority, Rights: From Medieval to Global Assemblages.* Princeton NJ: Princeton University Press.
Savage. M. 2011. *Identities and Social Change in Britain since 1940: The Politics of Method.* Oxford: Oxford University Press.
Sayer, A. 1992. *Method in Social Science: A Realist Approach.* London: Routledge.
Sayyid, S., and A. Vakil (eds). 2010. *Thinking through Islamophobia: Global Perspectives.* London: Hurst.
Schaffer, F. 1998. *Democracy in Translation: Understanding Politics in an Unfamiliar Culture.* Ithaca NY: Cornell University Press.
Scheffer, D. 2011. *All the Missing Souls: A Personal History of the War Crime Tribunals.* Princeton NJ: Princeton University Press.
Schluchter, W. 1981. *The Rise of Western Rationalism: Max Weber's Developmental History.* Berkeley and Los Angeles: University of California Press.
Schroeder, R. 1992. *Max Weber and the Sociology of Culture.* London: Sage.
Schulz, K. 2010. *Being Wrong: Adventures in the Margin of Error.* London: HarperCollins.
Schumacher, E.F. 1973. *Small is Beautiful: Economics as if People Mattered.* London: Blond & Briggs.
Scott, A. (ed.). 1997. *The Limits of Globalization: Cases and Arguments.* London: Routledge.
Scott, D. 1999. *Refashioning Futures: Criticism after Postcoloniality.* Princeton NJ: Princeton University Press.
Scott, D. 2004. *Conscripts of Modernity: The Tragedy of Colonial Enlightenment.* Durham NC: Duke University Press.
Scott, J.W. 2005. *Parité! L'universel et la différence des sexes.* Paris: Albin Michel.

Scott, J.W. 2007. *The Politics of the Veil*. Princeton NJ: Princeton University Press.
Scott, J., and D. Keates. (eds). 2001. *Schools of Thought: Twenty-five Years of Interpretive Social Science*. Princeton NJ: Princeton University Press.
Sen, A. 1983. *Poverty and Famines*. Oxford: Oxford University Press.
Sen, A. 1999. *Development as Freedom*. New York: Knopf.
Sen, A. 2009. *The Idea of Justice*. London: Allen Lane.
Sewell, W. 1980. *Work and Revolution in France: The Language of Labor from the Old Regime to 1848*. Cambridge: Cambridge University Press.
Sewell, W. 2005. *Logics of History: Social History and Social Transformation*. Chicago: Chicago University Press.
Shaikh, F. 1989. *Community and Consensus in Islam: Muslim Representation in Colonial India, 1860–1947*. Cambridge: Cambridge University Press.
Shankman, P. 1984. 'The Thick and the Thin: On the Interpretive Theoretical Program of Clifford Geertz'. *Current Anthropology*, vol. 25, no. 3.
Shapiro, I. 2007. *The Flight from Reality in the Human Sciences*. Princeton: Princeton University Press.
Shin, Chull. D. 2012. *Confucianism and Democratisation in East Asia*. Cambridge: Cambridge University Press.
Shore, B. 1996. *Culture in Mind: Cognition, Culture and the Problem of Meaning*. New York: Oxford University Press.
Silverman, D. 1997. *Qualitative Research: Theory, Method and Practice*. London: Sage.
Silvestri, S. 2011. *Europe's Muslim Women: Beyond the Burqa Controversy*. London: Hurst.
Simms, B., and D. Trim (eds). 2011. *Humanitarian Intervention: A History*. Cambridge: Cambridge University Press.
Skinner, Q. (ed.). 1985. *The Return of Grand Theory in the Human Sciences*. Cambridge: Cambridge University Press.
Skinner, Q. 2005. 'On Intellectual History and the History of Books'. *Contributions to the History of Concepts*, vol. 1, no. 1.
Skocpol, T. (ed.). 1984. *Vision and Method in Historical Sociology*. Cambridge: Cambridge University Press.
Skorupski, J. 1976. *Symbol and Theory: A Philosophical Study of Theories of Religion*. Cambridge: Cambridge University Press.
Smil, V. 1994. *Energy in World History*. Boulder CO: Westview Press.
Smith, K., and M. Light (eds). 2001. *Ethics and Foreign Policy*. Cambridge: Cambridge University Press.
Smith, T. 1994. *America's Mission: The United States and the Worldwide Struggle for Democracy in the Twentieth Century*. Princeton NJ: Princeton University Press.

Sollors, W. 1987. *Beyond Ethnicity: Consent and Descent in American Culture*. Oxford: Oxford University Press.

Sombart, W. 1967. *Luxury and Capitalism*. Ann Arbor MI: University of Michigan Press

Spivak, G. 1999. *A Critique of Postcolonial Reason: Toward a History of the Vanishing Present*. Cambridge MA: Harvard University Press

Starn, R. 2002. 'The Early Modern Muddle'. *Journal of Early Modern History*, vol. 6, no. 3.

Stigum, B.P. 2003. *Econometrics and the Philosophy of Economics*. Princeton: Princeton University Press.

Stove, D. 1973. *Probability and Hume's Inductive Scepticism*. Oxford: Clarendon Press.

Strong, T. 2012. *Politics without Vision: Thinking without a Banister in the Twentieth Century*. Chicago: University of Chicago Press.

Swedberg, R. 1998. *Max Weber and the Idea of Economic Sociology*. Princeton NJ: Princeton University Press.

Swidler, A. 1973. 'The Concept of Rationality in the Work of Max Weber'. *Sociological Enquiry*, vol. 43, no. 1.

Tai Hung-Chao, 1989. *Confucianism and Economic Development: An Oriental Alternative*. Washington DC: Washington Institute Press.

Taleb, N.N. 2008. *The Black Swan: The Impact of the Highly Improbable*. Harmondsworth: Penguin.

Taylor, C. 1985. *Philosophy and the Human Sciences: Philosophical Papers 2*. Cambridge: Cambridge University Press.

Taylor, C. 1992. *The Ethics of Authenticity*. Cambridge MA: Harvard University Press.

Taylor, C. 1994. *Multiculturalism: Examining the Politics of Recognition*. Princeton NJ: Princeton University Press.

Taylor, C. 2004. *Modern Social Imaginaries*. Durham NC: Duke University Press.

Taylor, M. 2006. *Rationality and the Ideology of Disconnection*. Cambridge: Cambridge University Press.

Tett, G. 2009. *Fool's Gold: How Unrestrained Greed Corrupted a Dream, Shattered Global Markets and Unleashed a Catastrophe*. New York: Little Brown.

Thaler, R., and C. Sunstein. 2008. *Nudge: Improving Decisions about Health, Wealth and Happiness*. New Haven CT: Yale University Press.

Thomas, G. 2007. *Education and Theory: Strangers in Paradigms*. Maidenhead: Open University Press.

Thompson, A. 2005. *The Empire Strikes Back: The Impact of Imperialism on Britain from the Mid-nineteenth Century*. London: Longman.

Thompson, J., and D. Held (eds). 1982. *Habermas: Critical Debates*. London: Macmillan.
Thompson, W. 1999. *The Emergence of the Global Political Economy*. London: Routledge.
Tibi, B. 1998. *The Challenge of Fundamentalism: Political Islam and the New World Disorder*. Berkeley and Los Angeles: University of California Press.
Tilly, C. 1984. *Big Structures, Large Processes, Huge Comparisons*. New York: Russell Sage Foundation.
Todorov, T. 1989. *Nous et les autres: la réflexion française sur la diversité humaine*. Paris: Seuil.
Tracy, J. (ed.). 1991. *The Political Economy of Merchant Empires*. Cambridge: Cambridge University Press.
Tu Wei-ming (ed.). 1996. *Confucian Traditions in East Asian Modernity: Moral Education and Economic Culture in Japan and the Four Mini-dragons*. Cambridge MA: Harvard University Press.
Turner, B. 1974. *Weber and Islam: A Critical Study*. London: Routledge & Kegan Paul.
Turner, S. 1980. *Sociological Explanation as Translation*. Cambridge: Cambridge University Press.
Turner, V. 1969. *The Ritual Process*. Chicago: Aldine.
Van Parijs. P. 1981. *Evolutionary Explanation in the Social Sciences: An Emerging Paradigm*. London: Tavistock.
Vincent, R.J. 1986. *Human Rights and International Relations*. Cambridge: Cambridge University Press.
Voegelin, E. 1952. *The New Science of Politics: An Introduction*. Chicago: Chicago University Press.
Vogel, H.U., and M. Elvin (eds). 2010. *Concepts of Nature: A Chinese Cross-cultural Perspective*. Leiden: Brill.
Volkan, V. 1988. *The Need to Have Enemies and Allies: From Clinical Practice to International Relationships*. New York: Jason Aronson.
Volpi, F. 2010. *Political Islam*. London: Hurst.
von Grunebaum, G.E. 1962. *Modern Islam: The Search for Cultural Identity*. New York: Vintage Books.
Vries, P. 2002. 'Governing Growth: A Comparative Analysis of the Role of the State in the Rise of the West'. *Journal of World History* 13.
Walker, R. 1993. *Inside/Outside: International Relations and Political Theory*. Cambridge: Cambridge University Press.
Wallerstein, I. 1974. *The Modern World System*, vol. 1. New York: Academic Press.
Wallerstein, I. 1980. *The Modern World System*, vol. 2. New York: Academic Press.

Wallerstein, I. 1989. *The Modern World System*, vol. 3. New York: Academic Press.
Wallerstein, I. 2011. *The Modern World System*, vol. 4. Berkeley: University of California Press.
Walzer, M. 1987. *Interpretation and Social Criticism*. Cambridge MA: Harvard University Press.
Walzer, M. 1988. *The Company of Critics: Social Criticism and Political Commitment in the Twentieth Century*. New York: Basic Books.
Walzer, M. 2004. *Politics and Passion: Toward a More Egalitarian Liberalism*. New Haven CT: Yale University Press.
Ward, H. 1996. 'The Fetishisation of Falsification: The Debate on Rational Choice'. *New Political Economy* 1.
Warda, H. 2007. *Communism and the Emergence of Democracy*. Cambridge: Cambridge University Press.
Warnke, G. 2007. *After Identity: Rethinking Race, Sex and Gender*. Cambridge: Cambridge University Press.
Wearne, B. 1989. *The Theory and Scholarship of Talcott Parsons to 1951*. Cambridge: Cambridge University Press.
Weber, M. 1949. *The Methodology of the Social Sciences*. New York: Free Press.
Weber, M. 1951. *The Religion of China: Confucianism and Taoism*. New York: Free Press.
Weber, M. 1958. *The Protestant Ethic and the Spirit of Capitalism*. New York: Charles Scribner.
Weber, M. 1964. *The Sociology of Religion*. Boston MA: Beacon Press.
Weber, M. 1966. *General Economic History*. New York: Collier Books.
White, H. 1987. *The Content of the Form: Narrative Discourse and Historical Representation*. Baltimore MD: Johns Hopkins University Press.
Whorf, B. 1956. *Language, Thought and Reality*. Cambridge MA: MIT Press.
Wight, C. 2006. *Agents, Structures and International Relations: Politics as Ontology*. Cambridge: Cambridge University Press.
Wight, M. 1991. *International Theory: The Three Traditions*. Leicester: Leicester University Press.
Wilkinson, R., and K. Pickett. 2010. *The Spirit Level: Why Equality is Better for Everyone*. Harmondsworth: Penguin.
Winch, P. 1958. *The Idea of a Social Science and its Relation to Philosophy*. London: Routledge & Kegan Paul.
Wiredu, K. 1980. 'How Not to Compare African Traditional Thought with Western Thought'. In Kwasi Wiredu, *Philosophy and an African Culture*. Cambridge: Cambridge University Press.

Wright, G. 1971. *Explanation and Understanding*. Ithaca NY: Cornell University Press.
Wright, L. 1976. *Teleological Explanations*. Berkeley and Los Angeles: University of California Press.
Young, R. 2004. *White Mythologies*. London: Routledge.
Zakaria, F. 2008. *The Post-American World*. New York: W.W. Norton.
Zeitlin, I.M. 1990. *Ideology and the Development of Social Theory*, 4th edn. Englewood Cliffs NJ: Prentice Hall.
Zelizer, V. 1994. *The Social Meaning of Money*. New York: Basic Books.
Zerubavel, E. 2006. *The Elephant in the Room: Silence and Denial in Everyday Life*. Oxford: Oxford University Press.

Index

abortion, 204, 209
Afghanistan, 19, 89, 113, 270, 271, 328
Africa/African, 5, 8, 10, 16, 18, 33, 52, 59, 84, 87, 88, 90, 91, 93, 97, 101, 103, 107, 109–10, 116, 118, 125, 127–8, 198–9, 257–60, 264, 274, 281–4, 295, 300, 301, 303, 333
African American, 139, 156
Afrikaans, 48
Afro-Caribbeans, 59, 65
al-Bashir, Omar, 84, 327
al-Qaeda, 54, 94, 165, 170, 173
al-Shabaab, 334
Albania/Albanian, 6
Algeria/Algerian, 1, 6, 8, 16, 47, 53, 190, 285
America, *see* USA
Anderson, Benedict, 40
Angola/Angolans, 6, 272, 300
'angry young men', 62
anti-Semitism, 137, 157
apartheid, 48
artificial intelligence, 186
Asia, 5, 8
Asian 'Tigers', 272, 273
Atatürk, Mustafa Kemal, 52, 320
Australia, 4, 5, 29
Austria, 72
autochthony, 20

'backwardness', 2, 57
Bamba, Amadou, 52
Bangladesh, 9
banlieue, 20, 21, 26, 64, 71, 135, 246
BBC (British Broadcasting Corporation), 63
Beckham, David, 58–61
Beatles, The, 62
behavioural psychology, 27
Belgium/Belgians, 5, 333
Berlin Wall, 88
beur, 1, 47, 61, 63, 64, 135, 174, 231
Big Brother, TV series, 12
Blair, Tony, 85, 97
blues (music), 64
Brahmins, 126
Brazil, 103, 301
Bretton Woods Institutions, 104
British National Party (BNP), 47, 134, 145
Britishness, 179–80
Buddhism, 18, 210, 232, 306
Bulgaria, 137
Burke, Peter, ix
burqa, 23, 39, 57, 65, 66, 141, 158, 323
Bush, G.W., 89, 90

California, 126
Caliphate, 51, 54, 94, 170, 205, 266
Cambodia, 270, 271

Cambridge, University of, 5
Cameron, David, 310
Caribbean, 61
Caucasus, 205, 265–6
Central Asia, 103
chador, 2
change, as a concept, 222–34
Chechens, 266
China/Chinese, 5, 9, 19, 31, 64, 70, 73, 74, 81, 84, 87, 89, 104, 108, 109–11, 147, 152–3, 161, 179, 220, 224, 232–3, 237, 284, 288–90, 303, 327, 330, 331, 332, 333, 334
cloning, 209
Cold War, 86, 87, 88
Commonwealth, 164
communautarisme, 139
Confucius/Confucianism, 109, 232
Congo, Belgian, 87
conversion, 1, 2
creationism, 142
Crusades, 52
Cuban American, 139
Cuban missile crisis, 263
cultural relativism, 66, 161, 289
cultural turn, in history, 182–3
Cyprus, 87
Czechoslovakia, 87

Darfur, 327, 331, 332
Darwin, Charles, 38, 122
Dawkins, Richard, 37, 214
décroissance, 75–6
democracy, how to export, 104–13
Democratic Republic of Congo, 274
Denmark, 45, 166
Dershowitz, Alan, 90
Deutschland schafft sich ab, 173
Dickens, Charles, 61
Durkheim, Émile, 181, 292, 313–14

Eastern Europe, 6, 205
East Asia, 29, 44, 73, 80, 101, 108, 133, 224, 232, 260
Egypt, 53, 290, 320
Einstein, Albert, 189
English Defence League (EDL), 134, 145
El Niño/Niña, 29
Enlightenment, the, 13, 25, 28, 37, 56, 80, 105, 119–20, 123, 194, 197, 204, 225

épater les bourgeois, 135
Estonia/Estonian, 159
ETA (Euskadi Ta Askatasuna), 90
ethnicity, 264–7
Euben, Roxanne, 290
European Exchange Rate Mechanism (EERM), 221
European Union (EU), 46, 73, 74, 89, 115, 137, 142
euthanasia, 200, 209

'fairness', 311–12
faith, as a concept, 204–15
fascism, 36
Fatah, 90
Federal Democratic Union (Switzerland), 50
female genital mutilation, 65, 66, 78, 134, 200, 227, 323
feminism, 66
Finland, 307
Foucault, Michel, 181
'Fourth World', 71
France/French, 1, 5, 8, 20, 21, 22, 23, 26, 41–7, 53, 55, 61–2, 64, 66, 71, 72, 86, 111, 137, 139–42, 171–2, 174–5, 190, 202, 205–9, 231, 246, 298, 300
France Culture (radio), 63
freedom, as a concept, 197–204
French Revolution, 183
Freemasonry, 55
Freud, Sigmund, 292
Fukuyama, Francis, 73, 105
fundamentalism, 2

G8, 97
G20, 221
Gaddafi, Muammar, 333
Geertz, Clifford, 125
genocide, 83, 85, 331, 333
Germany, 5, 7n, 53, 172, 190, 205
globalisation, 10–12, 69
Green Revolution, 281
Guantánamo, 89–90
Gulf states, 53
Gypsies, 191, 300

halal, 132
'hard sciences', *see* physical sciences
Harry, Prince, 62

Index

Hepton, Bruce, 58
hijab, 1, 2, 78, 200, 208, 213
Hinduism, 18, 210
Hitler, Adolf, 175
Hong Kong, 109
'honour' killing, 227
Huguenot, 230
human rights, 77–86, 321–8
Hungary, 87
Huntington, Samuel, 4, 6, 166–70, 173
Hutus, 274
hybridity, 317

imam, figure of, 1
IMF (International Monetary Fund), 104, 282
India, 9, 16, 70, 81, 115, 125, 224, 233, 285
individual, as a concept, 186–91
Indonesia, 125, 305
induction, as a concept, 257, 295, 300
Industrial Revolution, 91, 100, 120, 195, 197, 224
'In God We Trust', 207
International Criminal Court (ICC), 84, 323, 326, 328, 330
International Criminal Tribunal for Rwanda in Arusha, 85
IRA (Irish Republican Army), 90
Iraq, 85, 87, 89, 270, 330
Ireland/Irish, 47, 179
Irgun, 90
Irish Americans, 139
Islamophobia, 145, 165, 174, 208, 213, 321
Israel/Israelis, 84
Italian Americans, 156
Italy/Italians, 5, 6, 152–3, 230
IVF (*in vitro* fertilisation), 209

Jamaica, 12
Japan, 73, 108, 223, 232
jazz, 12, 64
Jews, 137, 142, 230
jihad, 94
jilbab, 2

Kabbalah, 116
Karzai, Hamid, 113
Keynesianism, 75, 218, 221, 299
Kenya, 99, 265, 271, 334

Kosovo, 205, 270, 330
Kurds, 95

Latin America, 5, 8, 19, 101, 167
Lebanon, 87
Lévi-Strauss, Claude, 116
Liberia, 327
Libya, 270, 328, 332–3
linguistic turn (in history), 182–3
Lithuania/Lithuanians, 159
Liu Xiaobo, 288
Lula da Silva, Luiz Inácio, 103

Macau, 109
Maghreb, 52, 90
Making Poverty History, 96–104
Malthus, Thomas, 196
Marseilles, 246
Marx, Karl, 122, 181, 292, 310
Marxism/Marxists, 53, 100
Maasai, 99
McKenzie, Paul, 58
Marianne, figure of, 207
market, as a concept, 215–22
meanings of Western rationality, 18–20
Mein Kampf, 175
Merkel, Angela, 231
Mexican Americans, 156
Mexico/Mexicans, 8
Michels, Robert, 181
Middle East, 5, 10, 19, 53, 104, 142, 205
Milosevic, Slobodan, 84, 265
Mogadishu, 333
Morocco/Moroccans, 1
Morris, Rosalind, ix
Moscow, 266
mosques, 50–58
Mouride (Brotherhood), 52
Mozambique, 101, 300
multiculturalism, 22, 39–50, 131, 231, 269
Muslim Brotherhood, 53

NATO (North Atlantic Treaty Organization), 87, 113, 328, 332–3
Nasser, Gamal Abdel, 53
National Health Service (NHS), 278–9
National Front, 133
Nazis, 36
Nehru, Jawarhalal, 107

Netherlands, the, 7, 42, 45, 72, 96, 166, 173
Newton, Isaac, 189, 307
Nigeria/Nigerians, 90, 91, 110–11, 126, 153, 302, 305
niqab, 129–31, 134, 141, 159, 171–2, 175–6, 201, 208, 213
9/11, events of, 8, 163, 166, 312
non-European perspective, vii
Northern Ireland, 205
Norway, 166
Nüremberg Tribunal, 84

Obama, Barack, 35, 89
OPEC (Organization of the Petroleum Exporting Countries), 17
Orientalism, 52
Ossetian, 266
Ottoman, 52
Oxford, University of, 115, 209

Pakistan, 9, 320
Palestine/Palestinians, 54, 95
Pentecostalism, 210, 301
physical sciences, viii, 27, 76, 145, 151, 186, 217, 219, 222, 226, 238–40, 255–6, 261, 267, 291–3, 296, 307, 309
plausibility, 294–7, 308
Poland/Poles, 6, 230
policing the world, 86–96
polygamy, 65, 133, 134, 190, 227, 322
Popper, Karl, 294
Portugal, 5
postcolonial burden of history, the, 14–17
post-traumatic stress disorder, 248, 310
Powell, Enoch, 163–4
Punjab, 115

Quick (restaurants), 132
Quran, 175–6

racism, 10
Ramadan, Tariq, 173–4, 201, 209, 213–14, 323–4
rap music, 12, 63, 135
rational-choice theory, 181, 183, 189, 262–3, 266
rationality, theory and thinking, 23–34
Readman, Paul, ix
Renaissance, the, 25, 116

Roma, 137, 169–70
Romania, 137
Room at the Top (film), 60
Rostow, Walter, 273
Russia, 89, 95, 205, 266, 330
Rwanda, 85, 87, 265, 274, 333
Rwanda Patriotic Front, 274

Sachs, Jeffrey, 245
Said, Edward, 15
Sarkozy, Nicolas, 22, 35, 132–3, 323–4
Sarrazin, Thilo, 173
Saudi Arabia, 53, 56, 205
Scandinavia, 7, 96, 193
Scotland/Scots, 47, 179
Scott, David, ix
Scott, Joan, ix
secularism/secularisation, 32, 160–61, 204–15, 318–21
Sen, Amartya, 250
Serbia, 87, 265
Shakespeare, William, 61
Sierra Leone, 270, 271
'silicon valley', 126, 228
Singapore, 232
Slovakia, 12
Small is Beautiful (Schumacher), 18
Smith, Adam, 220, 307
social engineering, 23
social sciences,
'scientific', the, viii
society, as a concept, 191–7
Somalia/Somalis, 91, 159, 253, 310, 333
Somaliland, 253
South Asia, 9, 59
South Korea, 73, 108, 223, 232, 233
Southeast Asia, 18, 44, 73, 81
Southern Sudan, 274
'Southern Theory', 290
Singapore, 73, 81
sovereignty, 328–34
Soviet Union, 80, 88, 89, 107
Spain, 5
Spivak, Gayatri Chakravorty, 118
Sri Lanka, 9
St George, flag of, 46, 180
Stasi Commission (France), 66
stem cells, 209
Stiglitz, Joseph, 250
subjectivity, 297–302, 308

Sudan (Sudanese), 84, 159, 327–8
Suez, 1956 crisis, 16, 87
Sufism, 52
Sweden/Swedish, 72, 152–3, 159, 165, 166, 193, 304
Swiss People's Party, 50
Switzerland/Swiss, 50, 72, 200, 305
Syed Khan, Sir, 52

Taylor, Charles, 327
telenovelas, 12
Thatcher, Margaret, 96
The Clash of Civilizations (Huntington), 4
The Empire Strikes Back (film), 15
The End of History (Fukuyama), 19
This Sporting Life (film), 60
Tibet, 87, 333
Travellers, 170, 191
Turkey/Turkish, 46, 53, 56, 172, 190, 211, 320

ummah, 191, 194, 201, 324
unemployment, 67–76
Universal Declaration of Human Rights, 77, 79, 82, 287, 322
USA, 5, 6, 8, 17, 19, 22, 23, 29, 30, 41, 42, 61, 66, 80, 84, 88, 89, 111, 127–8, 131, 134, 140–42, 149, 153, 155–6, 164, 168, 179, 193, 206–11, 221, 225, 280, 326

Vatican, the, 205
Vedic medicine, 116
Vietnam/Vietnamese, 16, 17, 73, 104, 108, 233

Wahabi, 50, 56, 205
Wales/Welsh, 47, 179
'war on terror', 77, 94
'Washington consensus', 232
Weber, Max, 13, 108, 109, 110, 181, 231, 292
West and non-West, 4–12
West Indians, 8
Western rationality, and postcolonialism, 13–23
Westernisation, 21, 56, 74, 93, 104, 111, 121, 126, 130, 149, 152, 228–30, 233, 316–17, 325
Westphalia/Westphalian principles in IR, 83, 87, 327, 328–31
Who Are We? (Huntington), 4, 167
Wilders, Geert, 40, 45, 173, 175–6
witchcraft, 63
World Bank, 104, 282

Yugoslavia, 166, 265

Zambia, 272
Zen Buddhism, 115

About Zed Books

Zed Books is a critical and dynamic publisher, committed to increasing awareness of important international issues and to promoting diversity, alternative voices and progressive social change. We publish on politics, development, gender, the environment and economics for a global audience of students, academics, activist and general readers. Run as a co-operative, we aim to operate in an ethical and environmentally sustainable way.

Find out more at
www.zedbooks.co.uk

For up-to-date news, articles, reviews
and events information visit
http://zed-books.blogspot.com

To subscribe to the monthly Zed Books e-newsletter send an email headed 'subscribe' to marketing@zedbooks.net

We can also be found on Facebook, ZNet,
Twitter and Library Thing.

www.ingramcontent.com/pod-product-compliance
Ingram Content Group UK Ltd.
Pitfield, Milton Keynes, MK11 3LW, UK
UKHW021914220326
469204UK00018B/73